Date: 8/28/17

BIO BUCHANAN
Strauss, Robert,
Worst. President. Ever. :
James Buchanan, the POTUS

Advance Praise for
Worst. President. Ever.

"One might put forth other candidates for the crown Mr. Strauss has bestowed on Mr. Buchanan, but one cannot dispute the élan with which he makes his case. This is history writing at it should be, but too often isn't: authoritative, yet lively and fun to read."

—David M. Friedman, author of *Wilde in America,*
The Immortalists, and *A Mind of Its Own*

"Authors who want to teach us the secrets of the best are a dime a dozen. Only Robert Strauss could show us what we have to learn from the worst. *Worst. President. Ever.* is a tour de force—entertaining and edifying in equal measure."

—Kermit Roosevelt, author, legal scholar, and
professor of law at the University of Pennsylvania

"If you despised W., if Obama fills you with loathing, if you fear apocalyptic consequences with the election of Hillary or Trump . . . then Robert Strauss is here with historical reassurance. A century and a half ago, America survived (just barely) a truly terrible president: a bungler of a politician who did next to nothing as the Union broke apart over slavery."

—David Kinney, author of *The Devil's Diary:*
Alfred Rosenberg and the Stolen Secrets of the Third Reich

"Was James Buchanan really the W.P.E.? And if so, what did he do (or not do) to deserve the designation? How does the peculiar business of presidential rankings work, anyway? To find out the answers to those and other questions, you'll need to read Robert Strauss's smart and very entertaining *Worst. President. Ever.*"

—Ben Yagoda, author of *Will Rogers: A Biography* and *The B Side:*
The Death of Tin Pan Alley and the Rebirth of the Great American Song

"President Buchanan had a great résumé, but in war, peace, race, religion, leadership, friendship, love, and honor he left much to be desired. Strauss weaves the history of this failed president with countless facts and observations about American presidents and his own lifelong fascination with the successes, failures, and foibles of our elected leaders."

—Rush D. Holt, former congressman, chief executive officer of the
American Association for the Advancement of Science

A daguerreotype of James Buchanan by Mathew Brady, probably done during Old Buck's presidency. He was still wearing high collars, a fashion of another age, when most men were seen in neckties. LIBRARY OF CONGRESS

An imprint of Rowman & Littlefield

Distributed by NATIONAL BOOK NETWORK

British Library Cataloguing in Publication Information Available

Library of Congress Cataloging-in-Publication Data

Names: Strauss, Robert, 1951- author.
Title: Worst. President. Ever. : James Buchanan, the POTUS rating game, and the legacy of the least of the lesser presidents / Robert Strauss.
Description: Guilford, Connecticut : Lyons Press, an imprint of Rowman & Littlefield, 2016. | Includes bibliographical references and index.
Identifiers: LCCN 2016023819 (print) | LCCN 2016024264 (ebook) | ISBN 9781493024834 (hardcopy) | ISBN 9781493024841 (e-book)
Subjects: LCSH: Buchanan, James, 1791-1868. | Presidents—United States—Biography. | United States—Politics and government—1857-1861.
Classification: LCC E437 .S77 2016 (print) | LCC E437 (ebook) | DDC 973.6/8092 [B]—dc23
LC record available at https://lccn.loc.gov/2016023819

∞™ The paper used in this publication meets the minimum requirements of American National Standard for Information Sciences—Permanence of Paper for Printed Library Materials, ANSI/NISO Z39.48-1992.

WORST. PRESIDENT. EVER.

James Buchanan, the POTUS Rating Game, and
the Legacy of the Least of the Lesser Presidents

ROBERT STRAUSS

Guilford, Connecticut

To my father, Samuel Strauss, who made me read every historical marker we ever passed, thus assuring me of a lifetime of winning trivia contests, and my mother, Edna, for teaching me how to laugh, especially at myself.

"Don't look back. Something might be gaining on you," attributed to Satchel Paige.

Contents

PREFACE

"WHAT BET DID YOU LOSE?"

The man at the other end of the phone worked in the Special Collections section of the Dickinson College library. I had just told him I had heard that Dickinson had digitized a lot of documents by or concerning James Buchanan, one of its early graduates, and I was wondering how to access them. I enthusiastically said I was doing a kind of biography of the fifteenth president.

A historian friend later said I should ask someone at the Historical Society of Pennsylvania, where Buchanan's nephew had donated many of the originals of those papers, just to see how often anyone had looked at them.

"Not very," was the reply.

Before I had put pen to paper for this book, but while I was thinking about doing so, I got an assignment from the *New York Times* for a special museums section on visiting sites concerning lesser-known presidents. Naturally, Wheatland, the home where Buchanan lived as a squire in his later years, was on the list. I called Patrick Clarke, the director of Wheatland, and while talking about the story, mentioned I was thinking of doing something larger on Buchanan. I asked him why there had not been much written about Buchanan, even after 150 years.

"You see, presidential biographies did not really start in earnest until the mid-to-late 1950s, when historians started thinking about Franklin Roosevelt, and his long tenure became of interest to them," said Clarke. "Naturally, authors gravitated toward the bigger names—Washington, Jefferson, Lincoln, Teddy and Franklin Roosevelt, but most historians agreed that Buchanan was a failure. As a result, why write about the guy? Why write about any loser?"

Around this time I also discovered that Buchanan's birthplace, a log cabin, had been moved in one whole piece to the rural campus of a nearby prep school, Mercersburg Academy, in central Pennsylvania. I had a friend who went there as a kid, so I asked her about it.

"Oh, yes, that is where people went to make trouble," she said. Not exactly Monticello, the cabin was a make-out and drinking spot. "Not many people cared about Buchanan, I don't think."

Being a contrarian, this disinterest, and even disdain, by the closest keepers of Buchanan's legacy made the subject ever more attractive to me. By the time I had done enough research, I could determine that he was clearly one of the worst presidents, with a good chance of being forty-third out of the forty-three (or forty-fourth out of the forty-four, depending on when you're reading this book). I would tell people I was going to do a book on Buchanan being that worst president, and I often got that kind of face where I knew people were hearkening back to high school to try to remember where Buchanan fit into the time line.

After hesitation many would come up with, "The guy before Lincoln, right?" Some of these folks knew every third-string catcher in the American League or all of the elements on the periodic table in order or the words to every Bruce Springsteen song. Buchanan, at most, was the answer to a $200 question on *Jeopardy!*

I was moving from that attracted contrarian to a frothing man of passion.

Worst or not, the man was president. Billions of people have now lived in the United States since Betsy Ross spangled those stars on the banner. As of this writing, only forty-three had made it to the top job. There are 118 elements on the periodic chart and dozens of third-string catchers every decade, and each Springsteen song seems to last an hour. Why the lack of interest in or knowledge of the guy?

My father was an American history nut, perhaps because he emigrated as a child from a repressive Ukraine and came to love his stars-and-stripes freedom all the more. In any case, he collected lots of books—I seem to doubt he read most of them—especially on presidents and about the Civil War; he was also a member of the Lincoln Civil War Society of Philadelphia. I inherited those volumes, and I have only now started to read them, especially the ones on obscure and denounced presidents—two on James Knox Polk, two copies of the same book on Warren G. Harding, the graying pages of one on Franklin Pierce, seven volumes of Woodrow Wilson's papers.

He collected none, though, on Buchanan. So I started to look through some of his other books to find what they said about the fifteenth president. There was *The Americans*, historian Daniel Boorstin's seminal trilogy about the American experiment—only one obscure reference, not even a full sentence, devoted to Buchanan. Bruce Catton's *The Coming Fury*, which was the official centennial history of the origins of the Civil War—a dozen references or so to Buchanan, whose term led to secession, the major topic of that Coming Fury. As other tomes showed similar lack of reference, the only conclusion I could make was that historians of the era were of the same mindset: "If you can't say anything nice, then . . ." I did find one title, *Great Presidential Decisions*, for which Columbia professor Richard Morris in 1960 picked three dozen landmark cases, mostly monumental in the positive—except for the two he attributes to Buchanan, which have the headlines "Buchanan Breaks Up the Democratic Party" and "Buchanan Confesses He Lacks the Power to Act."

My wife bought me a copy of *Buchanan Dying*, a play by the eminent author John Updike. Updike had grown up relatively near Lancaster, which Buchanan called home most of his adult life. In the notes to the last edition of the book, from 2000, twenty-six years after he published the play, Updike wrote that *Buchanan Dying* had been produced only twice: for a week in 1976 at Franklin & Marshall College, which Buchanan helped found, and in an uncostumed, unmemorized version at San Diego State University the following year.

If a play written by such an eminence as John Updike was brushed aside so monumentally, then that said something, though I am still not sure what.

Finally, there was karma. My daughter and her roommates moved to a new apartment in Charlotte, North Carolina, in the summer of 2015—on Buchanan Street, just up from Pierce Street and Fillmore Street.

There was no stepping aside now. No, I hadn't lost any kind of bet. My contrarian antennae had been raised to their acme. I had to tell the tale of the man whom I had determined was, as kids from my daughter's generation might put it, the WORST. PRESIDENT. EVER.

BUCHANAN TIME LINE

April 23, 1791: Born in Cove Gap, PA

Sept. 19, 1809: Graduated Dickinson College, Carlisle, PA

Nov. 17, 1812: Admitted to the law bar, Lancaster, PA

Dec. 6, 1814–Oct. 1815: Served in Pennsylvania House of Representatives

March 4, 1821–March 3, 1831: Member of United States House of Representatives from Pennsylvania

Jan. 4, 1832–Aug. 5, 1833: United States minister to Russia under President Andrew Jackson

Dec. 6, 1834–March 5, 1845: Member of United States Senate from Pennsylvania

May 29, 1844: Unsuccessful attempt to be Democratic nominee for president

March 6, 1845–March 6, 1849: United States secretary of state under President James Polk

May 25, 1848: Unsuccessful attempt to be Democratic nominee for president

1849: Retired to Wheatland, his twenty-two-acre home estate near Lancaster, PA

June 4, 1852: Unsuccessful attempt to be Democratic nominee for president

April 11, 1853: Envoy extraordinary and minister plenipotentiary to Great Britain under President Franklin Pierce

June 6, 1856: Nominated in Cincinnati, OH, as Democratic candidate for president

March 4, 1857–March 3, 1861: President of the United States

March 6, 1857: Chief Justice Roger Taney announces *Dred Scott* decision, declaring the Missouri Compromise unconstitutional

May 11, 1858: Minnesota admitted as the thirty-second state

Aug. 1858: Lincoln-Douglas debates

Aug. 5, 1858: Atlantic telegraph cable completed

Aug. 16, 1858: Buchanan and Queen Victoria exchange greetings on the Atlantic cable

Feb. 14, 1859: Oregon admitted as the thirty-third state

Aug. 27, 1859: Oil discovered in western Pennsylvania

Oct. 16, 1859: Harper's Ferry, VA, raided by John Brown

April 3, 1860: Pony Express started between St. Joseph, MO, and Sacramento, CA

Sept. 20, 1860: Prince of Wales comes to Detroit, MI, his first stop in the United States

Dec. 20, 1860: South Carolina secedes from the Union

Jan.–Feb. 1861: Mississippi, Florida, Alabama, Georgia, Louisiana, and Texas secede from the Union

Jan. 29, 1861: Kansas admitted as the thirty-fourth state

Feb. 4, 1861: Confederate States organized

March 4, 1861: Abraham Lincoln inaugurated

1866: Publication of Buchanan's presidential memoir, *Mr. Buchanan's Administration on the Eve of the Rebellion*

June 1, 1868: Died in Lancaster, age seventy-seven years and thirty-nine days

CHAPTER ONE

Introducing the Worst. President. Ever.

THE SNOW, GETTING HEAVIER AND HEAVIER AS THE CEREMONY WENT on, belied the anticipation. The Washington social world had been waiting for the inaugural ball of James Buchanan. There had been one minor slip-up early in the day, well before the snow started. Buchanan, or someone in his entourage, had forgotten to tell the presidential carriage driver to pick up incumbent president Franklin Pierce first. Pierce had stayed the night before at the stately Willard Hotel, across the way from the White House, from which he had moved out in anticipation of Buchanan moving in the next day. So the driver doubled back from the more raucous National Hotel a few blocks north and west, where the Buchanan bunch was bunking in. It delayed the ceremony about twenty or thirty minutes, but in the end everyone laughed about it and looked forward to a festive day, the kind the renowned party giver Buchanan was famous for.

Since the death of Dolley Todd Madison eight years before, there had been no focus for those who wanted to supplement Washington's dull government work and dubious living conditions with the lavish and fun times expected in a national capital.

Even after her son by her first marriage, James Payne Todd, had run through her money with his mounting debts and legal dustups, Dolley Madison was, essentially, America's Princess or maybe even Queen Mother. She had endeared herself to the masses for saving whatever she could, especially Gilbert Stuart's iconic portrait of George Washington, as the British burned the White House during the War of 1812, when her husband, James, was president. In fact, her popularity extended further back, to the Founding Father era in Philadelphia, when—with her first husband dying young during the 1793 yellow fever epidemic—James Madison, seventeen years older and by that time perhaps the most well-respected legal mind in the new nation, married her the next year.

With the capital moving from Philadelphia to Washington, President Jefferson, by then a widower and having appointed James Madison the secretary of state, asked Dolley to become what came to be termed First Lady—essentially the social chair of the government. Dolley's touch was perfect: a bit of the old world and a good dollop of the new. When it came to White House functions under Dolley Madison, everyone got a chance at the head table, political stances be damned. America's politics of the time generated what was called the "Era of Good Feelings," and it is hard not to give Dolley Madison's creation of a positive social atmosphere some credit for that.

After her husband's own presidential term, the couple retired to their country estate in Virginia, appropriately named Montpelier for the Francophile Madisons, and entertained dignitaries and local politicians alike for the next nineteen years, until James Madison's death. Dolley sold Montpelier, paid off James Payne Todd's debts, and returned to Washington, mostly serving as the doyenne to everyone else's parties, since she was, on her own, practically penniless.

By that time, though, the White House had ceased to be a party place. William Henry Harrison died a month after his March 4, 1841, election, so the John Tylers, who moved into the presidential home, felt too constrained by the first death of a president while in office to do much socializing. In any case, the first Mrs. Tyler, Letitia, was in ill health when Tyler took office, and she herself died in September 1842. Tyler was an embattled president—a Virginia Democrat who had been put on the Harrison Whig ticket to attract some Southern votes and then excommunicated from the Whig Party after his ascension to the presidency. The deaths of President Harrison and Mrs. Tyler notwithstanding, there was really little call for socializing in the White House during the unproductive Tyler years there.

Tyler was followed by James Knox Polk, whose wife, Sarah, was a strict Presbyterian, allowing no dancing, alcohol, cards, or, according to one historian, "loose joviality" in the White House. She was followed by Peggy Smith Taylor, the wife of General Zachary Taylor, who never appeared in public with her husband because "a Maryland blue blood, [she] thought commerce with politicians was degrading." By this time Dolley Madison had appeared at her last White House function, a dinner for President Polk just before his own death, which came only six months after his term ended. Then President Taylor died of cholera in July 1850. He apparently exacerbated the disease, which was not unusual in swamp-filled Washington, by attending a long, hot July 4 celebration at the still-unfinished Washington Monument. The Millard Fillmores, who came next, were never big party folks, Mrs. Fillmore being an incredibly shy and sickly woman, and they used those recent presidential deaths as excuses to tamp down any presidential socializing. Mrs. Fillmore died only three weeks after her husband's term ended, having caught a final chill during the inauguration of his successor, Franklin Pierce. Most tragic of all, Franklin Pierce's eleven-year-old son (his third child) died in a train accident while the family was traveling in the Northeast. Their first son had died in infancy and the second had perished when he was four—unprecedented that a president lost all three of his children before reaching the White House. Mrs. Pierce went into a mourning depression from which she never recovered, and was rarely seen in public during Pierce's term. Even then, she dressed entirely in black.

It had been a long, dreary haul for those who came through official Washington by the time Buchanan was elected in 1856. For the most part, Southern congressmen and high functionaries left their families at home, the legislative sessions normally not taking more than a few months. The Northern politicians were more often able to go in and out of the capital—train connections and roads being far better in their direction—while most of the Southern families had to come by river or sea at least part of the way.

There was every expectation that the Buchanan presidency would bring some calm and at least a modicum of levity to Washington. Buchanan had spent much of the previous four decades in the capital. He had first come to the town during the James Monroe administration, only a few years after the rebuilding following the War of 1812. Buchanan was a member of the House of Representatives from 1821 through 1831, then, following an interlude when he was minister to Russia under President Andrew Jackson, a United States senator from Pennsylvania for more than another decade, from 1834 to 1845. Then he was secretary of state under President James Knox Polk for the next four years, only moving back to Lancaster and his estate, Wheatland, in 1849.

Most of that time, Buchanan lived in boarding houses and moved in circles that were almost entirely Southern, despite his Pennsylvania provenance. He was a bachelor and often the mark for ladies who wanted to pair him up. In the mid-nineteenth century, bachelorhood was practically nonexistent. Only about three in a hundred able-bodied men never married, though, to be sure, childbirth being difficult, another sizable cadre were widowers. There was always some Southern congressman's wife looking to marry off a younger sister or plantation neighbor to a well-off bachelor like Buchanan.

Washington was probably America's first seasonal city. Most government functions, from legislative sessions to cabinet meetings to reception of foreign dignitaries, happened in the cooler months. When Buchanan was first elected, for instance, in 1820, he did not have his first session until December of the next year. It was an extraordinarily compact city, one with little business other than that of government and whatever retail and services were necessary to keep it going. Most congressmen and cabinet members had means, and their wives and children were used to comfort in their homes, so those families were less encouraged to trundle off to Washington, where there was little to attract them, especially in the sultry summer months.

Even fifty years into its existence, Washington was ill developed, only the area around the Capitol and the White House being much of a city at all. It was far more Southern than Northern, slow moving and not particularly sanitary, and though there was no slave trade anymore, there were, indeed, slaves. Nearby farmers let their hogs wallow even along Capitol Hill and near Judiciary Square, the closest thing Washington had to a civic commons. The nearby canal was often filled with discarded dead domestic animals and people routinely just threw their sewage into street gutters. Privy pits were still pretty much the order of the day and the springs and wells that provided the city's water supply were dicey at best. In fact, just days before Buchanan's inauguration, many who had dined at the National Hotel died or were sickened by what some believe was Republican poisoning, but was probably a dysentery caused by foul water in the kitchen. Buchanan himself had sweats and pains during the inaugural ceremonies and three congressmen, Buchanan's own nephew, and about thirty other people were said to have died from the mini-plague.

Those wives and older daughters of the distinguished congressmen and high officeholders who stayed in Washington did their best to be elegant, but it was an overwhelmingly male city. Even then, there was little to recommend a young single man there other than governmental ambition. There were no real gentlemen's clubs, though there were surely bordellos, and few restaurants or cafes that might have lined the byways of European capitals like Paris or London, or even Prague or Stockholm. Crime was rampant, with many of the Congressmen using their own slaves or servants for protection.

Dolley Madison, though, had shown that things in official Washington did not have to be grim. And now there was hope that Buchanan and his favorite niece and titular First Lady, Harriet Lane, would bring some luster back to the Washington scene.

The night of the ball, Harriet, whom several newspapers had already named "Our Democratic Queen," wore a white dress festooned with artificial flowers and a multistrand necklace of pearls. The new president was not feeling well yet, due to the residue of the National Hotel scourge, so he needed to retire early if he wanted to get some rest before earnestly starting his long-sought-after term. Harriet, who always stood on protocol, left the ball with Buchanan, knowing there would be many lively and lovely parties to come over the next four years.

The start of the Buchanan administration, at least his first unofficial appointment—niece Harriet as the White House hostess—was a success. The idea of one inaugural ball rather than several smaller affairs had been out of fashion since the inauguration of John Quincy Adams, but Lane and Buchanan decided to give the big celebration a comeback. A huge temporary structure—235 feet long, 77 feet wide, and 20 feet high—was erected on Judiciary Square, costing $15,000 alone, a huge sum in donations at the time. The white ceiling of the structure had a "sky" of gold stars, and the walls were red, white, and blue. The most glorious inaugural parade ever had finished only a few hours before the ball, with huge crowds along the route cheering outsized floats, some featuring model battleships, the Goddess of Liberty, and historical scenes.

Six thousand people crammed into the ball, cold and snowy as the evening was, dancing to a forty-piece orchestra. The feast was a gastronome's delight—four hundred gallons of oysters, five hundred quarts of chicken salad, sixty saddles of mutton and four of venison, seventy-five hams, one hundred twenty-five tongues, eight full steers of beef, twelve hundred quarts of ice cream, a cake four feet high, and wine costing more than $3,000, an unheard-of bar tab at the time.

Buchanan's first national mentor, Andrew Jackson, had opened the White House to "regular citizens" when he came to office, so Buchanan did it in a modified manner, offering to shake hands with anyone in the East Room starting at noon on March 5, the day after the inauguration. The next day, he gave his first "levee," an official state dinner with a name of French affectation.

Patrick Lynch, the *New York Times* correspondent, got to the levee at nine in the evening, while the president was in another several-hour ordeal of hand shaking. Even with Buchanan not in the main ballroom, Lynch was impressed:

As I approached the White House, sounds of music—the illuminated mansion—the flitting of fairy forms—the hum, the buzz, of a human multitude—infixed my attention. With my companion on my arm I ascended the steps of the Palace amidst the rolling of wheels, the prancing of horses, the cracking of whips, the loud voices or rather yells of the coachmen claiming places and precedence. The names of Governor this, General that, Judge somebody else; a Baron with a patronymic of garroting properties; a Lord from some petty German state, more remarkable for titles to words than to broad acres; a Polish Prince and a Russian Nabob; the Turkish Ambassador without his harem; together with a numberless host of Senators, members of Congress, ecclesiastics, editors and laymen, burst with indescribable effect upon my ear.

Harriet Lane was a stickler that everyone should be announced at their entrance, all being equal at least at the start of ceremonies, which the Timesman clearly thought a bit over the top with his ambassadors sans harems and judges-somebody-else. Still, he obviously thought this was a revolution in Washingtonian fetes.

We entered. Never did such a scene meet my astonished gaze before. The subdued murmurs of the human sea within—the swelling choruses of the bands—the promenaders swaying backwards and forwards—the anxiety of some to move forward—the painful desire of others to retire, which it was impossible to accomplish—the gentlemen protecting the ladies endeavoring to preserve their ornaments and jewels and dresses from injury—the stream going out meeting the stream coming in— combined to form a subject for contemplation not easily or soon to be forgotten . . . Everyone you met was superbly attired. I never was fortunate enough to fall in with such good humor under such circumstances . . . It was essentially a citizen meeting without reference to distinctions of rank. It was a display of democratic elegance and gracefulness of which any country, or nation or court in the world might feel proud.

The buzz around the party gave Buchanan's reputation a clear boost, which did not seem all that unreasonable. He knew and was on generally good terms with every president from James Madison to Franklin Pierce—as wide a set of personalities as could have ever held the office. He was a member of the Federalist Party when it still held a bit of sway, and he became a national leader in the Democratic Party immediately when he switched allegiances. Prior to his governmental service and during breaks from it, he was perhaps the most lauded attorney in Pennsylvania, handling difficult cases and smoothing the way for others. He came from little—his father owned what would now be perceived as a general store in an out-of-the-way crossroads town—and achieved much. His investments were sure enough that they survived his meager government salaries and were able to provide for more than a dozen nieces, nephews, and their progeny. Not everyone in high political places loved Buchanan, but all at least had a begrudging admiration for him, and even his political enemies never accused him seriously of profiting financially from his stations.

That same day of the levee, though, what Buchanan thought might become his signal achievement became public, and the public gaiety of the administration's first two days was immediately negated. It was perhaps the most notorious decision the Supreme Court has ever made, about the ownership of a man named Dred Scott, and all the barons' horses and all the nabobs' men would not be able to put together Buchanan's presidency again.

— ⁓ —

There seems to be little Americans like to do more than rank, rate, and compete—and then argue about those rankings, ratings, and competitions. Not that the rest of the world doesn't have its moments (the meanderings of the English soccer leagues come to mind), but in America it is a lifetime kind of thing.

Every Monday, for instance, sports fans, coaches, and players agonize over the polls of their favorite collegiate sports. Usually, there are at least two competing polls. College basketball, for instance, has the Associated Press Top 25, done by sixty-five writers and broadcasters, and the USA Today Coaches Poll, voted on each week by thirty-two college coaches. Never mind that these coaches are spending virtually every waking moment in season trying to get their teams good enough to be in the poll themselves and could hardly be watching enough games, even with the time shifting of TV, in earnest to make a really educated choice, or that sportswriters generally have only cursory knowledge of the game's nuances. It all hardly matters in hoops, since there is a sixty-eight-team, single-elimination tournament at the end of the season, endearingly referred to as "March Madness," which actually pits the teams together, essentially negating any in-season ranking.

Still, I will admit that I look each week for my two daughters' alma mater, Davidson, on those winter Mondays and if the Wildcats scratch up to, say, number 25, I will immediately e-mail my wife and daughters in celebration. Who knows whether the votes that got them there are from a coach who is a friend of the Davidson coach, or whether some voter confused their score from the past week with that of their near-homonyms, Dickinson or Denison or Dayton. The team is ranked, and presumably ahead of some college where a friend went, so I can gloat.

The obsession with polling for almost anything appears to be American, its leading popularizer being George Gallup, who likely would have said he never thought it would come this far. Ironically, Gallup is known far more for what he got wrong, albeit more than a half century ago. The famous photo of Harry Truman holding up the *Chicago Tribune* front page with the headline "Dewey Defeats Truman" is not particularly about Gallup's polling, but the general conclusion of Gallup, Roper, and other major polling outfits was that Thomas Dewey was going to slaughter Truman in the 1948 presidential race, which did not come close to happening.

Yet Americans blithely go on loving polls, not to mention other rankings—Scholastic Aptitude Test scores, *Jeopardy!* championships, beauty pageants, Nielsen ratings, weight-loss claims, circulation figures, figure-skating scores, and anything that makes a headline or a cocktail conversation winner. If God hadn't wanted us to know Big Data and its results, he wouldn't have created Wikipedia for us to look them up.

So it is only natural to rate the forty-three men who have been president to date as I write in 2016. It would not be stretching it too much to say that about half of Americans in 2016 thought that George W. Bush was the worst of presidents, and that a similar number on the other side would have given the dubious honor to Barack Obama. Our historical senses tend to be dulled. Looking back too far is either too difficult or too unpleasant.

There are historians, though, who, like those who debate the best left-handed baseball hitter or the most beautiful actress, go back beyond the Bush/Obama era to debate who really was the worst man to serve as president.

Most often, these lists and discussions tend to let William Henry Harrison and James Garfield opt out. Harrison lived only a month into his term and Garfield, being shot five months into his, lived just another month or so on his deathbed. The other forty-one, though, are fair game, and James Buchanan makes a good case for being that worst president.

———

It could not have been the best of days for Abraham Lincoln when he got a letter from his presidential predecessor, James Buchanan. It had been merely seven months that late October day since Lincoln had come to the White House as the first president from the new Republican Party. An arduous six months had passed since those first onerous shots back and forth between Charleston and Fort Sumter that officially started what was called the War of the Rebellion in the North and the War for Southern Independence in the Confederacy.

The Union army had been embarrassed and, frankly, a bit scared at the Battle of Bull Run—the first full-on battle of the war, in July—and was not successful at all in blocking shipping lanes to Europe from Southern ports. Funding from exports, particularly the hated slave-labor commodity, cotton, continued to accumulate in Confederate bank accounts. Talk of secession was still in the air in pro-slavery Maryland, its consummation meaning Washington would be surrounded by Confederate territory, and that would probably necessitate abandonment of the nation's capital by the government.

The same day Buchanan dated the letter—October 21, 1861—one of Lincoln's longtime political friends from back when they were both Whigs in Illinois, Edward Dickinson Baker, then a United States senator from the new state of Oregon, was killed in action as the militia he was commanding retreated along the Potomac River, just forty miles from the capital. Baker is still the only sitting member of the United States Congress to die in battle.

Buchanan, who—to be fair—would have been unaware of these unpleasantries, had something else on his mind. He felt compelled to write to Lincoln, not about how he might help save the Union, but about what he might be able to save before the White House possibly met its demise. It is the only letter from Buchanan in the Library of Congress's Lincoln collection, thus presumably the only one he sent to his successor, which makes it even more outrageous in its content.

"My Dear Sir," Buchanan started out. "Pardon me for requesting you to refer this note to your private Secretary.

"I believe that I left in the Library of the Executive Mansion Thier's History (in French) of the Empire (under Napoleon 1st) in some seven or eight volumes," wrote Buchanan. "It was covered in paper & has the name of its former owner, Geo. W. Barton, written in each volume. Should it be found I would thank you to send it either to the State Department or to Dr. Blake."

Buchanan did have a postscript asking that Lincoln "remember me kindly & respectfully to Mrs. Lincoln," whom he could have surmised was in one of her dark psychological periods as the crisis of the nation progressed.

The whole letter was just the sort of obliviousness Buchanan had displayed throughout his career. He was, after all, the man most responsible for the mess Lincoln inherited when he walked into the White House. Through a combination of hubris—maybe exacerbated by his readings on Napoleon—arrogance, misaligned affections, indecisiveness, and misreading of current events, Buchanan had brought on Southern secession and the Civil War as Lincoln's predecessor.

Those who study history should be careful about reading that history in the light of the future, yet it is often hard to think that Buchanan has any serious competitor for being the worst president of the United States. His role in the Southern secession—the war itself did not technically start until he was out of office for five weeks, but a half dozen states seceded on his watch—would have been fuel enough for his bottom ranking. At almost every turn, though, where there was a decision to be made during his term, Buchanan seemed to intuitively pick the wrong tine of every fork in the road. If there was ever a wrong man for the wrong time in American history, it was Buchanan.

Oddly enough, Buchanan may well have been the most qualified man—at least through his governmental resume—to ever run for president. Certainly this was so in his era in the early and mid-nineteenth century.

All the presidents elected before Buchanan, save James Knox Polk and Martin Van Buren, were either war heroes or Founding Fathers or both (John Tyler and Millard Fillmore were never elected on their own, but came to the White House when their predecessors died in office). Few had much legislative or executive experience in federal or state government—and even Polk and Van Buren, who did, were essentially handpicked by their mutual mentor, Andrew Jackson, to advance Old Hickory's legacy. Some of the most celebrated members of Congress of the nation's first seventy-five years never made it to the White House— Daniel Webster, John Calhoun, Henry Clay, Charles Sumner, Thaddeus Stevens, Thomas Hart Benton, Jefferson Davis, and William Seward among them. In fact, Buchanan's major competitor in the 1856 election, John Fremont, was the military governor of California after he led the battles to take it over from the original Bear Flag Republic government.

It is easy to conclude from those who made it to the White House in the early years of the Republic that "leadership" meant either a military history or a hand in the founding of the country.

Buchanan, then, was an anomaly: the first plodding-to-the-top president. By the time he actually ran for president in 1856, he had been a state legislator in Pennsylvania, a member of both the United States House of Representatives and Senate, minister to both Russia and Great Britain, and secretary of state. He was a serious candidate for the Democratic presidential nomination three times before he got the nod, and was said to have refused two different presidents—Tyler and Polk—who were willing to nominate him to the United States Supreme Court.

He had been hanging around so long in relative prominence that he had been a member of the long-dead Federalist Party early in his career, but switched over to being a Democrat, smitten by the charisma of Andrew Jackson and John Calhoun, two Southern slaveholders with fiery tempers and long memories. By the time Buchanan was finally on a presidential ticket, he was sixty-five years old. Only two presidents before him were elected at more than age sixty-one, and those war heroes—William Henry Harrison and Zachary Taylor—died within a month and a year and a half, respectively, of taking office. Not until Ronald Reagan would an older man be elected president, and more than a century later a man like Reagan in his sixties did not seem as ancient as Buchanan was apparently thought of in his time.

In truth, some historians have suggested that Buchanan's fumbling, or at least bumbling through, every major decision point in his presidency may have been due to some latent or perhaps undiscovered age-related dementia. Recent research, in fact, shows that Reagan's speech patterns during the latter part of his term presaged his eventual dementia. Buchanan's post-presidency memoir, though, was lucid—despite its complete reimagining of mid-nineteenth-century history—belying any full onset of that sort of disease. *Mr. Buchanan's Administration on the Eve of the Rebellion*, which was published five years after Buchanan's term was over, is not a stylish piece of work, but grammatical and with well-hewn thoughts. Ghostwriters were not the ubiquitous players in the late 1860s that they are today, so there is no indication it was written by anyone but Buchanan. In any case, Buchanan was known to be a prolific writer throughout his life. He loved gossip and was constantly seeking every tidbit from his well-connected correspondents.

No, it seems that Buchanan was just a bad president—a poor chooser of associates, a waverer when quickness was necessary, pompous when he should have been contrite, oblivious to both current events and public thought, and living in a sheltered past in an era when America was really burgeoning on the world scene.

His backroom deal to influence the Supreme Court to make the *Dred Scott* decision—it came out during the first week of the Buchanan presidency—sealed the split of the Union, effectively making the Democratic Party a Southern one, supporting the rights of slave owners to retain their ownership of black people even in free states and territories. He equivocated back and forth over what the disposition of slavery in Kansas would be, appointing governors and recalling them, never really giving either of two constitutional conventions in that border territory his imprimatur, and allowing a virtual prelude Civil War to start in the next territory looking to become a state. That indecisiveness in Kansas permitted the famed abolitionist John Brown to get a foothold in the crisis, and led to Brown's futile insurrection at Harper's Ferry, which was then part of Virginia and is now in West Virginia. The drama at Harper's Ferry made Brown a martyr and gave abolitionists a larger voice than in the past, particularly in the Republican Party, in turn giving Southern states' righters a reason to give a vigorous negative shout in response.

Buchanan presided over the Panic of 1857, a sharp descent downward that devastated more fortunes, large and small, on a percentage basis, than the onslaught of the Great Depression of 1929, in a faster, if less prolonged, decline. Every bank in New York City closed down its use of scrip, at least for a time, thwarting deposits, withdrawals, and, clearly, any forward movement of the nation's business. Buchanan decided to do nothing to have the government mitigate the crisis, as was his wont to pursue a hands-off attitude in most everything that concerned the federal government. That move further split the merchant classes of the North from their opposite numbers in the agricultural South, who used banks less and, thus, were not as affected in the Panic.

Despite the supposed international acumen Buchanan gained in his foreign service years, his main thrust in that area during his presidency was to try to purchase Cuba from Spain in hopes of making it a slave state, maybe even two or three, and using it as a buffer to Great Britain's supposed longings in Central America and the Caribbean. At the same time, Buchanan lamented Spain's military weakness in stopping potential slave revolts, presuming American slaves might take any type of slave uprising in Cuba as rebellious inspiration. Cuba was of little interest to most US citizens, save those Southern slave owners who wanted another state to add to their roster. Further looking south for more slave territory, Buchanan also tacitly supported what was then known as the "filibuster" by William Walker, a rabble-rousing quasi-military man who set out to conquer Nicaragua and Honduras with a band of mercenaries, either keeping it for his own dictatorship or, if he had to, handing it over to the United States as yet more slave-state territory. These were still swash-buckling times in the country, with more immigrants moving in and more Easterners pushing farther west in hopes of finding their fortunes. The greater part of the citizenry still thought of the United States as a country not yet complete. California had only recently become a state and Oregon would become so during Buchanan's presidency, but the extent of Manifest Destiny was not yet completely settled.

A large swath of land already part of the country was still not cut up into states, and Buchanan had grown up in government when there was more unity about how to incorporate it. By his term, though, there were established forces, especially in the North, that were tired of fighting for Texas and California, or even negotiating with the French and British for Louisiana and Oregon. The Know-Nothings, formerly known as the American Party, had formed to rein all of it in, keeping Catholics and

Hispanics and any sort of labor organizing to a minimum, if not completely eliminating immigration and organized labor altogether.

The times were complicated and, in some ways, invigorating, but over all of it hung the larger issue of slavery and its spread. For anyone to look to Buchanan for leadership, though, was futile, and all that Buchanan did to push the nation inexorably toward Civil War puts him at the nadir of presidential reputation. There was a longer time between the presidential election and the inauguration in the nineteenth century than now. Because of long-distance horse-drawn travel and the need to get everyone to Washington for the new administration, the usual date for the inauguration was not January 20, but March 4. In that long interim after Abraham Lincoln's election the previous November, state after state in the Deep South seceded under Buchanan's watch. His stand on the secession was odd in its philosophy and devastating in its execution. Buchanan determined by his strict read of the United States Constitution that states could not secede from the Union, but that he as president was powerless to do anything about it, that it was a states' rights issue or that Congress was responsible for figuring it out.

There were prominent people from many sides willing to spearhead a commission or even work in secret to prevent secession first, or at least find a way to avoid hostilities. Former president John Tyler, who eventually won a seat in the Confederate legislature from his native Virginia after it seceded, came to Buchanan, offering whatever he could do to bring South and North together. Edwin Stanton, who would serve in Lincoln's cabinet after being a late addition to Buchanan's when Southerners left to join the Confederacy, pleaded with Buchanan to do something, anything. Yet Buchanan stood by his originalist version of the Constitution—that he could do nothing, and that he would do nothing, to prevent what would become not only the breakup of the Union, but the onset of civil war.

Buchanan's diddling, furthermore, allowed the seceding Southern states time to prepare for war. Nearly every armory, garrison, and weaponry stockpile in those states was seized by state militias and governments. History remembers Fort Sumter because it was the one major garrison *not* seized by the new Confederacy, being well manned and well supplied. (There were three smaller ones that the US Army was able to keep off the Florida coast when that state seceded.) Even there, Buchanan issued an order for Fort Sumter to be evacuated, one ignored by its commanders under pressure from Stanton and other Northern cabinet heads and congressmen. In the meantime Buchanan gave orders not to thwart British and other European merchant ships from their usual runs into Southern ports, so as not to anger any European power into allying with the Confederacy if hostilities started.

In his memoir, *Mr. Buchanan's Administration on the Eve of the Rebellion*, which was published in 1866, only a year after the Civil War ended, with most everyone on the continent weary of that war and probably angry as well, Buchanan defended all of his actions, blaming the war primarily on Lincoln's election and the young Republican Party and its accomplices, the abolitionists, which he said incited the South by being so forward about wanting to rid the country of slavery. He claimed to be a Unionist, which he probably was in theory, but being the man who was in charge of saving the Union, he refused to admit that he blew every opportunity to do what was necessary to preserve it.

It is essential to put any kind of ranking in context. To call Buchanan America's worst president, there has to be some historical standard. In his book, *Where They Stand*, author Robert W. Merry tries to put the best/worst presidential surveys of historians in that proper context by going back to see how voters viewed those presidents during their elections. This method could be slightly simplistic, to be certain, but it at least does try to give a contemporary perspective contrasting the experts' opinions of the presidents over time. Since most people go to the polls every four years only "ranking" the current presidential candidates against one another, it may not quite entirely solve the issue of where presidents rate against each other throughout history. Those voting in the 1932 election, for instance, may have thought Herbert Hoover the worst president for presiding over the beginnings of the Great Depression, but the election was only against Franklin Roosevelt, not Franklin Pierce or Rutherford B. Hayes or Martin Van Buren, so that is how the electorate "ranked" him.

Still, Merry makes the point that no matter what we voters—or even well-educated historians—may say about the forty-plus US presidents today, looking back on their achievements and failures, we should at least take into account what voters saw in their times. On the historian side, Merry cites eight major surveys of mostly academics, journalists, and other prominent president watchers. The three most prominent were two by historian Arthur M. Schlesinger Sr. (1948 and 1962), and one by Schlesinger's son, author and Democratic presidential advisor Arthur M. Schlesinger Jr. (1996). Merry adds other surveys from places like the *Wall Street Journal* and *Chicago Tribune* from 1981 to 2005, thus encompassing all of the presidents, save Barack Obama, in at least one. Each survey had its own parameters, but all generally asked their interviewees just to list the presidents in order of competence or "greatness."

Oddly enough, in the first surveys—the Schlesinger Sr. ones of 1948 and 1962—Ulysses S. Grant and Warren G. Harding came out as the worst two presidents and Buchanan only made the "below average" category. In all the subsequent surveys, however, Buchanan and Harding were always the worst (with Richard Nixon sometimes in their midst, but more for his corruption in Watergate than his actual deeds in office otherwise, like opening China and starting the Environmental Protection Agency, which historians admit would raise him in ranking). Harding, though, served only part of a term, dying in office after a little more than two years, so it is hard to rate what might have happened had he lived and completed at least one term, as Buchanan did. In the most recent large survey, conducted in 2014 and thus not part of Merry's book, the American Political Science Association polled its members and the survey of 162 of them put Buchanan squarely at the bottom—and only one other of the bottom five, Franklin Pierce, his predecessor, served a full term.

Many other presidents' ratings fluctuate wildly. Coolidge, a pro-business president of the first order, rates as one of the worst in the *Chicago Tribune* poll, from a more populist paper, but much better in the one conducted by the *Wall Street Journal*, which is decidedly business oriented. Jimmy Carter looks better to historians as time goes on; Grover Cleveland, on the other hand, gets progressively worse. In every survey, though, Lincoln, Washington, and Franklin Roosevelt are the top three, in various orders, though Lincoln is number one in all but the most recent, the *Wall Street Journal* poll, in which he falls to second to Washington. It may be that Buchanan's negatives are exacerbated by being the precursor to the man presumed to be the best president, but it may be a better case to say that Buchanan had made a situation so dire that it gave Lincoln a low bar to start with, though one he superseded easily.

"Best" is far more available to historians and laymen than "worst." Third graders know of the myths and highlights of the best—Lincoln's Gettysburg Address, Jefferson's hand in the country's major forming documents, Washington's river-crossing coin toss, FDR's "fear" and "infamy" chats, the national and international mourning after Kennedy's assassination. Garfield and McKinley were assassinated, too, though, and Franklin Pierce was said to have given magnificent speeches (some maybe written by his closest college friend, the most popular author of the time, Nathaniel Hawthorne). When looking historically, most Americans will think of only the presidents who fulfilled, or seem to have fulfilled, the dreams and challenges of leading the nation.

Merry then takes a more populist turn, making a statistically based analysis of presidential election results. Though it may be flawed because it is, again, simplistic, Merry does take a shot to put ranking presidents to the whims of the electorate. If a president wins two terms, he gets some sway, and the best is when he wins two terms and a member of his political party wins the subsequent election. Similarly, serving only one term, and especially getting defeated running for a second term, is a clear path to the negative. The theory is that in the end, contemporary voters may be best at deciding who deserves kudos, and they get a chance to weigh in at regular, four-year intervals. Some presidents get mixed ratings. Truman, for instance, gets plusses for his first term, a shorter one because he was completing Franklin Roosevelt's term after he died. He got minuses for his second, since he did not run in 1952* and Dwight Eisenhower, a Republican, won, reversing the party in the White House.

What is striking, though, is how often Merry's voter-driven contemporary rating comes out negative. Precious few presidents were of the highest rank—two terms followed by a member of their own party: Washington, Jackson, Franklin Roosevelt, Reagan. The consecutive early presidents Jefferson, Madison, and Monroe are somewhat in that group, but they were in office when there was no opposition party, and Republican Grant was followed by Republican Hayes, but Democrat Samuel Tilden actually won the election's popular voting and had to compromise it away in a House of Representatives deal over Reconstruction.

There are many presidents, though, at the bottom, in fact nearly half—one-termers followed by those in the other party: John Adams, John Quincy Adams, Martin Van Buren, John Tyler, James Knox Polk, Millard Fillmore, Andrew Johnson, Chester Arthur, Grover Cleveland twice, William Howard Taft, Herbert Hoover, Gerald Ford, Jimmy Carter, George H. W. Bush, and, of course, Buchanan.

The question then becomes: Do we elect men destined to fail, or at least disappoint? Is there something about the American evaluative methods that makes us attack, rather than praise, our ultimate leaders? I once spent a couple of days with historical filmmaker Ken Burns for a newspaper story. Among the questions I asked him was how he chose his subjects, and whether he saw a theme in them. He answered that the Great American Story is the Rise, the Fall, and the Resurrection. It is what, he said, Americans love to watch, read, or hear. We can see it in the modern age with, for instance, Herbert Hoover, Harry Truman, Jimmy Carter, and George H. W. Bush. Each rode a different, but differently

---

* He was legally able, exempted as he was from the Twenty-Second Amendment, passed in 1947, limiting presidents to two terms.

wonderful, road to the White House. Each left under if not duress, then grand disapproval. Each, later on, established himself as a humanitarian or an innovator, and certainly someone whose wisdom was appreciated both in public affairs and among average Americans looking for a latter-day hero.

Americans seem awfully hard on their presidents. There is not just criticism, but vitriol. Protestors did not just disagree with Richard Nixon, for instance, in the wake of the Vietnam War and Watergate, but seemed to really hate him. It has become particularly virulent in the social media age, where instant and ubiquitous commentary seemed to build against George W. Bush and Barack Obama at wearying rates. There is no shortage of people who have called these men, each of whom has a Harvard graduate degree and an Ivy undergrad one, "dumb." Americans are surely difficult on the men who have led what they believe to be the most glorious country in earthly history.

—◆—

The late David H. Donald, a Harvard history professor, Lincoln expert, and Pulitzer Prize winner for his biography of US congressman Charles Sumner, said that when he met John F. Kennedy just after he became president in 1961, Kennedy told him that he, Kennedy, resented that historians rated the presidents against each other.

"No one has a right to grade a president—even poor James Buchanan—who has not sat in his chair, examined the mail and information that came across his desk, and learned why he made his decisions," Kennedy said, according to Donald.

Clearly, even Kennedy, loath to have anyone else rate his predecessors, was singling out Buchanan as the White House cellar dweller. To Kennedy's point, though, there have been extraordinarily few real biographies of Buchanan, either popular or scholarly. In 1883, late enough for Buchanan's life and administration to have fallen into historical repose, George Ticknor Curtis wrote the first one, *Life of James Buchanan*, for Harper & Brothers. Buchanan's family let Curtis have access to papers no one had seen publically and would not, if at all, for decades. The *Life of James Buchanan* was 664 pages, substantial enough, and as dry as late nineteenth-century writing could be. The ghosts of the Civil War, ended eighteen years before, were certainly still around, but by that time most Americans would have attributed its legacy to Abraham Lincoln, or at least the man who had left the White House six years before, its final general, Ulysses S. Grant. Even Ticknor Curtis's biography, though, was a bit suspect, since Buchanan's family authorized him to write it and gave him those secreted Buchanan papers with which to do research.

It took another eight decades for the next substantial Buchanan biography to appear, this one by Philip S. Klein, a historian who taught at Pennsylvania State University and Franklin & Marshall College, the latter not coincidentally in the hometown of Klein and adopted home-town of Buchanan—Lancaster, Pennsylvania. *President James Buchanan*, published by the Penn State University Press in 1962, was basically an apologia for Buchanan. Klein was apparently smitten—in the historical sense—with his fellow Lancaster citizen. He saw Buchanan as unfairly besmirched by the Civil War, especially, but also as a man, or at least a politician, of his age. Most centrists, and even conservatives of that pre–Civil War era, Klein would note, were Unionists, but were quite aware that the two competing sections of the country, South and North, were distinct. Many from the North were upset that slavery existed but were willing to let it ride, hoping to restrict it to the Southern states where it was legal at the time, and hoping further that it would die out soon enough, just as it had decades earlier in the North.

While those who criticized Klein thought him naïve at best, his was nonetheless the standard for Buchanan studies, such as they were, from then on. John Updike said it was "my main text, source and guide" for his play *Buchanan Dying*, and for his novel that incorporates the Buchanan presidency, *Memoirs of the Ford Administration*. Updike admitted, though, that he was smitten with Buchanan like Klein was, growing up as he did in central Pennsylvania, and he likewise presents an admittedly fictional version of Buchanan in a rosier light than most.

The only other substantial biography, *James Buchanan*, was that by Jean H. Baker, a history professor at Goucher College, written in 2004 for the Times Books series of presidential biographies, edited by Arthur Schlesinger Jr. Given the imprimatur, there had to be a Buchanan book to round out the series, and Baker's book is in that vein—pretty much helping fill in that time until we could get to a real president, Abe Lincoln.

The keeper of the Buchanan flame, Patrick Clarke, the director of James Buchanan's Wheatland, the plantation-like estate Buchanan called home in Lancaster, said he felt that the tone for presidential biography was set in the 1950s, when a number of historians, in the wake of Franklin Roosevelt's domination of the history of the 1930s and 1940s, delved into presidential studies. Those historians pretty much stuck to the "best" Presidents: Lincoln, Washington, Jefferson, the two Roosevelts, and, secondarily, maybe Jackson and Madison.

Most critically acclaimed biographies were proponents of the Great Man theory—that people like Washington and Lincoln propelled history forward in a way dramatically different than if even a merely good person were in place.

"Most historians agree Buchanan was a failure," said Clarke. "As a result, why write about the losers? Presidential biographers don't seem to want to study the alleged failures—why did this happen, what did his peers do or could have done differently, what can we learn from the mistakes?" That may have been why David McCullough's biographies of John Adams and Harry Truman became surprise best sellers. McCullough made heroes out of the previously lesser regarded, but he found heroic elements in his subjects, a hard sell for Buchanan.

What is curious is that while he is in office, the president of the United States—and it was so even in Buchanan's time—is the most well-known and probably the most talked-about person in the United States, if not the world. Buchanan, though, quickly became a virtual unknown. Those looking for Ken Burns's "Rise, Fall, and Resurrection" scenario avoided Buchanan, perhaps because they could only see the Fall. He was so uniformly disliked even immediately after his term that when he retired to Wheatland, his Lancaster estate, sadly and almost comically, people would come to the grounds and write graffiti on the fences and buildings or throw rotten vegetables at the house. Lincoln generously offered Buchanan armed guards, something that is standard for ex-presidents today, but never before thought of until Lincoln's time. Buchanan, who had hoped to do a bit of traveling in his retirement, stayed in Lancaster more often than not for fear of his safety and, as well, sad that he was so little lauded and so broadly vilified. Both North and South quickly tired of the Civil War, and, just as quickly, partisans on both sides overwhelmingly found Buchanan primarily to blame for it.

Buchanan wanted to engage several of his younger political colleagues to help write his memoirs, but they were unwilling to cast their mentor in the good light he wished to inhabit. As mentioned, those memoirs, not so subtly titled *Mr. Buchanan's Administration on the Eve of the Rebellion*, basically blame the Civil War on the abolitionists. Buchanan writes that he, above anyone else, did the most to try to save the Union and defer war. It sounds odd to those looking back at the war, but that was actually a standard line of reasoning for Southern-leaning politicians like Buchanan, at least through the early 1850s, before the war itself started. They felt that reminding Southern slaveholders of the moral implications of slavery, beating them constantly with it as the abolitionists did, made them just want to leave the Union and have their own slaveholding country. The theory held little water after "the Rebellion," but the much-battered ex-president continued to use it anyway in his own defense. Buchanan had hoped for a retirement of glory. He did get a few crowds cheering him on the train and carriage ride home from the capital and Lincoln's inauguration, but the first shots had not been fired at Fort Sumter yet. Those crowds turned out to be pretty much the last he would see through to his death in 1868.

———

In his short section in *Where They Stand* on why he feels Buchanan was regarded so lowly by both historians in surveys and the voters of his time, Robert Merry, otherwise an author of muted words, comes out with flailing fists:

> *Long before he became president, Buchanan demonstrated that he lacked the character required for strong presidential leadership. His weakness wasn't grubby venality; he had made a tidy fortune as an effective Pennsylvania lawyer before going into politics, and he felt no need to seek financial gain through public office. Rather, Buchanan was a man of no fixed principles and no consistent political or personal loyalties. With ease he could flit from one position to an opposing one without so much as an explanation to those left behind. Any contorted rationalization could justify in his mind whatever actions he considered in his interest at any time. And, while he took pride in his personal incorruptibility, he was not above corrupting others in pursuit of his policy aims.*

Today, researchers at the various modern political fact-check and gotcha organizations would be all over a guy like Buchanan for his incessant waffling and backtracking. For instance, when he was James Knox Polk's secretary of state, he brazenly opposed Polk's demand for the vaunted latitudinal boundary of 54 degrees, 40 minutes, far into present-day Canada, as the northern reach of Oregon in negotiations with England to turn over that land. Then he wrote an official report showing why 54/40 was the best option. He then refused to support that argument and advocated a compromise. Then, finally, he went back to supporting 54/40 and would not bow to Polk's demand to advocate the final compromise on the forty-ninth parallel—the one Buchanan had originally sought—to the Senate.

Buchanan was equally equivocal in regard to the Mexican War. First he pushed Polk to accept only limited annexations of Mexican land and then opposed Polk's idea to have a big peace commission, fearing it would not ask for enough territory. Finally in this exasperating sequence, he opposed giving the Senate the eventual treaty because it would only allow the annexation of enough—though far, far more than he initially suggested—from Mexico.

It is not surprising that Polk, in his diary, frustratingly wrote of Buchanan, "I cannot rely upon his honest and disinterested advice."

Nor, frankly, could anyone trust what Buchanan would say, even at the most prominent moments. During his inaugural speech, in the most egregious example, he made a big point of saying he would accept whatever the Supreme Court decided on the *Dred Scott* case. It was an ultimately important case, determining whether the Fugitive Slave Law was valid. Scott was a slave who had lived with his owners in free states in the North; he sued for his freedom when they returned to Missouri, a slave state. The problem was that Buchanan knew exactly what the outcome would be because he influenced justices to vote in favor of approving the recapture of Scott, thus nullifying the Compromise of 1850, which was the shaky lynchpin holding together the Union, disallowing as it did, slavery north of Missouri. He had, in fact, convinced at least two Supreme Court justices to decide that Scott was always a slave, no matter where he traveled, appeasing his Southern friends and figuratively crossing his fingers that the outcome would put the arguments about slavery to rest. The *Dred Scott* decision, though, coming out two days after Buchanan's inauguration, appeased no one, and Buchanan's presidency started spiraling down from that early juncture, his lack of foresight in how the reactions to slavery in both North and South had become irrevocably inflamed by a *Scott* decision he thought relatively innocuous.

In fact, Buchanan might have been prescient not too many years before. In 1850 he prophesized in a speech that within four years, there would be two independent republics where one had stood for nearly four score years (as Lincoln would later talk about at Gettysburg). He said he would not want that to happen, but that it seemed almost inevitable, although he hoped without a war. As usual, he took his assessment back when challenged and said his goal was to keep the Union, no matter what. Yet his failure to do so is the major factor in not only making him our Worst. President. Ever., but perhaps making his administration, ironically enough, the most important one in forming the American political psyche, the last one before Emancipation, perhaps, but one whose residue is clearly found in the civil rights struggles and unending nature of racial politics that have lasted into the twenty-first century and may infect the country forever.

CHAPTER TWO

The Young Buck

LIKE OTHER WELL-PRESERVED RELICS OF THE ERA IN THE GROVE IN THE middle of the Mercersburg Academy campus, where it was moved more than a half century ago, the log cabin birthplace of James Buchanan still looks fairly normal. Given the setting, on the grounds of a boarding school, the cabin mostly seems like a place where Santa Claus might sit during the holiday season, or where some docent in nineteenth-century garb might stoke a fire, roast something in a kettle above it, and tell tales of courageous pioneers heading west from Philadelphia, a hundred miles or so distant.

In reality, few people come by to look, as they might with Mount Vernon or Monticello or even the home of a similarly obscure president like Martin Van Buren in Kinderhook, New York, or James Garfield in Mentor, Ohio. Mostly, when visited at all, it is by Mercersburg schoolkids, sneaking in or under its shadows to engage in some minor mischief.

For a few decades before the 1953 move, the cabin was in Chambersburg, the Franklin County seat, used as the home of the county Democratic Party. It became obsolete because it was too small and not easily retrofitted for better communications lines. Back on April 23, 1791, though, it was more or less state of the art, with Elizabeth Speer Buchanan, age twenty-four, giving birth there to the second of the eleven children she had with James Buchanan, whom she had married three years and a week before.

The cabin sat on the crossroads of Stony Batter, about three miles west of Mercersburg, already a somewhat thriving community not far north of the Maryland border—what was to become the vaunted Mason and Dixon Line—not too far from midway between Philadelphia and Pittsburgh. The elder Buchanan had come in 1783 to Pennsylvania from County Donegal, where he was born in 1761, to make his fortune, much like immigrants before and since, in what had only recently become the United States. He picked a wife: Elizabeth Speer, the twenty-one-year-old daughter of a Scotch-Irish merchant who lived near Buchanan's uncle, a tavern owner in York, just down the road toward Baltimore. Buchanan picked, also, a spot on the trail west, in the small town of Cove Gap, in a place there called Stony Batter, and set up a trading business, what might have been called a general store in later days. He had worked for a man named John Tom there first, but opened his store a bit farther into the gap, where the road was rough and anyone really trying to get from Baltimore or Philadelphia to Pittsburgh that way needed to buy a lot of supplies.

At least one account said that there were days that one hundred horse riders came through Buchanan's Stony Batter store, which, to be sure, is far more than those who venture daily about a mile into the state park to see the obelisk marking the site where the younger Buchanan was born. There are few signs announcing it and not much of a parking lot for visitors anyway. It is one of two memorials endowed by Harriet Lane, the younger Buchanan's favorite niece, the other being in Washington, DC, built long after the president's death. The rise around the Stony Batter monument is probably little changed from when Buchanan was born there. It would seem to take an ambitious and hardworking man to make a business work there, rough as the road is even in the twenty-first century.

Before long, though, life became a bit less hardscrabble for the Buchanans. James Senior first bought a substantial farm—costing £1,500, a good sum of money in those times—near Mercersburg, about four miles away and the largest town in the area with about one hundred families. Then, in 1796, he decided it was time to move into town, buying a two-story house on the main street, opening up a store, and, eventually, becoming one of the richest men in the area.

James the younger was the second born—an older sister had died as a baby—but certainly the most favored, since the next five of James and Elizabeth Buchanan's children were girls. This was not a feminist age, so the pressure was clearly on from the boy's early childhood, at least when the family got to the relatively populated village of Mercersburg, that James would have to carry the Buchanan family forward into the new American century.

What is known about Buchanan's early life comes generally from an undated memoir given to George Ticknor Curtis by Buchanan's family. Twice during his post-presidential years, Buchanan tried to get friends to write an official biography, but in each case it did not happen. Various relatives and friends had kept Buchanan's extensive letters and jottings, and in the early 1880s, more than a decade after his death, they employed Curtis, who had written other historical pieces, to write a biography. Curtis wrote that he took as his mission to use primarily these papers—not other interviews or histories—to write the book, which came to 644 pages and appeared in 1883 from Harper & Brothers, the New York publishing house. Curtis said he did not apologize for rarely quoting anyone else. Though the family had not instructed him about that, he felt he had enough material from them to write a credible, if not completely objective, biography.

There is no reason to believe the otherwise unpublished memoir given to Curtis is anything but Buchanan's work, for it displays the often dispassionate writing typical of the many letters he wrote throughout his working life. There are only a few sentences of description of his father, with whom he sometimes had difficulties, according to later biographers, but those sentences praise him as a substantial man.

"My father was a man of practical judgment, and of great industry and perseverance," wrote Buchanan in the memoir. "He had received a good English education, and had that kind of knowledge of mankind which prevented him from being ever deceived in his business.

"He was a man of great native force of character," Buchanan continued. "He was not only respected, but beloved by everybody who approached him. . . . He was a kind father, a sincere friend and an honest and religious man."

Buchanan, though, was much more effusive about his mother and her influence on him:

My mother, considering her limited opportunities in early life, was a remarkable woman. The daughter of a country farmer, engaged in household employment from early life until after my father's death, she yet found time to read much, and to reflect deeply on what she read. She had a great fondness for poetry, and could repeat with ease all the passages in her favorite authors which struck her fancy.

She was a sincere and devoted Christian from the time of my earliest recollection, and had read much on the subject of theology. For her sons, as they successively grew up, she was a delightful and instructive companion. She would argue with them, and often gain the victory; ridicule them in any folly or eccentricity; excite their ambition, by presenting to them in glowing colors men who had been useful to their country or their kind, as objects of imitation, and enter into all their joys and sorrows.

Buchanan said that his father had always hoped she would stop doing domestic chores after he had made a lot of money, but she would not stop. Buchanan wrote that his mother believed religiously that those chores were what she was born to do.

"She was a woman of great firmness of character and bore the afflictions of her later life with Christian philosophy," Buchanan wrote, even then lamenting losing her. "It was chiefly to her influence that her sons were indebted for a liberal education. Under Providence, I attribute any little distinction which I may have acquired in the world to the blessing which He conferred upon me in granting me such a mother."

Buchanan was not a mama's boy, though. Early on, he became sure that he would be a success as an adult, whatever route he chose. Colleges had started springing up in the hinterlands. Most of the schools that had started in the eighteenth century were pretty much the male version of finishing schools for the elite: Harvard, Yale, Princeton, William and Mary, the University of Pennsylvania, Queens College (which eventually became Rutgers). As the nineteenth century started, however, families of relative means—like the Buchanans—began to figure that "college," whatever that really meant in further education, was something they wanted for their sons.* The University of North Carolina, Muskingum University in Ohio, Davidson College, Oglethorpe University, Bowdoin College (which educated Franklin Pierce, Buchanan's predecessor), and others sprung up in the West, the South, and northern New England.

For those in south-central Pennsylvania, the school of choice became Dickinson College, and that is where Buchanan's father induced him to go when he turned sixteen years old and had finished his studies at Old Stone Academy in Mercersburg. Buchanan, though, thought Dickinson to be pretty much a joke. Perhaps due to his mother's insistence on his reading the classics, Buchanan breezed through classes. The version of "college" at the time was a three-year course of study, and Buchanan had already entered as a junior, which was then the term for the second year.

Buchanan was a bit of a wastrel at Dickinson—well, no, he was a big pain in the neck. He started his lifelong habit of cigar smoking there; actually, in later years he was known to chew the ends of unlit cigars, much in the way movie sharpies and gangsters did in the early days of the cinema. Whatever his mother taught him about the classics, she certainly did not emphasize humility. Buchanan viewed himself as beyond reproach at Dickinson. Everyone acknowledged that he was the smartest student, but the administration, at least, did not appreciate his arrogance and flouting of the school rules. Colleges, especially those striving to make it in the early days of the nineteenth century, depended on almost

---

* The first coeducational college, Oberlin, did not open until 1833.

jackbooted allegiance and discipline. Dickinson was on the outskirts of civilization, west of Mercersburg in Carlisle, just short of the Appalachians, where only adventurers really crossed. It needed its reputation whole, not filled with hijinks (or even rumors of them), in order to attract the sons of the monied, or at least the money of those paying for them.

When Buchanan got there, though, Dickinson was going through a rather rough patch. In fact, it was almost on the verge of going under. The school had been run out of its original building, one that had been a grammar school before Dickinson's founding in 1783, and so the founder, signer of the Declaration of Independence Benjamin Rush, got the most prominent architect in Pennsylvania, Benjamin Latrobe, the designer of the US Capitol, to lay out a glorious replacement building, New College, in 1803. Unfortunately, that winter, a wind-driven snow storm came through the Cumberland Valley, apparently picking up some ashes from New College's basement and subsequently burning it to the ground.

Rush and the first president of the college, Charles Nisbet, rose like phoenixes. They lured sympathy from the high-standing. Latrobe offered to design yet another building and Rush got his old Revolutionary buddies, Thomas Jefferson and James Madison, to donate some money for its construction. Nesbit, who sought good relations among the faculty, students, and administration above all, died shortly after and the town-gown détente died with him. The new president, Jeremiah Atwater, said all that recommended Carlisle, still out on the frontier of sorts, were the sordid pleasures "of high life, of parade, of the table & ball chamber . . . Drunkenness, swearing, lewdness & dueling seemed to court the day." Dickinson students joined the rabble. "[They were] indulging in the dissipation of the town, none of them living in the college," said Atwater as he took over. No one, he said, could "expect that a college could flourish without a different state of things in the town . . . I hope that as God has visited other states, he will yet visit Pennsylvania."

Buchanan, though sixteen and younger than many of his classmates, was ready for that type of challenge on his first real time away from home. He did not want to appear to be some kind of self-absorbed nebbish, and later wrote that "to be a sober, plodding, industrious youth was to incur the ridicule of the mass of the students.

"Without much natural tendency to become dissipated," Buchanan wrote, "and chiefly from the example of others, and in order to be considered a clever and spirited youth, I engaged in every sort of extravagance and mischief." Perhaps his shining moment in that regard was at a Fourth of July celebration in his first year, 1808, when he downed sixteen toasts at a Dickinson event.

Buchanan didn't worry about that part of his reputation, since he had done well in his studies, until he was home in Mercersburg one September Sunday morning, when someone came to the door with a letter that his father opened and then threw at him. Picking it up, he saw the writing of the most sober of Dickinson professors, history and Latin teacher Robert Davidson, kicking Buchanan out of school for disorderly conduct. Davidson wrote his father that James would have been expelled sooner, but his scholarship itself was so high that the trustees just had to wait it out a bit.

James, as we would say in the twenty-first century, freaked out. His father said he had only one choice: to supplicate to Davidson and the board and give up all his degrading behavior, at least until he graduated the next year. He went immediately to John King, the Presbyterian minister in Mercersburg and, as a Dickinson trustee, the man who had recommended Buchanan go there. Buchanan pledged calmness and sobriety if King would convince Davidson to rescind his dismissal. Davidson figured Buchanan had been scared straight, so the board let him back in, and Buchanan pulled his celebrating back a few notches for the year.

Yet when it came time for honors to be given for the graduating class—the biggest one being a speaker at the graduation ceremony—Buchanan was nixed by the trustees, even though he had the best grades in the class, for a student who was a bit more subdued and respected by the teachers personally. He wrote to his father in anger, but the old man was unmoved. Buchanan's dad told him to take his punishment and move on, but Buchanan, the bull head, decided to write a graduation speech anyway.

In the meantime, a friend who had been given the second honors—more or less what a salutatorian would have today—offered Buchanan his spot on the dais, a move that pleased neither the trustees nor Buchanan, arrogant as he was, who said he would not take a second-fiddle spot but wanted the first honor he thought he deserved.

In the end, on September 19, 1809, Buchanan got to speak as an official nonhonoree. He read his "The Utility of Philosophy" oratory in an extra slot between his friend and the third student in line in academics. Buchanan never did forgive Dickinson, writing later that he departed Carlisle "feeling but little attachment towards the Alma Mater." He must have known, though, that cleaning up his act while at Dickinson would serve him well as he went on to the next phase of his life, training for the law in the rambling town of Lancaster, the largest inland city in the United States, with a population of six thousand.

Buchanan's father had occasion to see the attorney James Hopkins of Lancaster in the court near Mercersburg and suggested to his son that he see if Hopkins would be his preceptor—an apprenticeship being the normal way of becoming a full-fledged lawyer. Hopkins did, indeed, accept the fellow who was the top academic student at Dickinson just down the road, and by December Buchanan had found a room at the Widow Duchman's Inn on fashionable East King Street, across the street from the mansion of his mentor, Hopkins, and only about two blocks from the courthouse.

While Buchanan did take advantage of the plethora of taverns near his boarding house, he also decided the two years he would be with Hopkins were a time to study the preceptor's courtroom and business style and the law itself. Buchanan prided himself, even to a fault—or many faults—on being a strict constructionist when it came to law, which he credited to his early studies at Dickinson and Lancaster.

Buchanan was not in Lancaster by chance. It was the capital of the commonwealth at the time and he had decided his career, while in name would be the law, would be, in reality, politics. Lancaster had actually been the capital of the United States for one day, September 27, 1777, when Congress escaped Philadelphia as the British approached. Congress then decided it was not far enough away from the British advance and moved on west to York the next day.

Lancaster was no half-baked place, however. The first asphalt-paved road in the United States was built from Philadelphia to there, designed by John Loudon McAdam, the Scottish engineer.* The Conestoga wagon, the seminal cloth-covered vehicle taking pioneers west, named for the Conestoga River that bisected the town, was manufactured in Lancaster. So was the Pennsylvania long rifle, invented by Lancaster's US congressman William Henry. Meriwether Lewis trained as a surveyor in Lancaster, and much later, in the 1870s, Franklin Winfield (F. W.) Woolworth opened his first general store in Lancaster.

Lancaster had perceived of itself—since at least the time of the Revolution—as the key to the West. It had boosters and promoters, bowing neither to Pittsburgh, perhaps the real key to the West, nor Philadelphia, which while now superseded by Washington politically was still far more important than the upstart Lancaster.

The doubt today that a village of six thousand inhabitants was in any way important forgets that the vastness of America was rural, and that the population of the whole country when Buchanan got to Lancaster was only five million—smaller than the population of twenty-three states in 2016, and about that of present-day Alabama. For a kid from Mercersburg and Carlisle, this was a boomtown, a place with people of means and a border spreading out.

In his field, the law, there was no better place to be other than maybe Philadelphia or New York. The commonwealth capital had business, politics, civil matters, and property law, all running out of the courthouse at King and Queen Streets. People came from all over to adjudicate their problems and would need local lawyers to solve them.

Buchanan agreed with his father's assessment of James Hopkins, especially when he saw that mansion across from his boarding house.

---

* Thus was the place from which the word "macadam" emanated.

He was only eighteen when he got to town, but he saw the future ahead of him, and after three years of grinding research and soliciting clients for his preceptor, in 1812 he passed the bar. The future seemed bright for the brightest twenty-one-year-old lawyer in the commonwealth capital.

But just as he was about to step out and start to roll, the commonwealth legislature voted to move the capital down the macadam a couple of hours to Harrisburg, the break point for river vessels coming from the south and land-only freight coming from the north along the strategic Susquehanna River. That made Harrisburg a better place for a trading center, a gathering place for businessmen who might better use a courthouse and legislative system at that spot. That was how state capitals seemed to be going—Trenton was that point on the Delaware; Richmond, on the James River; Hartford, on the Connecticut; Providence inland to the bay and its islands; Albany, on the Hudson.

Buchanan thought it almost a personal insult. He had done the groundwork diligently and here were these fool legislators mucking up a good system—for him, at least. He first went, though, to the man who had been his least sympathetic ear—his father. He scrambled back home to Mercersburg and, in his wailing about the move of the capital, caught his father off guard for a short time, perhaps because the elder Buchanan had seven children still at home to be concerned about.

His father had used some of his general-store profits to invest in land in the new western state of Kentucky, which had become romanticized by the adventures there of another Pennsylvania boy who tripped out West, Daniel Boone. The land, 3,600 acres, though, was tangled up in deeds, trust problems, and liens. The senior Buchanan thought he had a good lawyer down in Kentucky working on it, though the lawyer had been handling the issues more slowly than desired.

Young James was a cocky sort and saw an opening. He told his father he could personally solve those problems, and he quickly got a horse, riding down to Kentucky against his father's wishes. He told the older man he was going to Kentucky for his health, that it would be a vacation.

The father knew that was all hokum, but after two months of trying to dissuade his son, he gave up and hoped for the best.

When James got there, though, it was not the hayseed territory he thought. It was near the capital at Elizabethtown, and when he got to the courts, all the giants from the area were there—most significantly a man he would tangle with later in life, Speaker of the United States House of Representatives Henry Clay, and all his political associates. Buchanan was not quite in his element—and below water in theirs.

"I went there full of the big impression I was to make—and whom do you suppose I met?" Buchanan wrote later with the perspective of time burnishing his humility. "There was Henry Clay! John Pope, John Allan, John Rowan, Felix Grundy—why, sire, they were giants, and I was only a pygmy. Next day I packed my trunk and came back to Lancaster—that was big enough for me. Kentucky was too big."

The lawyer his father had employed told him not to worry, that it was all under control and his father would soon have clear title to the land. It was better handled locally, Kentucky being a state where personal contact mattered.

When Buchanan hightailed it back to Lancaster, he went back to his preceptor, Hopkins, asking him for a permanent job. Hopkins found him something even better—a government sinecure. The northern part of Lancaster County, which had been primarily rural, but full of land speculators who wanted to see it otherwise, was split off and made into a new county called Lebanon, after its main village.

The development gave politicians in Lancaster an opportunity to throw out some patronage, and Hopkins's good friend, Attorney General Jared Ingersoll, was in position to dispense it. Lebanon County was going to need a young, vibrant assistant prosecutor, and Hopkins, who did not really want the job himself, got Ingersoll to send it his protégé Buchanan's way. It was not a full-time job but earned Buchanan a base pay—perhaps $1,000 or $2,000 a year, enough to cover at least rent and board—and got him started on what to him was a surprising turn, a political career.

He had studied mostly property law under Hopkins. "I determined," he wrote later, "that if severe application would make me a good lawyer, I should not fail in this particular . . . I studied law, and nothing but the law." After studying, for a break he would walk out past downtown to the west, along an area called Chestnut Hill, and look into the sunset— perhaps into the future—and go over in "speeches" what he had taught himself during the day. Buchanan knew the area around Lancaster was growing and, not that he was particularly venal or mercenary, he wanted to make a good living through the law. Public office did not seem to be the way to do that, so he never professed an interest in it.

It turned out to be a good thing, since his meticulous records show that he made $938 in 1813, his first year of law practice, and a raise to $1,096 the next. The usual way for a young lawyer to get started—not too far different from those in individual practice in the twenty-first century—was to take whatever odd case an older lawyer would proffer his way. They were usually cases either too small or too inconvenient for an established lawyer, and no doubt Buchanan was happy to have whatever an established lawyer—either a mentor or a possible connection later— would hand off to him just to get started.

By 1814, though, the Lebanon County assistant prosecutor thought it was time to move it along. Buchanan would visit home every so often, and when he did he found himself talking politics with his father. Both of them professed to be Federalists, the party out of power, and complained about how the Madison administration was bungling the hostilities with Great Britain, the "War of 1812" already in its third year. The best news at home over those times was that his favorite sister, Jane, had gotten married to Elliot Lane, a man he liked. Though he wrote nothing about it, he probably came home to Mercersburg for the 1813 wedding ceremony.

Lancaster was a Federalist island in the Democratic sea that was Pennsylvania. George Washington had titularly been a Federalist, but in reality John Adams was the party's only president. With Alexander Hamilton, the party's rising star, killed in a duel with his Democratic rival Aaron Burr, the void of leadership was dissipating enthusiasm for

Federalist issues—primarily a strong federal bank and tariffs, which would finance infrastructure projects desperately needed in a growing nation. The young political leaders in Pennsylvania flocked to the Democrat-Republican Party of its heroes, Thomas Jefferson and James Madison, but Buchanan wanted to rise in his adopted town, so he threw in with the local Federalists, much as his father had. Later in his career, when he became a Democrat, he defended his Federalist youth by saying he was a product of his father's influence, an entirely excusable trait when it came to the citizenry—which then was still primarily monied white men—who would be voting.

Buchanan joined the Washington Association, which would have been much like the Young Republicans and Young Democrats of the current day. He had moved up to the presidency of the organization and, at a Fourth of July barbecue, gave a rousing speech that was deeply critical of Madison's seeming bungling of the war effort. Still, he said, Federalists should not shy away from getting into the fight to reverse the war's course.

Whether it was intended by Buchanan or just fortuitous, the speech got good notice from the older Federalists in Lancaster. On August 24 the British won a crucial battle at Bladensburg, outside of the nation's capital, and marched on Washington, burning public buildings, including the White House, with the Madisons barely escaping from the conflagration.

That same day, a Lancaster Federalist leader, Peter Diller, nominated young James Buchanan to be the Federalist candidate for the Commonwealth Assembly, and the twenty-three-year-old lawyer accepted. The nomination would be tantamount to election in November in the Federalist stronghold, and despite his father's consternation that he was giving up his concentration in property law for the vagary of politics, the son convinced his father that the connections he would make in Harrisburg would enhance his law practice.

The next day, August 25, there was a rally in downtown Lancaster for war volunteers. As the new prospective assemblyman, Buchanan gave a speech and became the first to sign up to be a volunteer in whatever regiment was going to mount itself out of Lancaster. Though they had no standing in either the federal army or the local or state militias, about two dozen young men from Lancaster, under the direction of another lawyer, Henry Shippen, got their horses, pistols, long arms, and swords and rode off to Baltimore as the Lancaster County Dragoons.

When they got there, Major Charles Sterret Ridgely, the Third Cavalry Regiment commander, asked for ten volunteers to go on what he told them would be a secret mission. The regulars, perhaps, would have found this to be code for a step backward, but the Lancastermen, whatever they thought of the war, envisioned the opportunity to become war heroes, valuable in politics, business, and party talk. The men excitedly riding in from Lancaster were eager, and Buchanan was at the front of the line to volunteer for the mission.

Ridgely told them to go to a point four miles from the city and then open his sealed orders. Shoulders slumped as they found out that Ridgely wanted them to seize—read that *steal*—about sixty good horses in the outlying town of Ellicott Mills, "always preferring to take them from Quakers," who presumably hated the war the most and needed to suffer for it.

Buchanan and his fellow future horse thieves hoisted their tents for the night as a deluge of rain came, soaking Buchanan, who drew the proverbial short straw and got the bunk next to the porous tent wall. The next day, they rounded up the required horses, angering the populace of Ellicott Mills, no doubt, and started marching them back to Baltimore. There, as they paraded down Market Street, the Lancaster volunteers who had managed to avoid going on the secret mission greeted them with loud laughter—the "heroes" losing a bit of their enthusiastic standing. By early September, after the famed Fort McHenry bombing by the British, which inspired observer Francis Scott Key—a young lawyer like Buchanan—to write "The Star-Spangled Banner," the British left Baltimore and the Lancaster County Dragoons, their dreams of war heroism deflected, but all their limbs attached, went home.

His war service was, perhaps mercifully, short, and Buchanan easily won his first real election, but as usual, there was the inevitable note from his father seeing the dark when everything to him was bright: "I hope you will make the best of the thing now," wrote the elder Buchanan. "I am fearful of this taking you from the bar at a time when perhaps you may feel it most."

Still, Buchanan took off for Harrisburg for the three-month legislative session with his usual youthful upbeat thoughts. When he got there, though, he found that the Pennsylvania Assembly was not the glorious body he might have thought. There were a lot of local petitions and because the commonwealth's courts were so ponderous and piled up with cases, many of those petitions were asking for private bills, their constituents figuring they had a better chance of personal legislation than a victorious or swift court case.

Buchanan, though, wanted to see through the morass. He discovered quickly that those in the assembly who got noticed were the men who delivered speeches, not necessarily the grinds who got those petitions moved to the floor. There were those who could speak off the cuff, but Buchanan decided he would craft his speeches, leaving nothing to chance. He chose immediately to be a bit controversial.

Though the War of 1812 was almost over, Philadelphia still worried about being attacked again by the British. The United States Congress had rejected a bill that would have had some sort of universal conscription, but the Pennsylvania Senate decided the federal government could not defend the city's port properly and passed its own conscription legislation. The scheme was that all the commonwealth's men age twenty-one and over would be divided into groups of twenty-two. One of those men would be drafted and the other twenty-one would ante up to pay for a $200 "bounty purse" to pay for the unlucky conscript.

Buchanan rose in the assembly on February 1, 1815, and attacked the legislation, suggesting instead that the militia from the commonwealth be entirely voluntary. It looked like the British did not have their hearts in continuing the war anyway—in fact, peace came two weeks later—and to expend such effort to defend Philadelphia should not be part of the commonwealth's agenda.

Though he had hardly planned it to be so, the speech turned out to be an auspicious introduction to the larger world of politics for young Buchanan, and would have repercussions for the rest of his political life. Buchanan had wanted to make clear the Federalist view of the war, and was concentrating on this bill alone.

When it came down to the reality and the debate, though, the speech was like a stone thrown into the lake, with ripples pulsing out farther and farther. This new member of the assembly had taken on Philadelphia, the real seat of power in the commonwealth. That meant also that he was firmly putting the interests of the western part of the commonwealth over the rich and powerful eastern section. Further, he was championing the poor over the rich entirely—a poor man could not pay the "bounty purse" and would have to be the one in the twenty-two to serve.

It is hard to believe Buchanan's speech was calculated to be so populist, but it set him apart from most of the Federalists, who, despite otherwise being against the war, would rather have seen men be able to pay a fee if they did not want to serve and, further, would want Philadelphia defended, since that was not only the seat of the Bank of the United States, but also, with New York, one of the two largest merchant centers in the new country.

According to Buchanan's own private papers given to his authorized biographer George T. Curtis, the Democratic state senator from Mifflin County, William Beale, probably in deep sarcasm, saw the speech as being so far from the usual Federalist stance that he suggested Buchanan join his party at once, thus not having to change his principles and views one bit.

Buchanan, who had thought he would be making at least a splash of some grandeur, was mortified. When the measure came to a vote in the assembly, he was absent. Fortunately, the issue died when peace was declared with England those few weeks later. That was the only speech Buchanan made in the term, and he even doubted himself, a rare occurrence, and decided not to run again. His father, true to his contrary nature, said to forget the speech and its effects and re-up for the assembly. This time his father was the more optimistic, saying that having another term would enhance his chances to go to the US House of Representatives. He would always have opposition, but the best course was to regroup, refresh, and move onward.

Buchanan was overjoyed at the unexpected kudos from his father. As part of the beginning of his new campaign for the assembly, he went back to the Fourth of July rally for the Lancaster Washington Association, held in front of the courthouse. That was Buchanan's neighborhood. His boarding house was only down the street, and his office was kitty-corner from the big public square on which the courthouse sat. He and Lancaster's prothonotary, John Passmore, a mountain of a man at about four hundred pounds, had bought the building where they both had offices and apartments, not to mention a small tavern below, for $4,000 in cash the year before, with a mortgage of another $1,000. Chances are his father fronted him the money, much as a father would in modern times.

This was going to be his real coming-out party. Buchanan was well prepared this time. He would be, he believed, preaching to the converted. This would be an audience, he felt sure, that would treat him with kindness, a local boosterish crowd.

❦

The portraits of Buchanan in his later years make him appear to be a stuffy man, starched collars and dour looks, not a smile or a looseness about him ever. That is probably more a sign of the age—painted portraits being formal and photographs taking a long time to produce, thus needing the subjects to sit motionless. There are not, for instance, portraits of Lincoln giddily giggling or Robert E. Lee or Ulysses S. Grant riding sidesaddle with a skewed hat. The stiff later Buchanan runs against all physical descriptions of him as a young man.

Buchanan was said to be distinguished looking, with blue eyes, wavy blond hair, and broad shoulders. He apparently had a disease that prevented him from developing body or facial hair. That would not have done him much good in the age of the bearded presidents of the later nineteenth century (Lincoln, Grant, Garfield, Hayes, Benjamin Harrison), but clean-shavenness was the order of his day. He had a sonorous, deep voice and a quick gait. He was at least six feet tall, which was not quite a giant in those days, but just the right above-average height for a sturdy man.

Besides his lack of body and facial hair, he had one other odd physical attribute. He was nearsighted in one eye and farsighted in the other, and was also a bit wall-eyed, his pupils wandering sometimes as he tried to stare. Thus, he often cocked his head when talking to others—just so he could see them better—which gave the impression that he was so interested in them he needed to get close. His second biographer, Philip Klein, who sincerely thought Buchanan's reputation had been besmirched over the years, wrote that this physical gesture was "a perpetual attitude of courteous deference and attentive interest. The mere appearance conveyed so definite an impression of assent and approbation that many people, on early acquaintance, sincerely believed that they had completely captivated James Buchanan and reciprocated by attentions to him which he attributed to traits more complimentary to him than a wry neck. Partly because of this physical peculiarity, Buchanan made a good 'first impression' on almost everybody he met."

Buchanan's reputation as he prepared to speak on July 4, 1815, was solid. His strength as a lawyer was that he knew the law. He did not show off his intelligence, but his stick-to-itiveness. He was well prepared when others were haphazard, tireless when others would tend to slack. He was also the epitome of the "hale fellow, well met" in social situations. He was never too forward, nor would he recede into the crowd. He was fond of cigars, the blacker the better, and drank maybe a little more than he should have, but only a little, mostly Madeira, which was the drink of the colonies, so perfect for a Federalist.

The speech he planned was the speech he gave, in both word and spirit. He was not thinking about, as Senator Beale from Mifflin County had chided, converting to Democrat-Republicanism, and his verbiage could have been that of any presidential candidate in a primary fight in the modern era. It was full of invective, partial truths, and over-the-top partisanship. He called his opponents "demagogues" and "functionaries," "friends of the French" who were plagued with "diabolic passions." He even claimed the Democrats did not believe in the Constitution because they formed their party calling themselves the "anti-Federalists."

The Democrats, he said, were the party of anarchism. They had disbanded the navy when they took power in 1800, thus leaving merchant ships unprotected, and went further to kill off commerce by their insistence on embargos. They attacked the Bank of the United States, further weakening the formation of businesses, and stopped the national tax, which provided for the young country's infrastructure.

As a final proverbial nail in the coffin, Buchanan shouted, they declared war, a war they could not finance. Instead of our natural allies being brought close to the breast, the English were the bad guys and the Democrats gave themselves over to the wastrel French. Napoleon Bonaparte was the titular leader of the Democratic Party, and James Madison served to profit personally from the alliance.

To propel the war forward, the United States had to borrow, and since it was desperate, the rates were usurious. Indignity followed as Washington itself was invaded and set aflame.

"The very capital of the United States, the lofty temple of liberty, which was reared and consecrated by Washington, has been abandoned to its fate by his degenerate successor, who ought to have shed his last drop of blood in its defense," said Buchanan, moving ever deeper into hyperbole. "Thanks to Heaven that we have obtained a peace, bad and disgraceful as it is. Otherwise, the beautiful structure of the federal government, supported by the same feeble hands, might have sunk, like the capitol, into ruins." He called Thomas Jefferson's ideas wild projects and sarcastically referred to him as a "philosophic visionary."

For local politics, the speech was a success, with the Washington Association printing copies of it and sending it around the commonwealth. Buchanan got his renomination and reelection, but also the enmity of the Jeffersonians, the Democrats particularly of Lancaster County and nearby.

His father, once again, took the contrary stance. He wrote his son that he was a bit too severe in his putting down of the Democrats. His father reminded Buchanan that he had friends in the opposite party and that Lancaster was too small to let those associations drift apart.

This time it might not have mattered, since he was going to be elected as a Federalist. But that party was dwindling in influence. Buchanan would be ready for that, but this speech and the reputation he set for himself that day would serve him ill later on, the Democrats from the commonwealth having long, long memories.

In any event, his assembly career came to an end the following year. Tradition among the Lancaster Federalists was that someone served at most two terms and then ceded his place to someone else—in this case it was his friend Jasper Slaymaker. Buchanan had started to become as exasperated with the Federalists as he was with the Democrats. The former seemed to always want to protect the rights of the rich and the latter appeared to him to be always looking to stir the rabble. He needed time away from politics for that reason—and also to devote some time to law work, as his working capital was still rather low.

Buchanan started plugging away at his law practice, becoming as much of a general practitioner as anything else. His reputation stayed as it was when he was a young apprentice—he studied every issue meticulously and always came to court well prepared. He was not flashy, but in any case where he had a chance, he usually won. Eventually, as fortune would have it, he got a case that put him on the star track.

Because judgeships were generally lifetime appointments, there were still many Federalists on the bench, especially in the higher commonwealth courts, left over from the Washington and Adams presidential years. When Jefferson and Madison came to power, though, the Democrats targeted the courts, knowing that their most prized legislation could easily be overturned by vestigial Federalist judges.

So the Democrats took another tack: figuring out how to prove those judges did not display the "good behavior" necessary to keep their lifetime appointments, thus making them eligible for impeachment. One of those judges was Lancaster-based Walter Franklin. Since Lancaster was still Federalist territory, getting a Federalist judge out and replacing him with a Democrat would be a coup.

With the war against Great Britain still raging, the Pennsylvania militia was amalgamated into the federal army, but in July 1814 a young Lancaster man named Houston decided he did not want to serve. The Pennsylvania militia court-martialed him and he was convicted, but he appealed to Franklin's court and the Federalist judge ruled that since the Pennsylvania militia had by that time become part of the federal service, it had no authority to try young Houston.

The case went all the way to the United States Supreme Court, which overturned the verdict, and in 1816 the state legislature, which had turned Democrat decisively by that point, impeached Franklin.

Looking for a lawyer who could win his case, Franklin settled on Buchanan. It would have been unusual even in those times for a judge to throw his chances to save his reputation to a twenty-five-year-old lawyer, but there were at least three possible reasons, according to Buchanan's advocate biographer, Philip Klein. The easiest is that the two were apparently friends from being downtown Lancaster neighbors and fellow Federalists. When he was in the Pennsylvania Assembly, Buchanan had been consternated about the Democratic witch hunts of judges. Buchanan throughout his life claimed to be a strict constructionist when it came to the Constitution. He had his slippages later on, especially as president, but clearly he saw the separation of the three branches of government in this case being violated horribly by the legislature. Finally, Buchanan had only recently left the legislature himself and Franklin knew Buchanan was well liked personally by members of both parties.

Buchanan kept to the separation of powers argument and did not indict anyone personally in his defense of Judge Franklin. He noted that the case against Judge Franklin was brought only because the Democrats did not like his decision, not because they could find him derelict in making it. His fairly dispassionate argument was a popular winner. The impeachment managers had the trial adjourned for several weeks before they came back and gave a weak prosecution, so the state senate had no choice but to acquit Franklin.

Still, there was a bull's-eye on Franklin's judicial robes. In February 1817 the Pennsylvania Assembly again impeached Judge Franklin, this time because he had ruled that two Lancaster lawyers were able to keep a $300 judgment they had won for a plaintiff, since they were owed that amount as legal fees. Buchanan brought in his old mentor, James Hopkins, to help him after the lower house voted two to one against Franklin, and together they convinced the state senate to acquit him.

It did not take long for the legislature to target Judge Franklin again, another impeachment about a decision, not about Franklin's character or malfeasance. This time, Buchanan really did get lucky. The assembly and the senate got into a snit over who had precedence over which chamber would host the impeachment. It got so rowdy that at one point, the assembly members stormed the senate chambers, some members even climbing through the windows, to disrupt senate business, even just to shout at each other.

When things calmed down a few weeks later, the impeachment got started, but by that time Judge Franklin had become a minor player, and the legislators were more concerned about their own infighting. Buchanan won Judge Franklin's third acquittal in a breeze.

While the publicity surrounding the three impeachments certainly shined up Buchanan's legal reputation, Judge Franklin's fees made him more than solvent. Buchanan's income in 1815 was a decent $2,000. In

1818, the year of the last trial, it had quadrupled to $8,000. This put him in the pantheon of the Lancaster legal community—an aesthetic and financial success while still in his mid-twenties.

Buchanan had stepped up far further than even his father would have imagined. His mother might have wanted him to become a minister, but as much as he admired her, he was quite happy to have chosen law. He was ready to take the next step, whatever that might turn out to be, and that might take him farther from Lancaster than his current observers would have predicted.

When he was in the assembly and soon after, Buchanan would end the day often with a visit to one of the local downtown Lancaster taverns. As would be with a young professional in the modern day, he was most comfortable with the age-appropriate members of his profession. He admired those whose station was a little higher than his, like his first Lancaster friend, Jasper Slaymaker, whose family had become wealthy in business and speculation, and Amos Ellmaker, who had gone to prestigious Yale University in Connecticut and then came to study with James Hopkins alongside Buchanan.

One of Ellmaker's friends from Litchfield, a town nearby Yale where he had studied law initially, was Molton C. Rogers, the son of the governor of Delaware. Rogers, according to Patrick Clarke, the director of Wheatland, the mansion that was the last home of Buchanan in Lancaster, "was born with a silver spoon in his mouth and was already tied to the high society crowds of Lancaster and Philadelphia," as was Slaymaker.

Not necessarily because of that, Buchanan decided to form a sort of partnership with Rogers in 1816. They had become close from eating at the same "bachelor mess," a loosely organized men's dining club, and found each other's views on life to be similar, even though they came from different upbringings. According to Clarke, Rogers was from money and tone, "but Buchanan was not. Buchanan was from mountain stock. His father was successful to a degree. He was not wealthy like Rogers and his crowd. He had eleven kids, with a lot of mouths to feed. He made an OK living, but, well, he was a grocer."

Rogers and his crowd were happy to bring Buchanan along. Rogers moved his practice into Buchanan's East King Street building and, in turn, got him accepted to, such as it was, Lancaster society. By October Buchanan was one of the managers of the annual Lancaster society ball. The next month, Rogers and John Reynolds, an officer of the Farmers Bank, sponsored him for the Masonic lodge, to which he was initiated in December. The Masons, a somewhat secretive organization, were instrumental in politics and business relationships. George Washington was a Mason, as were many of the Founding Fathers and presidents down through the centuries. Buchanan stayed with the organization for the long term, eventually becoming deputy grand master in his district.

Soon Buchanan's social scene changed from the back rooms of taverns to the parlors of the fashionable and wealthy in Lancaster and sometimes Philadelphia. His earnings increased, and the reputation of his masterful maneuverings for a respected judge made him a prized invitee. There is little doubt that he was probably seen as Lancaster's most eligible bachelor, and many of his invitations were no doubt to have families introduce their marriageable daughters to him.

About a year after the two men formed their business partnership, Rogers started dating Eliza Jacobs, the daughter of Cyrus Jacobs, whose fortune came from iron works. Eliza's brother was a student of Buchanan, as Buchanan had become one of the go-to lawyers to whom to apprentice in town. One day, Rogers suggested that Buchanan escort Eliza's cousin, Ann Caroline Coleman, to a party, and Buchanan accepted without hesitation.

The grocer's son had just stepped up to the big prize. Ann Coleman's father, Robert, was one of the richest men in the United States. Like Buchanan's father, he had emigrated from Ireland in the mid-eighteenth century, getting his start as a laborer and clerk for an ironmaster in Reading, a bit north of Lancaster, and marrying the master's daughter. By the time John Adams was president, Coleman owned a half dozen iron businesses and was probably one of the young country's first self-made millionaires.

By all accounts he was obsessively possessive of his daughter. She was said to be gorgeous and mercurial—sometimes sedate and sometimes a wild child. She was twenty-two when she met Buchanan, which at the time was getting along as an unmarried woman. Robert Coleman, who had come from nothing, was not going to let his daughter make some disadvantageous marriage. His oldest daughter—he had four daughters and five sons—had married Judge Joseph Hemphill of Philadelphia, who had served in Congress before his judicial appointment. When Ann started getting serious about Buchanan, Coleman, now seventy-one, was none too sure he was the right choice.

Buchanan seemed to have his doubts as well, not so much about Ann, but about whether he was meant for the then nouveau riche. The American wealthy were still trying to figure themselves out. This was hardly England, Spain, or France, with barons and earls, fortunes of centuries' standing, and rigid rules about who could even come into contact with whom. It was not as if Buchanan had to slay a dragon or find some royal blood within to jump up a bit in society, but he surely did not know whether he was comfortable being treated to so much when he came to someone's mansion party, and not have the means to treat back. The Coleman family's influence was widespread over eastern Pennsylvania, so sometimes the invitations spanned days, with feasts and parties constantly. Buchanan liked it for the time being, but he knew if he married Ann Coleman, he would have to be the instigator for some of these galas, not just the recipient.

Nonetheless, Buchanan asked Ann to marry him in the summer of 1819, just as his buddy Molton Rogers became engaged to Eliza Jacobs. The news of both potential unions buzzed Lancaster. Would there be a double wedding? Would one of the families try to outdo the other? Would one of the young lawyers abandon the law and go into iron instead? Word was, though, that the Colemans were dubious of their potential son-in-law. Coleman was a trustee at Dickinson College and knew well of Buchanan's untoward reputation there. A strict and hard-working man, he also may not have liked the antics of Buchanan and his young friends in Lancaster, who drank a lot, reveled in practical jokes, and often spent their money unwisely.

Still, Buchanan continued his courtship. In late 1819, though, the country went into a financial panic. Buchanan, back to being a property lawyer, was snowed with work, as land was bought and sold quickly and bankruptcy and foreclosure proceedings filled the courthouses. Buchanan was doing a lot of work with the Farmers Bank and a friend there, William Jenkins. He was back and forth to Philadelphia frequently, putting a crimp in his partying in Lancaster with his betrothed.

His political scene was in disarray as well, since the Federalist Party was dwindling in popularity. For the first time, Buchanan got involved in a national issue, getting on a party committee with Jenkins and his preceptor, James Hopkins, to try to convince the commonwealth's members of Congress to vote against the intended Missouri Compromise, which would allow Maine to break off from Massachusetts and become a free state, but allow Missouri to come into the Union a slave state. This was Buchanan's first public stand against slavery, in fact his first public stand on anything nationally controversial.

Gossip being what it always is, and certainly so in the high-society circles that had time to think about such things, Buchanan was taking a hit from some of the cattier women in Lancaster. One of those women pulled out her claws and wrote to her husband that "Mr. Buchanan did not treat [Ann Coleman] with that affection that she expected from the man she would marry, and in consequence of his coolness she wrote him a note telling him that she thought it was not regard for her that was his object, but her riches."

Ann did write with that sentiment to Buchanan, which flummoxed him. He figured that if he dropped business and rushed to daily courting again, he would fall prey to having people, including Ann, believe he was only out for her father's fortune, so he apparently wrote to her only that he was sorry, but business was tough, that he apologized for his absence but hoped she understood that he was innocent of those money-grubbing charges.

Then came the cataclysmic event that today might find its way to the public via BuzzFeed, TMZ, or *Entertainment Tonight*. At the end of November, returning from out of town, Buchanan stopped by casually to see the Jenkins family before going home. While he was there he met Mrs. Jenkins's sister, Grace Hubley, who was visiting. Needless to say, Grace was indeed graceful and pretty; had she been old and haggard, perhaps the fate of America forty years from that day would have changed considerably.

Instead, someone told someone who told Ann Coleman about Buchanan's alleged eyeing of Grace Hubley, and she became incensed that Buchanan would have stopped off anywhere before seeing her, but certainly not someplace such a woman as Grace Hubley would be. Ann immediately fired off a letter breaking off the engagement—a letter supposedly delivered to Buchanan at the courthouse, where he was said to turn pale. His feelings shattered, he did nothing immediately.

Ann was apparently upset, though, and decided to go, at the suggestion of her mother, with her younger sister, Sarah, to see their older sister, Margaret, who had moved to Philadelphia. They left Lancaster on December 4, but she caught a cold on the way to Philadelphia, where she had hoped to see some plays and operas. Apparently she did not, mostly just resting at her sister's place.

Two days later, Buchanan got a settlement in a big case, saving the Columbia Bridge Company, a business in which several of his friends had an interest. This was on a Monday, and Buchanan apparently had business to fill the week, but may well have thought he would try to get back in good graces with Ann by the weekend.

That was never to be, however. Thursday morning, Buchanan heard the news that convulsed Lancaster and Philadelphia—Ann Coleman was dead. Judge Thomas Kittera, a friend of the Colemans, and later of Buchanan, wrote this in his diary:

At noon yesterday [December 8] I met this young lady on the street, in the vigour of heath, and but a few hours after[,] her friends were mourning her death. She had been engaged to be married, and some unpleasant misunderstanding occurring, the match was broken off. This circumstance was preying on her mind. In the afternoon she was laboring under a fit of hysterics; in the evening she was so little indisposed that her sister visited the theatre. After night she was attacked with strong hysterical convulsions, which induced the family to send for physicians, who thought this would soon go off, as it did; but her pulse gradually weakened until midnight, when she died. Dr. Chapman . . . says it is the first instance he ever knew of hysteria producing death. To affectionate parents sixty miles off what dreadful intelligence—to a younger sister whose evening was spent in mirth and folly, what a lesson of wisdom does it teach. Beloved and admired by all who knew her, in the prime of life, with all the advantages of education, beauty, and wealth, in a moment she has been cut off.

Since there was never a public autopsy, there was no evidence of Ann Coleman committing suicide, though Judge's Kittera's mention that her doctor had never seen any case of hysteria causing death certainly leads to a suspicion that she might have taken her own life. In any case, there was clearly talk that whatever the clinical circumstances of Ann's death, many blamed it on Buchanan and his apparent neglect of his affections.

It is clear that the Colemans must have felt that way. Buchanan wrote them a heartfelt note, which read in part, "It is now no time for explanation, but the time will come when you will discover that she, as well as I, have been much abused. God forgive the authors of it . . . I may sustain the shock of her death, but I feel that happiness has fled from me forever." Apparently, the Colemans never saw those words, since they refused the note when it was delivered by a messenger and sent it back unopened. Buchanan asked to see her corpse and walk with her casket as a mourner, but the Colemans refused him. He bunked in with Judge Franklin, his erstwhile client, who lived next door to the Colemans, but even the judge could not shake the Colemans' disdain of Buchanan. Buchanan tried to write a memorial to Ann to appear in the local paper, but in the end he was overcome with grief and Judge Franklin composed a rather mundane one for him.

For the rest of December, Buchanan laid low. He visited his home in Mercersburg and, most likely, took a little break from work, the courts slowing for Christmas and the New Year anyway. He may have been mourning or regrouping or seething that the Colemans were so cold to him.

He must have known, even then, that this would be a turning point in his life. He would have to recover both from Ann's death and from the whispers about him that flew around Lancaster and Philadelphia. Strangely, though, in the end Ann Coleman's death may have led him down a path he might otherwise not have trod.

For those who have picked up this book, it is probable that they have given at least a passing thought to James Buchanan and the other men who have reached the presidency. I got the bug early—mostly because I had a bug.

Actually, it was tonsillitis, and I was not yet to my fifth birthday. The doctor who was going to take those vestigial inflamed tonsils out of me sent me to the huge municipal hospital in Philadelphia, where I was placed in a room packed with cribs. It was the 1950s and the babies of the baby boom seemed all to be getting their tonsils out at once.

My father, an American history buff, had already taken me to the Liberty Bell and Independence Hall and a few other minor halls nearby—Carpenters' Hall, basically a union meeting place, was my favorite, mostly because no one else ever seemed to be visiting there—in Philadelphia's Independence National Historical Park. One of the first books he bought me was a Disney version of *Ben and Me*, where an absentminded Ben Franklin was guided in his discoveries and diplomacy by Amos the mouse, who rode in Franklin's hat and told him how to handle fellows like "Red"—Amos's name for Thomas Jefferson, based on Jefferson's red hair. Dad and I also visited Christ Church, which Ben and Red and General George Washington attended when they were in Philly. Amos, the fictional mouse, grew up there with his siblings "poor as church mice," Amos said. "In fact, we were church mice." Amos was one of twenty-six children, the oldest, his name beginning with A. So, he had to go out to seek his fortune, eventually finding Ben. Those who go to the Franklin printing shop re-creation on Market Street in Philadelphia can, if they look closely in a crack in the brick wall, see a gray mouse head sticking out.

I had to wait in that children's ward for several days while the inflammation subsided, and one morning, my father came to see me with a big smile. Knowing I also had become a sports fan—starting to memorize the statistics of every Philadelphia Phillie baseball player—he handed me what is still the favorite book I have ever received, *Facts About the Presidents*, compiled by Joseph Nathan Kane. Its pages are not just yellow, but burnt sienna now. It could have been the tablets from Mount Sinai and not influenced me more.

In its pages, which—given when I got it—only go up to Dwight Eisenhower, are stats and quick anecdotes and little almost-nothings about The Guys, as my father and I called them. There are birth and death dates not only of the presidents, but of the first ladies and vice presidents and parents and children of The Guys. The statistics are all over the place, almost willy-nilly. "Nine of 33 had fathers who married twice." "Two of 33 were posthumous children." Causes of death: "Wilson—Apoplexy, paralysis . . . Jackson—Consumption, dropsy . . . T. Roosevelt—Inflammatory rheumatism." Relative longevity of the presidents and their parents: "J. Adams—90 years, 247 days; 70 years, 106 days; 98 years, 43 days . . . Monroe—73 years, 67 days;" and then the unfound parents' ages still listed but left like this "____; _____."

Kane gave me a visual place to go: "Hayes—Height 5 feet 8½ inches; weight 170 pounds; dark brown hair; sandy red beard; deeply set blue eyes; large head, high forehead, straight nose, curling brows; mild but very audible voice." Or the biggest of The Guys, "Taft—Height 6 feet; huge frame; weight 300–332 pounds; deep-set eyes; ruddy complexion; turned-up mustache." And an idea of their secret passions and hobbies: "Poker—Harding, Truman . . . Jujitsu—T. Roosevelt . . . Indian clubs—Coolidge . . . Mechanical horse—Coolidge . . . Pitching hay—Coolidge." Even a five-year-old could appreciate how nutty this seemed, a president who loved pitching hay, riding a mechanical horse, and throwing Indian clubs, but, then, a few pages away was the notation that Coolidge was also the only president born on July 4—to the White House born, so to speak.

Dad had me hooked. Yes, he took me to ball games and theater, but anyone might go there. We didn't travel much, but when we did, there was no historical marker he didn't stop at and have me read with him. When I was ten he had some business in North Carolina, and we went there over Christmas vacation, stopping along the way at Civil War sites then celebrating the war's centennial.

On the way back he headed northwest to the town of Staunton, Virginia, so we could go to Woodrow Wilson's birthplace. We got up to the door, my father almost salivating at the thought of visiting someplace he had never dreamed he would get to.

The door was locked.

Crestfallen, my father went to the side of the building, where there was a note on the side door. The birthplace was closed because, that very day, December 28, 1961, Edith Bolling Galt Wilson, the president's eighty-nine-year-old widow, had died and the place was in repose in her memory.

Undeterred by his bad luck, my father motored across the Blue Ridge highlands the ninety minutes or so to Charlottesville. Before we could visit Ash Lawn, James Monroe's house, or Monticello, Jefferson's estate, my father had his own personal mission. We headed directly to the University of Virginia library and bounded up to the collections room. No visitors were there but we two, my mother opting to stay in the library lounge. My dad had his big box camera at his side and went immediately to the librarian in charge.

"I'm Judge Strauss from New Jersey, and I need to see President Jefferson's will and photograph it," he said, then invoking the name of a judge he knew in Virginia, or at least a judge he said he knew, as a reference.

The incomprehensible burbling from the librarian's mouth somehow indicated this was not something the library was supposed to be doing. My father's agitated reference to the Virginia judge over and over again—I think even I was laughing a bit at this point—saw the man cower farther and farther into the stacks. After what seemed like an endless back-and-forth, the man retreated, went to the vault, or wherever he had to, and brought out the will, spreading the five pages out on the table for my father to photograph. I know it is five pages because on the top shelf of my office bookcase, I have that photographed Jeffersonian will in two frames, just as my father did during his lifetime.

I have another presidential keepsake that I like for the story value as well. It is a T-shirt from the bookstore at Calvin Coolidge's birthplace in Plymouth Notch, Vermont.

My wife and I made that pilgrimage after leaving our two daughters, then sixteen and thirteen, for a week's internship at our friend's refugee resettlement agency in New Haven, Connecticut, while we tootled around New England.

But the story really starts just a few years after the gift of *Facts About the Presidents*, when my father brought home a set of white plastic statues. All about four inches or so high, they were likenesses of the presidents—by this time going from Washington to John F. Kennedy—all standing on platforms that had their last names on the front and their terms of office on the back in raised letters. Some kids had toy soldiers. Girls of my era may have had Barbie dolls. But I had my Guys. Dad even bought an extra Guy later—Lyndon Johnson when he came to office and to that four-inch-high plastic form.

After I had grown up, my mom obviously put them in a brown wooden cigar box and added them to "Robert's things." I found the box after she died, and I put them away again—until it was time to indoctrinate

Sylvia, my younger daughter, maybe when she was about seven or eight years old. One day a few years later, I noticed that she had taken seven of them out and put them on her nightstand, all in a row—save that William Howard Taft was a few inches in front in his place in the horizontal row. There were five back to his left and one to his right. So I asked Sylvia what was up.

"It's Friday," she said.

"Friday? So why Taft?" I asked.

"Sixth in the row. Friday," she said, exasperated at me for not recognizing the calendar she had made out of The Guys.

One day in 2004, when she was thirteen, Sylvia and I went to see the remake of *Around the World in 80 Days*, starring Jackie Chan. At some point in the movie, which is set in the late 1870s, someone mentions President Rutherford B. Hayes.

"Nineteen," Sylvia said in a whisper while leaning over to me.

"Nineteen?" I asked back.

"Yes, nineteen," she said assuredly.

I don't think I said anything more, but she could feel that I didn't have a clue what she was saying.

"Rutherford B. Hayes, the nineteenth president," she said, and then went on to cheer some antic Chan was doing on screen.

Sylvia, now an adult, still pretends that she is nothing like me, and it was even more her belief back in her teenage years. She was a pretty good athlete then, doing at least one sport a season. One thing, though, was that she was determined to do as little running as possible. When she found out that shooting three-pointers in basketball meant that she had to run only between those outer curved lines, she became the team shooting guard. In soccer and lacrosse she was most often a goalie, recognizing quickly that goalies rarely run during a game and, thus, are often exempted from doing so even in practice.

So when I got to the Coolidge birthplace bookstore, I could not help but notice that T-shirt, one emblazoned with a portion of a famous Coolidge quote: "I do not choose to run . . ." Coolidge used it to say that despite being eligible to run in the 1928 election, he had determined he would retire—and maybe pitch hay or ride that mechanical horse more.

I thought it was perfect for Sylvia and her non-running sporting proclivities, but when I gave it to her, I merely said it was her presidential present from our trip. Even at thirteen, she knew better. She looked at the T-shirt and threw it back at me in disgust.

There is little in presidential oddball minutia and detritus that has not attracted me, the more random and serendipitous the better. I have seen Grover Cleveland's cancerous jawbone tumor (in the Mutter Museum, a collection of medical oddities in Philadelphia) and the pieces of his wedding cake his sister preserved (at his birthplace, the only presidential one in my home state, New Jersey). We passed close to Herbert Hoover's birthplace in West Branch, Iowa, and stopped to see the most impressive thing there, the family chicken coop. Woodrow Wilson's crib, George Washington's false teeth, Grant's Tomb . . . I have collected memories of them all.

We tried to go to John and John Quincy Adams's house on Presidents' Day—and it was closed, who would have thought, because of Presidents' Day, a federal holiday. I was in between interviews during a book tour in Charlotte, North Carolina, and noticed that James Knox Polk's birthplace was just south of the city. No one else was there and the shelves in the small bookstore looked like they had not been stocked in years. I bought a coffee cup with Polk's visage (and about a half inch of accumulated dust) for a friend. Several months later, my daughter was having a college interview at Vanderbilt University in Nashville, so while waiting, I walked the few blocks to the Tennessee State House. To my surprise, on the grounds was Polk's tomb. I had seen the bookends of a presidential life in the space of mere weeks. How fortuitous.

I became imbued with the spirit of James Buchanan in the late 2000s, when I discovered that the bulk of his papers were housed in the ornate red brick building on the southwest corner of Thirteenth and Locust Streets in Philadelphia, the Historical Society of Pennsylvania. It is on or near that corner that I have parked my car for the two decades

I have played in the early-morning full-court basketball games at the Sporting Club, the somewhat fancy gym a block away. For at least two generations, that corner has been the center for transvestite and transgender prostitution pickups. That sad pickup scene is often still going on when I reach the corner at about five thirty in the morning, an urban quirk that makes city living either endearing, exciting, or reprehensible, depending on your point of view.

It is also the corner, the southeastern part of it, that is the site of what is probably Philadelphia's most notorious killing. On December 9, 1981, in the chaos that used to be the bar-closing time on that well-trod corner, police officer Daniel Faulkner made a traffic stop of William Cook, the brother of radio reporter Mumia Abu-Jamal. Faulkner was shot and killed in a melee afterwards, and in a circus trial Abu-Jamal was convicted of murder and placed on death row. His case became a cause célèbre for political activists and death-penalty opponents worldwide.

Next to the Historical Society is another of Philadelphia's repositories of history, the Library Company, founded by Benjamin Franklin in 1731, a collection of important and rare papers and tomes, like the Mayflower Compact and first editions of *Moby Dick* and *Leaves of Grass*. In the first-story window separating the two buildings is a marble statue of Franklin, Philadelphia's somewhat patron saint, incongruously in a toga. The entirety of this—Ben in a toga, Mumia and Faulkner, transvestites awkwardly soliciting, me parking for early-morning basketball, and, to be sure, Buchanan's writings behind the red brick wall—inspired me to think about Buchanan's legacy. It seemed entirely appropriate to me to have it somehow embedded on this crazy city corner.

Years later, the editor of special sections for the *New York Times* asked me for ideas for a Museum section. I was pondering presidential at the time, so said it might be fun to do something on sites connected with lesser presidents. Among those I chose was the estate of John Tyler, Sherwood Forest, in rural Virginia. I called over and the executive director said, excitedly, "Oh, you will just have to talk to Mrs. Tyler."

Tyler may not have been the most significant president, but his historical paternity is without equal. Late in life, post-presidency, he had several children with his second wife. One of those boys followed the same pattern, having children in his dotage with a second wife. Two of those children were still alive when I did the story in 2015, and one of them, Harrison, was still living in the original John Tyler house with his wife, Frances Payne Tyler.

I am not always dazzled by celebrity, having been both a sportswriter and a TV critic in my time in journalism, but those serendipitous moments have their hold on me. I am a basketball gym rat and, at different pickup games, I have had to guard comic Kevin Hart and actor Will Smith. Hart was short and quick but could not shoot well. Smith was in his young *Fresh Prince* days in that time and dunked backwards over me. Another time a friend was in a play with Elizabeth Taylor that was going through Philly during her birthday, so he brought me to the hotel where they were staying for her small birthday gathering and the only seat was next to her on the couch, where I sat gape-mouthed the whole evening.

The chance to talk to the president's granddaughter-in-law, though, now that was a major kick. I could not get her off the phone, nor did I want to. The stories flowed. How she was sunbathing one day in the garden of the Tyler home, said to be the longest house in America—230 feet long with thirty-three rooms—when a group of older folks wandered down and started staring at her. "I wasn't going to kick them out, Robert, but it was then I decided we should give tours and make a little money out of it," she said. She also said she loved riding horses on the family plantation in South Carolina, but when her father, her riding partner, died when she was twelve, his best friend, who did not have horses himself, volunteered to come ride with her every few weeks or so. The best friend? The Honorable Strom Thurmond, who himself ran for president in 1948.

Despite her disdain for that Coolidge shirt, Sylvia was with me on my first trip to Wheatland, the Buchanan estate, when I did a story for the *Philadelphia Inquirer*'s Weekend section about what to do in Lancaster. We bought a simple souvenir postcard, not a T-shirt.

Sylvia could only laugh in derision, though, when I told her a few years later that Sue, my wife, allowed me ninety minutes to go to Rutherford B. Hayes's home in Fremont, Ohio, a few miles off the Ohio Turnpike, on our way to my mother-in-law's house in Michigan. During the tour—there were only two other people with us in the thirty-plus-room house—the docent asked if we would like to see Hayes's billows-driven harpsichord. She pulled it out and looked at me gazing at the machine.

"Would you like to play it?" she asked.

It could have been Mozart's own instrument and I would not have been more anxious. I pressed the bellows with my feet and played, I think, "Take Me Out to the Ball Game."

I would like to believe Hayes would have appreciated my enthusiasm.

Chapter Three

Up from Lancaster

THE DEATH OF ANN COLEMAN NO DOUBT DEVASTATED JAMES BUCHANAN personally and the gossip around it could not have pleased him. It didn't affect his lawyering, though. Not only did he continue with the work he had, his reputation was, almost counterintuitively, enhanced by the affair. The thought may have gone like this: If, indeed, Ann Coleman went hysterical because Buchanan was working so hard, and he clearly would not have had to do so if he were going to marry the daughter of the richest guy around, then he must really, *really* be a hard worker. Thus, his practice thrived in the months following her death. Even Cyrus Jacobs, the father of the woman who had introduced Coleman to Buchanan, made Buchanan his legal advisor for his vast iron holdings.

Had Coleman lived and become Mrs. Buchanan, it may well have placed Buchanan in the position he originally sought in the law. Edward Coleman had his own sons to give the business to, but it seems apparent that Buchanan would have become the company's legal counsel. Politics would probably have been too dirty or maybe even too demeaning, and certainly less lucrative, so his career would no doubt have gone a different way.

Now when the Federalists of Lancaster were looking for a congressional candidate to run in the district that included Lancaster, Dauphin, and Lebanon Counties, they asked Buchanan, the erstwhile Commonwealth Assembly Federalist, whether he would run, and he had nothing in mind that would now bar the way.

Buchanan's two assembly contests had been relatively clean, so he was probably unaware that he could be besmirched running for Congress. To be sure, his opponents dredged up every negative aspect of the Coleman death, and then circulated false rumors that Buchanan accused Governor William Findlay of owning a slave. That "slave," a woman named Hannah, had been Buchanan's nurse when he was a boy, and when her employment there was done, Buchanan's father found her work with the Findlays, who lived nearby in Mercersburg. Even though Findlay was a Democrat, the opposite party, Buchanan had long been instructed by his parents to be respectful of everyone, and he was angry that he would be castigated for writing something nasty that he had not done. One of Buchanan's best traits throughout his life, especially with all the political infighting he was involved with, is that he never publically insulted anyone. It is true that he did have his hatreds—Stephen Douglas being the most prominent—but he always found something positive to say, or just did not say anything.

This first congressional campaign may have been influential in that. Buchanan won and Findlay lost, but Buchanan kept his cool. He made no stump speeches and allowed others to campaign for him. His law partner, Molton Rogers, actually ran for state senate on the Democratic ticket but lost to Buchanan's running mate, a Dauphin County man. That Rogers and Buchanan continued being the best of friends and law partners would attest to Buchanan's clean campaigning.

During the Jeffersonian Democratic era, Congress met only a few months out of the year, and Buchanan's first term, though it now would seem strange, did not begin until December 1821, more than a year after he was elected. That was good for him, since it gave him time to clean up a lot of law work and make some money before his paltry congressional salary would start. It also had him home in Pennsylvania when his father died on June 11, 1821, in what must have been a gory accident. The elder Buchanan was apparently almost home in his Mercersburg driveway when the horse towing his carriage bolted and he flipped out of his seat, his head striking the carriage's iron tire, killing him. The young

James went home to take care of his family's affairs, setting up finances to care for his mother and the five younger children still at home. Later on, Buchanan would "adopt" his nieces and nephews, keeping as many as twenty of them afloat financially at one time or another.

Buchanan came to a Washington that was still trying to get things together from the War of 1812, though it had been nearly seven years since the British had burned buildings during their attack on the city. The White House had been rebuilt. The Capitol building was still unfinished, however. The congressional chambers were like an old, bad baseball park—pillars blocked the view of the Chair for many members and the gallery was only a raised platform behind the floor, usually populated by women, who, no matter what their station, were little more than celebrity hunters wanting just a chat or a smile from a distinguished representative.

Buchanan was at least as starstruck as those women, hardly believing he was in this glorious place and not yet thirty years old. When someone of any fame showed him any courtesy, Buchanan felt humble and impressed. John Randolph, the venerable Virginia congressman, often called "the Showman of Congress" for his oratory, greeted him warmly early on, and John Sergeant, the Philadelphia congressman who was chair of the Judiciary Committee, took him aside to tell him about the personalities of his new compatriots. He sought out Ninian Edwards of Illinois, a fellow Dickinson alumnus, and introduced himself to every other freshman, just hoping he would be accepted into the fraternity.

Always wanting to have a model, Buchanan chose William Lowndes of South Carolina to emulate. Lowndes was a master speechmaker, displaying not the showiness of Randolph, but just the qualities Buchanan hoped he would have—lots of research, a sincere demeanor, no bad words for an opponent, and preciseness rather than generalities. Even Randolph liked the guy.

So, a few weeks after Buchanan came to the House, when Lowndes was ill and wanted to make sure his views on a particular piece of legislation—the War Department Deficiency Bill—would be heard, and his aides asked Buchanan to make them into a speech, he was floored with excitement.

It was a delicate operation. Secretary of War John C. Calhoun had asked for $170,000 to pay the bills of the Indian Bureau in his department, but there was a faction in the House, much like the twenty-first century Tea Party, calling itself the Radicals, that wanted to limit the federal government from doing much of anything, and that also particularly hated Calhoun, who had long wanted to be president himself. The Radicals would allow the House to appropriate only $100,000 for the bureau for 1821, half of what the budget was the year before, and $70,000 less than Calhoun said he needed. Lowndes, being a South Carolinian like Calhoun, wanted him to have at least that extra $70,000—the War Department deficiency of the bill's title.

Though he was speaking for Democrats, Buchanan reveled in the opportunity. His talk was successful, as the deficiency bill passed overwhelmingly. Oddly enough, in the meantime, William Findlay won a Senate seat overwhelmingly in Pennsylvania, the first Democrat to take Lancaster, and then the whole state. Buchanan's Federalist Party was dwindling to little, or nothing, at least outside of New England. The reelection season was coming up quickly and Buchanan had already gotten used to thinking of himself as a congressman.

He surely was not a Radical, and he had gotten kudos from Lowndes and Calhoun, who both had their eyes on the presidency, which would not again be up until 1824. Buchanan had already started thinking about whom to support—not unlike today, when it seems the next presidential race starts only a few days after the previous inauguration. He had been elected, though, as a Federalist, and switching parties immediately did not seem to be the right way to win reelection.

Then circumstances interceded and Buchanan was free. The national Federalists indicated that they would not be fielding a candidate in the 1824 presidential election. That allowed Buchanan to stand for Congress in 1822 as a Federalist, but start working toward getting on the side of a Democrat for the next presidential cycle. As a Federalist, he realized, he could be wooed by just about anyone. Being from Pennsylvania was a good thing as well. Massachusetts, New York, and Virginia had pretty much dominated national politics in the nation's first fifty years. Virginia would take the presidency—only John Adams's four years interrupted that—while New York, starting with Alexander Hamilton, got the bulk of the federal patronage administrative jobs.

So Pennsylvania politicians, now pretty much coalesced into one party, started to think of alliances of midlevel states to break into that upper realm. Buchanan decided to get into the thick of the new coalition, bringing his mentors from South Carolina, along with his neighbors to the west, Ohio, into an influential triumvirate. Lowndes had fallen ill, so had taken himself out of consideration for the next presidency, and Calhoun moved into the forefront in the new three-state cadre. Through one of his chieftains, he asked Buchanan to suggest someone from Pennsylvania who might become secretary of the navy, since President Monroe had an opening in his cabinet there, and though the incumbent, S. L. Southard, decided to stay instead of taking Monroe's offer of a Supreme Court seat, the exchange further connected Buchanan with Calhoun, the presumptive front-runner for the Democrats.

Buchanan, though, wanted to make sure first he was reelected in 1822, which meant staying a Federalist, loyalty at home being more important than worrying about the next president. He concentrated on constituent service—sending newsletters to be copied and distributed about what Congress, and Buchanan, were doing; submitting minor bills to help out his area; making sure both Democrats and Federalists liked what he was doing in Washington. He won reelection easily, and then started to see where he was going to be headed in 1824.

The Federalists were clearly on the wane by then. What remained of the party endorsed Buchanan for a third term—the first time the Federalists in Lancaster had ever done that. Buchanan saw that there would never be a fourth term if he did not move himself along from the Federalists. He ran on a ticket with the name "Federal-Republican." As often happened in that time, the congressional election was held in

October, three weeks before the presidential election. Buchanan was still a Calhoun man, as were many of the influential people in the Pennsylvania Democratic Party.

By late 1824, though, Andrew Jackson had become the favorite of most of the Southern-leaning movers of the Democrats, which was essentially the only party left in presidential terms. In an election that seemed more European—with four candidates—than American, which more often than not only had two major ones, Jackson got the most electoral votes, with ninety-nine, but not nearly a majority. John Quincy Adams, the son of the former president, got eight-three; William Harris Crawford of Georgia, the leader of the Radicals who plagued Calhoun, got forty-one; and Henry Clay of Kentucky, who would soon start the Whig Party, got thirty-seven. Crawford was not going to get any more than he had, but was not ready to throw his weight to anyone. Clay, though, was an up-and-comer and anxious to bargain his votes for something, presumably the post of secretary of state.

The election would be thrown into the House of Representatives, as the Constitution mandated, with each state getting one vote, thus presenting compromise almost everywhere. The supposition was that if either Jackson or Adams offered Clay that cabinet post, that man would have the presidency.

Buchanan, then, made his first real national headline. He asked Jackson, then an incumbent senator from Tennessee, but really running as Old Hickory, the hero of the War of 1812, if he could have an audience. Jackson granted a meeting, mostly because he may have thought that Buchanan represented Pennsylvania's vote in the House runoff, a toss-up at that point.

Buchanan had been enamored of Clay ever since he met him in Kentucky, when Buchanan was trying to help his father with the older man's real estate claims. He knew Clay was not going to win in 1824, but maybe if he would help Jackson now, he would put himself in position for a coming election. The last three presidents had been secretary of state, as had John Quincy Adams, so that seemed a likely road for Clay.

Like in a latter-day spy novel, when Buchanan reached Jackson's apartment, the former general asked him to take a walk in town. Jackson was known to be quick tempered—he had already killed a man in a duel—but loyal to allies and vicious to opponents. He was not devious, and often direct, too direct if the person challenged him. Buchanan had to be careful, but Jackson was not a man for small talk. From his gut he asked the question: Had Jackson already made a deal to make Adams secretary of state, and, if not, would he make that deal with Clay? Buchanan said he had no particular influence with Clay, but complimented him. It was December by now, and the House vote would be in a couple of weeks. Buchanan said he wanted Jackson to be president, and thought that having Clay as his secretary of state was a good move in many ways. Jackson was noncommittal, saying he was keeping his own counsel, but Buchanan was free to report his nonanswer back to his compadres.

Buchanan was proud of himself. He was now on good terms, he thought, with the three most powerful men in politics: Jackson, Clay, and Calhoun. By January 24, though, he had reason to second guess, for that day, Clay's Kentucky delegation and the Ohio delegation his people controlled pledged their votes to Adams, and a few weeks later, Adams won in the House and immediately made Clay his secretary of state. There was talk of violence in Washington if Adams prevailed, but after some loud words, nothing happened.

Buchanan had now become a politician for good. His first move was always how to retain his seat or, later, when he was in appointive office, his station, while looking forward to the next time around. Whatever had been left of the Federalist Party was now gone with the election of Adams, a former Federalist, who was now a Democrat both in leanings and in name.

Buchanan had always been a good budgeter, keeping meticulous records down to the penny. It came as no surprise, then, that Buchanan knew just how many votes every power in every township he represented controlled. His congressional power, then, was dependent on pleasing those men, often individually. Was there a judgeship he could assure? A job he could offer? A favor for a farmer? A meeting he could attend, for substance or show? A loan a businessman needed? A legal issue he could arbitrate?

He was the ultimate fixer, taking not a cent for a fee, but hoping for a vote in the next election. Buchanan was never vicious. He would not know, after all, the secret ballot of anyone whom he helped, but he knew in general that if he remained affable and productive, the result would be positive from below.

From above, well, that might be a different story. Seeing Adams as a temporary obstacle to his other presidential favorites, Buchanan started a party in Pennsylvania he called Amalgamation. It was primarily formed from his old Federalist friends and his Scotch-Irish landsmen, farmers who had long been Democrats, especially from the western part of his district. These groups had a couple of things in common: They loved Jackson and they hated the Philadelphians who were trying to control the commonwealth.

Buchanan had clearly drawn his line. He may have realized that the Philadelphia Democrats, particularly the patrician George Mifflin Dallas, who would become vice president under James Knox Polk, would control much of the patronage in the commonwealth without him, so the only way he could have influence there would be to find power in Washington, and Jackson seemed to be the man in the future. Adams, whom merchants in the cities favored, had won the last election by wheeling and dealing, not popularity. If only Jackson and Adams ran, it would be not much of a race the next time around, Buchanan felt.

Then a bombshell came. Buchanan's furtive meeting with Jackson before the 1824 House vote became the subject of gossip. It became "apparent" that Buchanan had gone to him to deal for Clay's position in a presumed Jackson administration. Buchanan was hoping, according to this line of thought, that Jackson would have a one-term presidency and the way would be cleared for Buchanan's former favorite, John Calhoun. The Philadelphia group loved the intrigue. Jackson, of course, said that nothing happened at the Buchanan meeting, but Buchanan was now in the position of embarrassing Old Hickory. Buchanan had loved being in the middle of the presidential scene, but now he could anger the very people he was trying to help.

His old friend and law partner, Molton Rogers, long a Democratic power broker, taking over from his Delaware governor father, said Buchanan had to apologize to just about everyone at once. As good a writer as he was, Buchanan managed the feat, at least to a degree. The Philadelphia Democrats really could have not cared less, just that they kept their patronage power. Calhoun knew the whole mess was untrue, but just needed assurance that Buchanan never spoke against him. Jackson was appeased but never again trusted Buchanan. Jackson would need Buchanan's support in the 1828 presidential campaign, but knew him now a bit weakened in the commonwealth. Buchanan's seat in Congress was safe, but Jackson was determined not to cede him any influence if he did not have to.

Still, as sometimes happens, that Buchanan's name was now on the national scene, even if somewhat negatively, seemed to prove the old dictum that keeping his name out in public was better than no publicity at all. The plodder in Buchanan realized he would have to make this a lesson. He would no longer stick his neck out, about nearly anything, even when it seemed he would have to.

—◆—

Whatever the outcome of the affair, Buchanan was now a firm Jacksonian Democrat. For the first time in his five terms in Congress, he took the floor on February 4, 1828, to make a political speech, a mild one compared to other Jacksonians, but clearly condemning the Adams administration as being too preemptive and taking too much power away from Congress. Jackson wanted to always seem a man of the people and, despite suffrage in America being white, male, and fairly affluent, the "people" were those who knew their congressman, not their president.

Buchanan and several others who had long campaigned against each other as Democrats and Federalists over the years formed a new

Jacksonian wing of the Democratic Party. Those who never did like the Jacksonians became Adamsites, whether they wanted to be or not. Either they did not like Buchanan, like E. C. Reigart, who always wanted the congressional seat but always had to step aside for Buchanan, or they thought that the Adams wing was more civilized, connected to influential Philadelphians who could assure them jobs.

Buchanan, though, thought things would cool down when Jackson became the obvious choice for the Democratic nomination. He was unprepared for the viciousness that ensued. He gave three speeches in disparate parts of his district on July 4, giving the people what he thought they wanted to hear, his political accomplishments and views. He emphasized how he had helped out constituents for a decade now—getting duties on iron and hemp and liquor, getting the Irish in his district an easy road to citizenship, being on the side of both farmers and manufacturers, and espousing better education. These were all things he could continue to do if Jackson were elected.

The opposition, though, was ruthless. They brought up his Federalist past, not as something good and sane, but wildly anti-Democrat. The Adamsites went back to his old handbills, which promoted his presidency of the old Lancaster Washington Society. They said he was an advocate of slavery, and the slave trade itself, something not really true, but something Buchanan could not refute because he had never before taken a public stand. There were enough Pennsylvania Dutch and Quakers in the area that any connection to slavery would hurt Buchanan. The *Marietta Pioneer*, for the village near Lancaster, wrote a story quoting people who said they heard Buchanan say that Qunicy Adams's wife was born out of wedlock. Reigart, his old nemesis, was the editor of the paper, so when Buchanan asked for an apology, he got only a qualified response.

His detractors pulled what would be a modern charge—that he had not been in Washington for business often enough. Fortunately, Buchanan's penchant for keeping meticulous records helped him there, as he showed a diary of every day he was in Congress, and even had the Treasury withhold his pay for each session he may have missed.

Still, the vicious fight drained Buchanan. He won his seat handily, but with little enthusiasm for the infighting he knew would continue with vigor with the Family, as the Philadelphia-oriented Democrats called themselves.

In the spring of 1830, Buchanan announced his retirement from politics, but he knew damned well this was not the end, just a temporary stay on the sidelines. There had already been promotion of him as a potential vice presidential running mate for a second Jackson term, a term that now seemed more likely than before.

The original thought of backroom movers was that Jackson's first term was merely a holding pattern for John Calhoun. Calhoun was the Democratic senatorial star, the big thinker sometimes opposed to but often in collaboration with the Whig's Daniel Webster and Henry Clay. The power of the time was in Congress, despite Calhoun, Webster, and Clay often seeking the presidency. Jackson was just the way for his version of the Democrats to knock the Adamsites, who were essentially Federalists in disguise, out of the White House and clear the way for a new generation. Old Hickory was a hero and a winner, but he was, indeed, getting old by early nineteenth-century political standards, ascending to the presidency just a week before his sixty-second birthday. Jackson's wife died in December, not two months after his election and well before the inauguration, so most assumed Jackson would acquiesce to his caretaker role, bridging the early presidencies of the Founders and the next-gen group of those born after the Revolution.

Jackson had other ideas. He was a general and loved being in charge. Further, he was miffed about how the previous election had come out, with Adams and Clay back-door dealing, which he presumed meant that they thought him not smart enough to be the big boss. Jackson, despite his real-life patrician's bearing, transformed himself into America's first president of the people. Nothing confirmed this more than the inauguration week chaos at the White House.

Because his wife had died, Jackson planned no pomp as part of the inaugural festivities. Somehow, though, circumstances made it one of the most remembered inaugurations in history. Adams, like his father before him, chose not to participate as the outgoing president in the inauguration. Adams never liked Jackson and was not going to dignify him at the end of his own presidency. The move backfired, however, as it gave the regal-looking Jackson the whole stage, even to the point of his being given the oath of office by the last politically active Founder, Chief Justice John Marshall.

It was a beautiful March day in Washington, and military veterans used the inaugural parade to honor the general. There were thousands of them, from those who had served in the Revolutionary War down to active military men of the peaceful 1830s, and especially those who had served under Jackson at the Battle of New Orleans, which had kicked the Europeans out of the country for good.

The reception at the end of the parade was supposed to be swift and informal. Instead, the veterans and others stormed the house. Estimates of more than twenty thousand "visitors" came from news accounts. They danced, drank, and otherwise caroused, breaking glassware and dishes, missing spittoons with the droppings from their chaw, and tearing up the rugs Dolley Madison had bought to fix the place back up from its British burning in the War of 1812.

While the whole scene may have horrified the patricians, it endeared Jackson to his electorate. It gave force to his dissolution of the Bank of the United States and then his standing up to South Carolina, when the state tried to nullify tariffs imposed by the administration. Unlike Buchanan later on, Jackson took the affront personally and threatened military action against South Carolina, not only if it tried to secede, but in its quest to avoid the tariffs.

That tariff tiff, but also the whole strong Jacksonian presidency, doomed Calhoun.

Though he was now part of the administration as vice president, he was identified with the anti-tariff movement in his home state. Jackson had already become a master of patronage, doling out jobs to both friends and foes—good ones to loyalists, dead-end ones to the troublesome, so they could never say he ignored them. He loved his role and his partisans saw him as almost godlike, a George Washington with tobacco stains and dueling in his past.

Though Calhoun was one of his first mentors in Congress, Buchanan quickly saw promoting him further was not going to get him much of anywhere. When Buchanan heard his own name proffered as a potential new running mate for a potential second Jackson term, he said nothing but thought, "Well, retirement from politics sounds good, but the vice presidency sounds better."

He had ended his decade in Congress on a high note. There had been a move among some Democrats to reduce the influence of the Supreme Court, even going so far as to allow state courts to decide which federal laws were valid in their jurisdiction. Buchanan, though, had solidified his stance as a strict constructionist in constitutional matters, believing that the document had given federal courts, and ultimately the Supreme Court, jurisdiction in "all cases in law and equity, arising under this Constitution, the laws of the United States, and treaties." The Judiciary Act of 1789, especially its Section 25, further defined this phrase as meaning cases where a state court ruled on a piece of federal legislation, those where a state law might violate the Constitution, and those which reached appellate courts in similar matters of state versus federal legislation.

His defense of Section 25 was grounded in the idea that the Constitution had superseded the Articles of Confederation, which gave almost all of the judicial power to the states. That could only foment chaos, argued Buchanan, since if each state court had say over every piece of federal legislation, the country could not be united, which was the whole point of having a constitution. Sure, no one wanted to give up too much sovereignty, especially to a court of fewer than a dozen men, but that is why the United States was formed. Each colony could have been its own country, but that is not how it came out. Buchanan won the dubious Congress over, the House adopting his report almost two to one.

In a final rush Buchanan took the floor as manager for the impeachment of Judge James H. Peck of Missouri. Peck had disbarred and thrown into prison a St. Louis lawyer merely because that lawyer, Luke E. Lawless, had written newspaper articles criticizing Peck's opinions. Buchanan was able to get close to ousting the jurist—a rarity in impeachment cases against judges—but Peck survived, winning acquittal only twenty-two to twenty-one.

Buchanan's mother, now age sixty-six, was ecstatic that Buchanan was going back to the law. The extended family needed him at home, she told him, but also needed him to provide for them, as he had promised to do. Buchanan was surely willing to acquiesce to that—but just for the time being. He had drunk the proverbial Kool-Aid of national politics. He knew the president, the senators, the ambassadors, and the backroom bosses as well. He would be back—or, with staying behind the scenes in Pennsylvania Jacksonian circles—never far away.

Jackson had a bit of a surprise for Buchanan, and it was not going to be the vice presidency. Buchanan, perhaps unknowingly, had made a misstep. Early on in the Twenty-First Congress—in December of 1829—he had chafed at a move by James K. Polk, a young congressman from Tennessee, which would have tabled a motion on a minor bill without anyone able to speak on the matter. Buchanan thought that an impolitic move by such a novice member of the House, and he forced a vote on it, which embarrassed Polk, even though it amounted to nothing in terms of legislation.

Polk, however, was a protégé of Buchanan's hero, President Jackson. That Polk was from Tennessee should have tipped Buchanan off. It was just another check mark on the ledger against Buchanan for Jackson, who was about as hands-on a president as the nation had ever had. Still, Buchanan did have some power in Pennsylvania, so Jackson could not quite call him out in a duel.

Instead, Jackson dispatched one of his closest advisors, John Henry Eaton, to offer Buchanan the job of minister to Russia. A letter from Eaton, as the offer came, was tantamount to an edict from Jackson. Eaton had been the focus of another of America's tabloid piece of politics. His first wife had died when both were young, and in 1829, when Eaton was just finishing his career in the Senate from Tennessee on Jackson's say-so, he married the beautiful Peggy O'Neill Timberlake, whose husband had just died. Florida Calhoun, the vice president's wife, saw this as an impropriety and refused to befriend the new Mrs. Eaton. That split the wives of the higher levels of the government in what became known as the Petticoat Affair. Eaton, though, was a part of Jackson's Kitchen Cabinet, which did, though infrequently, meet in the White House kitchen to avoid suspicion. Eaton got a promotion to secretary of war and Calhoun lost even more favor. In fact, the Petticoat Affair probably got Martin Van Buren, another Kitchen Cabinet member, the presidency, since his wife sided with Mrs. Eaton and Jackson eventually chose Van Buren as his vice presidential running mate in his second term.

No accounting for how pettiness—or petticoats—can change the course of American politics.

Jackson was the Don Corleone of his day. He gave offers no one was allowed to refuse. Buchanan must have realized that this was one of those offers. Jackson had jettisoned all the members of his cabinet loyal to Calhoun, including Secretary of the Treasury Samuel Ingham of Pennsylvania. Buchanan thought he could fill the hole created by Ingham's demise as the leader of the Jacksonians in Pennsylvania, but to do that, he had to get out of going to Russia. Eaton's letter indicated the offer was confidential, so Buchanan could not talk about it to anyone, which confounded his plans completely.

Buchanan pleaded off to Eaton by saying he had restarted his law practice and leaving would put his clients in jeopardy. Further, he said, he did not know French, the language of diplomacy, and taking classes in French would arouse suspicions of the savvy, who would know Jackson had tapped him for some foreign post. In the end Jackson told Eaton to tell Buchanan he could delay his leaving for Russia until the end of 1831 or early 1832, several months hence, and if he had to take French classes, well, so be it, but just not to talk to reporters about the appointment, since

John Randolph of Virginia was still in Russia anyway. No announcement of his appointment would be made for a while.

"Jackson really disliked Buchanan and distrusted him," said Wheatland overseer Patrick Clarke. "It had never become apparent to anybody how much until Jackson was almost on his deathbed and his biographer was interviewing him, and got into the early presidential years. [The biographer] asked whether it was true that Jackson had sent Buchanan off to Russia on purpose. Jackson said, 'If I could have sent him further away, I would have.'"

By all accounts, however, his time in Russia was Buchanan's high point in terms of unalloyed success in governmental service. Before he left he put his real estate and financial holdings in the care of friendly attorneys and cautioned his relatives and friends that he might have spent the last of his days in Lancaster. He had amassed a fortune by that time—the equivalent of $4.5 million today—and assumed that his career would now be in appointed service, no longer in law, and thus probably in Washington or in foreign lands.

Beginning in early April 1832, he took twenty-five days to get from New York to Liverpool on the *Silas Richards* and then spent two weeks in England. He took a railroad for the first time in his life—from Liverpool to Manchester, thirty miles in eighty-five minutes, an unheard-of speed in Pennsylvania. While seeing the mother country was invigorating, he was anxious to get on with things in Russia.

Buchanan's imprimatur was almost entirely to get a trade agreement with Russia, not just to babysit the eastern flank of Europe. He knew he had to make the United States look worthy in the eyes of Czar Nicholas, so he rented a villa for the legation off the St. Petersburg harbor. It had a courtyard, stables for six horses, and all sorts of bronzes, marble sculptures, crystal, and solid kitchenware, enough for a party of thirty diplomats had he needed it.

He presented his credentials to the czar in mid-June and, to his surprise, Nicholas I and the empress greeted him warmly, even coming down from their thrones to shake hands. Buchanan thought his French poor, but he got through the day without it hampering international relations.

Russia's big beef with the United States was a tariff imposed in 1828, which the Russian ministers said severely hampered any trade between the two countries. Buchanan knew the ways of international relations required patience, so he spent that summer primarily studying French and international law, writing letters, and going to whatever social function was necessary.

Buchanan found, though, the life of a foreign diplomat far different than that of a Lancaster attorney or even a member of Congress. Everything was pomp, glorious and seemingly decadent. He wrote a long letter to his friend, John Reynolds, about the change in circumstance in early August:

> *I must submit to the established customs, or forfeit many of the most essential privileges of a foreign minister. If I were to drive through the streets of Lancaster in the same style I do here, I should soon have a mob of men, women & children in my train. I must drive four horses; otherwise I could not go to court. My driver like the rest is a Russian with a long flowing black beard, dressed in the peculiar costume of his country. There is a postilion on the leader; but what is the most ridiculous of all is the Chasseur who stands behind. He is decked out in his uniform more gaudy than that of our Militia Generals with a sword by his side & a large chapeau on his head surmounted by a plume of feathers. The soldiers at their stations present arms to the carriage, on the streets they take off their hats to it & it is everywhere received with so much deference, that I feel ashamed of myself whenever I pass through the City. It is ridiculous flummery.*

Buchanan was used to the directness of American politics and society in general. When people wanted to say something to you, they found you and told you what it was. People were direct, even abrupt, but deviousness was not expected. In European courts, though, everything was wrapped in mystery and deception, or at least indirectness. Buchanan was there to get Russia to be what would now be called "a favored trading partner." England, Austria, and France were still the strong countries in Europe, but Russia, especially under the new czar, was pushing westward, in both territory and presumed influence. Both France and Britain did not like this. Russia had put down a rebellion in Poland with great force and loss of life, and France and Britain were using the negative publicity of the Polish fighting to isolate Russia commercially.

So the timing of his entry to St. Petersburg was fortuitous. Buchanan had essentially been exiled there by Jackson, who knew that Russia had never had a hard business treaty with a Western government. There had been some trade with the United States in recent years, mostly raw sugar coming from America through Black Sea ports and carried north to be refined around St. Petersburg, but this was a trickle, almost an anomaly. Russian diplomats were looking longingly at the discussions around a tariff bill that might lower the heavy tariffs passed by Congress in 1828.

Jackson had sent Buchanan to Russia not so much to fail, but to stagnate. Jackson figured there was no chance the Russians would agree to anything substantial, and Buchanan would be there virtually incommunicado and receding from American political memory.

Then, on August 19, an American ship came to St. Petersburg with news that the Tariff of 1832 had passed both houses of Congress—passed indeed without Jackson's signature. Duties on iron went down by 20 percent and on hemp by a third, while most anything else Russia could care about was down at least 15 percent. Buchanan immediately got word to the palace—and then heard nothing for six weeks.

Buchanan went into full party mode. He used his own money to give a series of parties for the men of Russian and expatriate authority. He employed French cooks, which the higher-ups loved. When he invited women he found they loved stories, so he told them fictional tales. The Russian nobles did not drink much and sat around in mixed company after dinner—not smoking cigars and telling ribald stories as Buchanan was wont to do in Lancaster and Washington.

In October Buchanan got the answer from the czar he pretty much suspected, that he was not going to negotiate that trade treaty. The point was, though, that Buchanan was going to have to defend himself and look like he would be acquiescent to the czar. Buchanan wrote in some minor modifications and waited the typical foreign diplomat's wait. The last boat back to America left the already ice-laden waters of the St. Petersburg port in November, but Buchanan, the nervous American politician, still wanted things expedited. He forced the issue by a formal request that the treaty be signed on the czar's birthday, December 18, always a big event in St. Petersburg, and in this case the treaty would make it an even more special occasion.

The czar loved the idea. The big party came at the palace, and as the czar greeted the foreign ministers, he spoke right to Buchanan. "You may judge of my astonishment," Buchanan later wrote, "when the Emperor accosting me in French, in a tone of voice which could be heard all around, said, 'I signed the order yesterday that the Treaty should be executed according to your wishes.'"

The coup had been made, whether by circumstances or fact. England and France had only recently reached an agreement on some diplomatic issues surrounding Belgium, so Russia needed some alliance to counteract that. The United States seemed as good as any, given that its trade would all be by water, and thus be able to circumvent English or French territory, at least via the Black Sea, where Russia wanted more development anyway.

Buchanan had to stick around for a while, since the signed agreement back from Washington could not occur until the port was open after the winter. Buchanan started to get invited to more parties, and at any of them the czar and his wife attended, they gave their attention often to Buchanan. The czar loved to walk the streets of St. Petersburg in pedestrian dress, and when he would see the American minister, he would shout out, "Buchanan!" and engage him in conversation. The empress was big on dancing, and Buchanan was the same, so the czar often ceded his place on the dance floor to them.

At some point in the winter, a cache of mail and newspapers showed up at the American legation. Only then was Buchanan assured, as he suspected, that everything sent to him was read first by someone in the czar's employ. He was glad that he was always reserved in his writing, no matter what he thought. Finally, in the summer, the treaty was finalized and Buchanan planned his trip back home. Along the way he stopped at several of Europe's big cities, which he had not before seen—Hamburg, Amsterdam, Brussels, Paris, Edinburgh, Glasgow. He got to London and presented himself in court there, meeting all the right folks, from Lord Palmerston to Tallyrand. He stopped off at Ramelton, Ireland, from whence his ancestors came. "There I sinned much in the article of hot whiskey toddy which they term punch," he wrote to his friend Reynolds in Lancaster. "The Irish women are delightful."

"When Jackson sends him to Russia, those missions were supposed to be three-year missions," said Wheatland curator Clarke. "He completes it in a year, partly by luck and partly by his personality. He wooed the czar. He just charmed the czar. Instead of taking two years and possibly failing, he succeeds in securing the first commercial treaty Czar Nicholas had done with any country.

"When he stops in England, he becomes aware of the fact that the United States' interests are not well represented there at all, and there is this thing called the Crimean War going on," said Clarke. "He steps in without even thinking about it and negotiates to protect the interests of the United States. So then he comes home and he is this big deal here—so Jackson, who exiled him to be forgotten, says, 'Jesus.'"

Buchanan came back to Lancaster and settled some affairs—a sister had married, a brother had died, his investments were just fine and his friendships were intact. He had gone from a minor player in Washington to a man known in the courts of the powers of Europe.

"The emperors and empresses, the dukes and counts, the chancellors and ministers who wore the medals and ribbons seemed to him not much better informed than he was," wrote Buchanan's advocate in biography, Philip Klein in his *President James Buchanan.*

"For the first time in his life he began to think seriously about the presidency," wrote Klein. "Why not? He could do it."

———

Stereotypical though it might be, every modern profile of Buchanan, including this one, at least mentions that he might have been gay. Here he is, a foppishly well-dressed man who never marries; loves to give parties, always hanging out with the most beautiful women there; and seems ambivalent just at the crucial moment in his engagement.

Bachelorhood in middle-class and upper-class America in the nineteenth century is a complex topic. According to Clarke, Buchanan would not have been seen as a pariah for being a bachelor.

"To be a bachelor in the mid-nineteenth century was not a really big deal," Clarke said. "The Republicans tried to make it a big deal during the campaign, though. There is a political cartoon that came out and showed Buchanan sitting on a bench, and he has these sort of patched-up, tattered clothes on. He has his coat, which he is holding up, and it has its patch that says, 'Ostend Manifesto' and another that says, 'Cuba,' with the implication that he has no wife to sew his clothes." Yet, Clarke reiterated, "It was not any problem not to be married."

That began to change in the late nineteenth century. As the world started to industrialize, the intact family was an important part of being a real man. Grover Cleveland was elected as a bachelor, but it was well known that he was looking for a wife, and he did get married while in the White House. Clarke believes it would be impossible for a bachelor to be elected in the twenty-first century, given the sanctity most voters feel about family life. Divorce is OK, even being gay would perhaps be OK, so long as there was a committed relationship in there somewhere. "Unmarried people today are dangerous, and that has been so for a long time now," Clarke said. "Buchanan's bachelorhood was just not a real enough problem in his time."

On the other hand, Buchanan was shaken by the events of December 1819. It is unclear how and why Ann Coleman died, and nothing in the written record gives a thorough conclusion. It is difficult to give a truly modern spin on matters of social mores and sexuality two centuries past, but given the silence of the main characters, it seems all the more likely something different than usual was up.

According to Judge Thomas Kittera's diary entry, the only real contemporaneous accounting of Ann Coleman's death, the attending doctor had never heard of "hysteria producing death," but that is what he concluded happened. Ann's hysteria no doubt came because of her confused relationship with Buchanan, whether he loved her or not seeming to be the main factor. There has definitely been speculation that she committed suicide in some way—self-poisoning or maybe even some sort of violence, especially since it is unlikely that if she was feeling fine during the day, as Judge Kittera suggested, and if her sister felt comfortable enough with Ann's condition to go to the theater in the evening, that she would die of natural causes a few hours later.

Shocking as it may sound to those who think premarital sex started with the birth control pill, it seems more than possible that Ann and James had sexual relations during their courtship. They spent weekends at multiday soirees together and she was no longer a teenager, which would have been generally the time for marriage for someone of her station and purported beauty. There was something about the single life that she must have liked, and she was free enough to go between Philadelphia and Lancaster and the outer reaches of the region on her own. There are many letters to and from Buchanan over the years indicating that Buchanan loved associating with women at parties, many of those letters and dispatches commenting on his graces, his gentility, and his willingness to believe women were men's equals, at least in intelligence.

Ann and James had not been dating a long time when they became engaged, so it is possible that her "hysteria" might have been caused by an early pregnancy. Women in the early nineteenth century, high station or not, tended to get pregnant early and often. James was one of eleven children and Ann was one of ten. At twenty-three, her age at the time of their engagement, how was she going to keep up with that pace if she did not start quickly? If she could get pregnant, perhaps she could move up the wedding. If she could get pregnant, perhaps she could get her father off her back and finally let her marry someone. Yet if she got pregnant and she lost the guy, as she may have seemed to, what could she do?

Then, to be sure, there was also the chance that she really did think Buchanan was gay, but that seems unlikely. It is difficult to project homosexuality looking at it through modern society's norms. For the last century, Freudian psychology, with its emphasis on sexuality, has been the center of such discussion. In the nineteenth century, though, women were generally not perceived to be sexual beings in the first place—save if they were prostitutes—and, in addition, men talked and wrote about other men in terms of love that may have had some sexual overtones, but was really more ethereal. Men ruled the world, so men talked more about other men than women in every way.

Buchanan's apologist, Philip Klein, cites a flurry of "misfiled" letters between Buchanan and Mrs. George Blake, one of his dining companions in a Washington boarding house during his first two years in the United States House of Representatives, just after Ann Coleman's death.

"Mrs. Blake teased him about his apparent aversion to the fair sex, persuaded him to escort her to public functions in Washington, and conducted a vigorous campaign to find a wife for him," Klein wrote in his biography of Buchanan. He was supposed to visit the Blakes in Boston early that summer, but his law practice kept him in Lancaster. "[Buchanan] wrote Mrs. Blake in midsummer that Lancaster was as dull as could be and that, like the children of Israel in the wilderness, he longed after the fleshpots of Egypt."

Klein then goes on further about what Buchanan, the new guy in town, saw in the nation's capital:

He had been having a good time in Washington where, among the ladies, the knowledge of the Ann Coleman affair had given him a kind of romantic appeal. He had not forgotten Ann, nor had he lived the life of a recluse. Washington was full of lovely maids and matrons, but personable young bachelors were few. Buchanan knew the Van Ness girls, Cora Livingston and Catherine Van Rensselaer of New York, the Crowninshield misses from Vermont, Priscilla Cooper, who became the wife of his friend Robert Tyler, the Caton sisters from Baltimore, and many others, including a sprightly Julia and a giddy Matilda about whom he wrote glowing encomiums. He spent August with the Blakes in Boston; but despite the best efforts of his kind hostess, he returned home no closer to matrimony than he had been before.

Given the roster of available women—the names Klein gives, like Livingston and Van Rensselaer, bespeak money and fame—Buchanan's lack of betrothal could lead to the supposition he was gay, but he was also that new guy in town, surveying the scene and not willing to commit to the social future, when his political future may have been paramount in his mind. He roomed with other congressmen in a boarding house from the start, so he was conscious of his station and no doubt happy just to be in the social whirl.

Klein also points to letters Buchanan wrote to Judge Kittera, with whom he had become friendly after Ann Coleman's death, which had what he called "cryptic" phrases like "be particular in giving my love to my intended." Judge Kittera lived in style at 518 Walnut Street in Philadelphia, only a block from Independence Hall. His sister Ann and two of his nieces lived there with him. Klein posits that Buchanan may have been attracted to, or even started a relationship with, one of those women, who may be the "intended" he mentions. But Buchanan's life soon switched away from Pennsylvania, back to Washington as he became a US senator, and any relationship, if there was one, dissipated without much of a trace.

Certainly there were homosexuals in that age, but it is not apparent because of their writing or even their habits—particularly men sleeping in the same bed. Hotels and boarding houses had only so many rooms. Gigantic Marriotts and multistory apartment buildings were a long way off. Sleeping in the same bed was a matter of convenience, not sexuality. Surely some of those men who slept in beds together for years were gay lovers, but there were too many of them to think that all were.

For more than a decade, while they were in Congress—the play on words is delicious here, but may not lead anyone to Sodom—Buchanan and William Rufus DeVane King of Alabama shared living quarters when both were in Washington, for they were also diplomats, high-ranking officials, and businessmen in their home states as well, so not always in the capital. Andrew Jackson, who hated Buchanan, called Senator King "Aunt Nancy" and the law partner of Jackson's protégé, James Knox Polk, wrote of him as "Mrs. James Buchanan."

While they were in Washington, though, Buchanan either dated women or at least talked about the possibility of doing so to friends. There is no evidence King ever did. So it is possible, say, that King was homosexual and Buchanan was not, yet they were still fast friends and on tight budgets in Washington, so lived together. Further, they were in government service a long time, while others may not have been, so just that they, coming from such different backgrounds and so disparate geographically, survived national politics for so long as friends made people notice.

"They certainly didn't have the word 'gay' back then," said Paul F. Boller Jr., professor emeritus of history at Texas Christian University and author of several books on presidential politics, including *Presidential Campaigns: From George Washington to George W. Bush.*

Boller said Washington insiders, even at the time, speculated over whether King and Buchanan's well-known close friendship had evolved into a romantic relationship.

"I don't think the word *homosexual* was used either," Boller said. "So they'd sort of use the term 'a little feminine' and all of that."

Another piece of "evidence" of Buchanan's gay relationship with King was a sentence in a letter Buchanan wrote to another friend when King became minister to France in 1844: "I am now solitary and alone, having no companion in the house with me," Buchanan wrote. "I have gone a wooing to several gentlemen, but have not succeeded with any one of them." Were this actually a fast homosexual relationship, and not clearly a plea for a roommate to split the bills King no longer did, it would seem unlikely Buchanan would broadcast it like this.

Yet there is the case of the paucity of correspondence between King and Buchanan, given their long relationship of whatever sort it was. Wheatland's Clarke, citing research at the Buchanan estate about the rumor that King's and Buchanan's nieces conspired to burn their correspondence after King's death, said there is no evidence of that happening. King died only weeks after he became vice president under Buchanan's predecessor, Franklin Pierce. He developed an infection and went to Cuba in the winter in hopes of recovering from it. He actually was inaugurated in Cuba, but while still sick, he returned to his home in Alabama, where he died forty-five days into his term.

King clearly influenced Buchanan's political views. He had been born in North Carolina and he served as a congressman from that state until quitting Congress to take a foreign service post. He then bought land in the Alabama Territory and founded the town of Selma, where he became wealthy as a slaveholder and farmer. His Southern views no doubt had an influence on Buchanan, who was often castigated as a "Doughface," a Northern politician who, his face and brain malleable as dough, had overwhelmingly Southern sympathies, particularly on the existence, if not the approval, of slavery. King was a Unionist, which made him a moderate in the South. He fought against the idea of secession, even coming as he did from the Deep South, always trying to find ways to somehow reconcile slavery and keep the Union intact.

As a moderate Democrat, King became an early supporter of Andrew Jackson's quest to become president, his official US Senate biography says. The biography quotes an unnamed critic of King as describing him as a "tall, prim, wig-topped mediocrity," noting that King wore a wig "long after such coverings had gone out of fashion."

Another section of the official biography has this description from a fellow senator about King's easy personality: "He was distinguished by the scrupulous correctness of his conduct. He was remarkable for his quiet and unobtrusive, but active practical usefulness as a legislator . . . To his honor be it spoken, he never vexed the ear of the Senate with ill-timed, tedious or unnecessary debate."

The *Encyclopedia of Alabama* says that rumors were around in Washington about King's sexual orientation even before his rooming with Buchanan, but then grew after Buchanan and he became close.

"Neither man ever married, and by 1836 they were sharing a residence in Washington," the encyclopedia entry reads. "Any negative reactions to their relationship appear to have had little effect, and the men continued with their living arrangement and their work as legislators."

After King's election the county in the Washington Territory that eventually housed Seattle named itself King County in his honor. Ironically enough, given King's founding of (and burial in) Selma, where Martin Luther King Jr., made a name for himself, King County, Washington, later changed its honorary patron from William King to Martin Luther King Jr., the 1986 proclamation reading in part:

> *WHEREAS, the County of King in the State of Washington was named after William Rufus DeVane King by the Oregon Territorial legislature in 1852, and . . .*
>
> *WHEREAS, William Rufus DeVane King was a slaveowner and a 'gentle slave monger' according to John Quincy Adams, and WHEREAS, the citizens of King County believe that the ownership of another human being is an injustice against humanity, and WHEREAS, William Rufus DeVane King earned income and maintained his lifestyle by oppressing and exploiting other human beings, and . . .*
>
> *WHEREAS, Reverend Dr. Martin Luther King, Jr. believed that liberty, justice and freedom were the 'inalienable rights' of all men, women and children, and WHEREAS, Reverend Dr. Martin Luther King, Jr. was a spiritual man who believed all people were created equal in the sight of God . . .*

*The King County Council, hereby, sets forth the historical basis
for the 'renaming' of King County in honor of Reverend Dr. Martin
Luther King, Jr., a man whose contributions are well-documented
and celebrated by millions throughout this nation and the world, and
embody the attributes for which the citizens of King County can be
proud, and claim as their own.*

No matter what his relation with King, Buchanan survived it and
soon became president. In later years he continued to be rumored to be
dating or about to marry one or another woman, but never another man,
remaining a bachelor to his death. Abraham Lincoln and James Garfield
had some claiming them gay because of letters that professed "love" with
other male friends.

As uncertain as the claims of Buchanan's homosexuality are, it is
also quite likely that one or another president may have been gay, or at
least had homosexual relationships, just by the odds. If such rumors were
believed or proven, no eighteenth- or nineteenth-century presidential
candidate would have survived politically. In his historical and sex-filled
novel *The American People, Volume 1*, gay activist Larry Kramer posits
that several presidents were at least bisexual, if not gay. He describes a
long-term relationship Andrew Jackson may have had with another man
and then says it was apparent Franklin Pierce was always in love with
his best friend from Bowdoin College, Nathaniel Hawthorne. Finally,
he gets to Buchanan, both on his failed presidency and his sexual orientation:

*Another gay president! Two in a row! Pierce's successor, James
Buchanan (1857–1861), is a bungling, unattractive Pennsylvanian
also too fond of slavery for the country's good. What did he and Pierce
before him do in Washington for eight years? How does a country piss
away eight long and entire years? Where is everyone and anyone?*

*Three homosexual presidents, Jackson, Pierce, Buchanan, almost
in a row ... What is happening and why is it happening now? Even*

today, there is not a major piece of historical work about these three gay presidents that makes mention of the foregoing revelations.

This does not make Buchanan's potential homosexuality—whether it be fiction or Kramer's opinion—either true or, on the other hand, out of the question. The evidence of his homosexuality seems greater than that of any other president, but it seems more likely that in terms of sexuality, he could not get over the death of Ann Coleman and was too driven as a politician to form any real intimate relationship of any sort—gay or straight.

Biographer Jean Baker wrote that Buchanan "propagated the myth" that he stayed a bachelor because he had only one love—"the earthly object of my affections"—Ann Coleman. Baker wrote that Buchanan told a friend when he was in his forties, in 1833, that he would marry soon, but she implies that he did that only because he was running for the US Senate and it would look good for his candidacy. This happened again when he hoped to get the presidential nomination in the 1840s. He thought about getting married to Dolley Madison's niece, Anna Payne, Dolley being perhaps the most popular woman in Washington for decades, but since Anna Payne was nineteen and he was in his fifties, he said he decided against it and wrote a poem about it:

A match of age with youth can only bring
The farce of winter dancing with the spring.

Buchanan realized, wrote Baker, that he had good intentions, but also knew he just wanted companionship, that it was "not good for man to be alone, and [I] should not be astonished to find myself married to some old maid who can nurse me when I am sick, provide good dinners for me when I am well, and not expect from me any very ardent or romantic affection."

In fact, his relationship with his niece, Harriet Lane, provided enough of a distraction. They apparently adored each other—presumably in the proper familial way—and certainly were devoted to each other from the time she was an adolescent until the day he died. He took care of her finances and social education from the time she was his ward, and she took care of him when he got older and was the keeper of his legacy for decades after his death.

It is only a parlor game to speculate what Buchanan's legacy would be if he were gay. There has certainly also been speculation about Abraham Lincoln's relationship with a longtime friend, Joshua Speed, and it is only fair to think that if someone wanted to have a gay role model as president, he or she would certainly pick Lincoln over Buchanan. If somehow a cache of letters would turn up giving further proof that Buchanan was, indeed, gay, it would no doubt further besmirch his presidency to those unsympathetic to homosexuals, but it would be fascinating to see how gay advocates might embrace this worst president.

CHAPTER FOUR

The Man Who Would Be President,
Again, and Again

AFTER HIS TIME IN RUSSIA, BUCHANAN CAME BACK TO LANCASTER A man full of himself. In what could be called a passive-aggressive move, he bought the Coleman house on East King Street—the place where his dead fiancé had grown up and where he courted her. It was a big home for a single guy, but it was his, as if in replacement for his lost alleged love.

But how long would he live there? He saw himself blocked from the US Senate seat up for 1833 either by the timing of his return from Russia or by internal state Democratic politics. And he had grown weary of the usual cases he might try as a lawyer in Lancaster.

He started to think of other options.

The Democratic faction based in Philadelphia and headed by George Dallas, who would eventually become James Knox Polk's vice president, would make it difficult for Buchanan to become much of a legal force in the commonwealth's biggest city, so he contemplated finding some legal sinecure in New York or Baltimore.

He made one foray to Washington, though, to check in with President Jackson. While he had been away in Russia, there were two big political issues. The first was Jackson's veto of a bill to recharter the Bank of the United States. Jackson hated the idea of a central bank, thinking it limiting in the expansion of the nation and, in any case, run by enemies, and Jackson, if nothing else, felt himself a benevolent dictator, smarter than the average man and wanting to keep control, at least in politics.

The other issue was one with which Buchanan wrestled. It was South Carolina's nullification of the tariff agreements of 1828 and 1832, so integral to Buchanan's treaty with the czar. Buchanan had thought often about whether a state could negate a federal law and what would happen if it decided to leave the Union instead. His strict constructionist interpretation of the Constitution did not make clear what the solution would be. He was a Union man, though, and when Jackson said he would contemplate military action to force South Carolina to accept the tariffs, and the state then caved, Buchanan was relieved.

He knew, too, that in order to curry favor with Jackson, he would have to be both anti-Bank and anti-nullification. The latter was easy, but being a former Federalist and in favor in general of a centralized economy, he tried to find a middle ground on the bank issue. He admitted to Jackson that he held those old Federalist views, but told him that because he believed in the general, he would not say anything about a central bank, one way or the other. Dallas and his Philadelphia allies were pro-Bank, since that bank had long been in Philadelphia and important in its local economy. Jackson was cool to them because of that.

Jackson himself was in a bind. He never loved Buchanan, but he hated the Bank-loving Philadelphia faction of the party even more, since they could actually stand in the way of something important to him—the demise of the Bank of the United States. William Wilkins had voted for the recharter of the Bank in the Senate, so Jackson had it in for him. Buchanan may have come back from his Siberian exile a hero, but the circumstances were now so—with the mercantile treaty signed—that it was not going to happen again. So off went Wilkins to the St. Petersburg mission, leaving an opening with which to reward Buchanan a bit—and have him beholden to Jackson and his anointed successor, Martin Van Buren. Instead of looking for an attorney's office in New York or Baltimore, Buchanan was headed back to Washington, to complete the two years remaining of Wilkins's United States Senate seat.

Buchanan was now back on the road he hoped to be. Sure, Van Buren was next in line, but Buchanan was only forty-three. He could wait a bit, move the way he was used to, lumberingly and with measured steps. Even his apologist, Philip Klein, wrote in *President James Buchanan* that Buchanan was no mercurial guy: "James Buchanan always did things the slow way, the hard way, the sure way. He had no talent for the sudden devastating move, the brilliant stroke, the daring gamble, or the quick quip which by-passed a problem in a gale of laughter. He did not try to change his own position or to give new meaning and direction to the Pennsylvania Democracy. He began laboriously to rebuild his power from the bottom up, starting again in Lancaster County."

In the meantime Pennsylvania seemed to be turning Whig, which would surely impinge on Buchanan's chances to be reelected to the Senate in 1836, but Buchanan, ever taking the long view, perhaps even knew that something would blow his way. This time, it was the arrogance of the other political giant to come out of Lancaster, the boisterous and self-assured Thaddeus Stevens, who had also gravitated to Lancaster as a lawyer and by 1835 was a member of the Commonwealth Assembly.

The Whigs and Anti-Masonic Party controlled seventy-six of the one hundred seats in the Pennsylvania Assembly, the Democrats failing because of the Jackson-induced schism in the bank and tariff dealings. Stevens saw this as an opportunity to plague the Democrats even more, connecting them to the elitist, secretive, and feared Masonic movement. In December 1835 Stevens started an investigation of the Free Masons, calling every prominent Democrat to testify in Harrisburg. Buchanan was able to avoid this issue—he was, indeed, a Mason—because he was already in Washington. The whole thing completely boomeranged on Stevens and the Whigs. It was obvious what he was doing, and it was thoroughly useless and vindictive. It caused the Democrats to reunite and even angered fellow Whigs, who distanced themselves from the Anti-Masons, weakening whatever coalition they may have had.

While Buchanan had done nothing of significance in his first months in the Senate other than constantly speaking in favor of whatever Jackson favored, the overreaching by Stevens worked to his advantage. Buchanan aligned himself with Van Buren for the 1836 presidential race and hung on to his coattails hard. Van Buren squeaked out a victory in Pennsylvania by a mere 2,183 votes and the Whigs could not come up with a decent opponent, so there was only token opposition to Buchanan by some Bank-leaning Democrats.

Buchanan was now set—elected by his entire state, so in effect the leader of his party there. He had for the first time a long-view job, the six years of a full term in the Senate, just the thing for a guy who "always did things the slow way, the hard way, the sure way."

When he got to Washington, he looked up his old acquaintance, Senator William R. King of Alabama, and they agreed to room together. Whatever their relationship sexually—and there has been plenty of speculation about that in the 180 years since—they were part of a cadre of Southern gentlemen and the Northern Doughfaces, the term for Northern politicians who could be molded to Southern views, who admired them.

Most of the more prominent Doughfaces—Buchanan and Franklin Pierce, two eventual presidents among them—were not from prominent social families and were not particularly appreciated by those in the North who were. When they went to Washington, they gravitated to the Southerners, who, whether they were rich or not, had different social graces, which led them to accept virtually anyone to their social circles in the capital. Friendship, then, may well have superseded previous political leanings. Buchanan had no history of being for slavery—or even thinking or writing about it—before his Senate terms. King, however, had many slaves back on the plantation in Selma, Alabama, and was probably part of the slave trade in his native North Carolina before it was outlawed. Most of King's Washington friends were Southerners, and they became the bulk of Buchanan's social circle.

In fact, Buchanan had, only a few years before, in 1834, bought the freedom of two slaves, a mother and daughter, of the Virginia-based family of his brother-in-law, the Reverend Robert Henry, husband of his sister Harriet. At the time, Buchanan was beginning his political comeback from his Russian foray, and he understood being seen as a

Northerner with slaves that near to him was untenable. He arranged to buy their freedom himself, and for a time the daughter worked for him as a household servant—but a paid servant.

About this same time in 1834, Buchanan made another seemingly small move, but one that would be an important personal one through to his death. He realized that he would need someone to take care of the old Coleman mansion that he had bought, since he figured some job would take him to Washington or beyond. One of his favorite restaurants was the White Swan Hotel, right on the courthouse square nearby his home. The proprietor's niece, who had just turned twenty-eight, had started cooking and cleaning at the hotel, and Buchanan asked her if she would not mind staying at the house—whether he was there or not—and making sure it was clean and ready when he would come home from his Washington duties. The niece, Esther Parker, known as Miss Hetty, would be his housekeeper and closest confidante, or maybe second eventually to his niece Harriet Lane, for the next thirty-four years, and probably the person to whom he said his last words.

Those last words would be a long time off, though. Buchanan was on the rise. He was voted the chair of the Senate Foreign Relations Committee, his Whig opponent being the formidable former secretary of state Henry Clay. His station was even more assured when another of his Pennsylvania rivals, George Dallas, was given that old exile post—the ministership in Russia. Buchanan did his usual plodding job, making sure bills were paid and the president was apprised of what Congress thought of his foreign policy, but there was little dramatic in his senatorial life.

Presidential politics, though, was clearly on his mind. Van Buren was likely to try to have a second term—every incumbent before him had run again, though John Adams and his son, John Quincy, had failed to win—but he was likely to dump his running mate, Richard M. Johnson, whom he blamed for bringing down the ticket in 1836.

Buchanan made a deal with his best buddy, King, who had served as president pro tempore of the Senate. He would push for King to be the new vice presidential candidate and King would then make it clear that, if elected, he would not run for president when Van Buren's presumed second term was up in 1844, paving the way for a Buchanan candidacy.

Buchanan's scheme, as would be his usual thought, was based on whose "turn" it would be by that time. Van Buren was from New York, so that state had had a decent run. Johnson was from Kentucky; Jackson, from Tennessee; Calhoun, Jackson's first vice president, from South Carolina; Adams, from Massachusetts, and the three presidents previous to him, from Virginia. King's nomination would take care of the Deep South. Pennsylvania was the second most populous of the states, and it had seen no one in national executive office, barely even a cabinet member.

It would be Buchanan's turn, to be sure, in 1844, it would have seemed.

Buchanan's scheme never came to fruition. Van Buren remained loyal to Johnson, even though the election was doomed from the beginning. There had been a depression in 1837, which worked against the Democratic battle to kill the Bank of the United States, deemed to be the bastion of economic stability by both the merchant and working classes. The Whigs gained momentum in the off-year election in 1838, and then decided to do a quite Jacksonian thing, nominating a war hero, William Henry Harrison, as their 1840 presidential candidate.

Not only did he not get his scheme into action, but Buchanan also saw the Whigs' presidential ticket take Pennsylvania—albeit by only 350 votes out of 300,000—in the 1840 election, which nationwide was a landslide for Harrison, on whose coattails the Whigs carried both the United States House and Senate.

When Harrison died a month after his inauguration, and John Tyler, really a Democrat in Whig clothing, took over the presidency, speculation started earlier than ever about who would run for the Democrats in 1844. The field was wide open, with influential senators like Thomas Hart Benton and Calhoun; the former president and vice president, Van Buren and Johnson, respectively; and even the much-loathed Tyler—who had been seen by many to have usurped a presidency not nearly his—as the favorites.

Buchanan could hope for that nomination, but the odds were long, and he had not had the usual time he needed to think of a new scheme. In a way it was strange that Buchanan could even entertain the idea of becoming president. By the time he was reelected senator in 1842, he had spent nearly two decades as a congressman, either in the House or Senate. His contemporaries included five future presidents (Van Buren, Tyler, Polk, Fillmore, and Pierce) and major luminaries, from Webster, Clay, Calhoun, and Benton to his friend King, Jefferson Davis, and, in his post-presidential career, John Quincy Adams. He had never had his name on any piece of major legislation nor given any prominent address nor even been anything but a bit player in any significant debate. His most heralded achievement—his maneuvering to have the trade treaty with Russia—was mostly due to timing, but even if he were given all the credit for it, this was Russia, not Great Britain or France or even Spain or the Netherlands.

Despite all that, Buchanan's name was often in the mix whenever positions of prominence were in the air, if not at the current moment, then looking toward the future. It seems, looking backward, that Buchanan's strength was, in fact, his lack of aggressiveness. He was loyal, hardworking, and congenial. He had become Congress's most faithful conservative—not in the sense of right or left, as modern "conservatism" would want—but meaning steadiness.

He would almost always take the middle ground in any argument, just in case the winds would sway one way or the other. For instance, incongruously, he disliked both free trade and protective tariffs. He said one or the other would make one part of the nation or the other suffer, but then he did not come up with a solution. He would vote for something and then condemn it, like the 1842 tariff bill, and the Bank of the United States dissolution, where he felt the state should have some say in regulating banking, but he wanted a currency that could stretch. He believed in Manifest Destiny, yet voted against the Webster-Ashburton

Treaty, which would have had the British cede thousands of square miles of Canadian territory to the United States.

It is not that Buchanan wanted to be everybody's friend, just that he often would make a decision and then rethink things, which frustrated even his purported patrons, especially Andrew Jackson and James Knox Polk. He often demurred when it came to deciding whether to run for an office or acknowledge that he was interested in one job or another in higher administration.

In 1844, though, he was ready to go all-in for the Democratic presidential nomination. Once again, his early waffling did him in. Buchanan continued to gauge whether Pennsylvania's political men would think him ready for the job, so he supported all of the bigwigs, without yet asking for favors.

Meanwhile, fate dealt Buchanan another low hand. On February 28 the secretary of state, Abel P. Upshur, was killed by an accidental gun explosion on the USS *Princeton*. President Tyler basically then took over the department and, in a ruling that he thought would get the Democrats to renominate him, appointed expansionist John Calhoun secretary of state and decided to annex Texas. This was tantamount to starting a war with Mexico but was acclaimed in the South, because Texas would no doubt become a slave state. By mid-April former president Van Buren had weighed in, condemning the annexation. The same day, Henry Clay wrote a broadside saying the same thing. It catapulted Van Buren back into the race, since the Northern Democrats believed the whole incident and annexation were arranged by Southerners just to spread slavery.

Van Buren's newfound popularity, and the possibility that Whigs like Clay would support him, put Buchanan in the backseat among Northerners. Then, at the Democratic Convention in late May, Buchanan and the Pennsylvania delegation pushed for, and won, a resolution that the presidential candidate needed a two-thirds majority of delegates to get the nomination. That effectively killed Van Buren's candidacy, since it was a sectional vote. Buchanan, who had supporters in both the North and South, seemed a likely compromise.

Then reared the graying mane of the man still the most popular politician in the country, Andrew Jackson. He was seventy-seven and only a year away from his own death, but still a driving force in the Democratic Party. He had long been a supporter of Van Buren, his former vice president, but Jackson was in favor of annexing Texas, so he could not let him be president. As for supporting Buchanan, well, that was never going to happen.

So Jackson picked a neighbor of his, the former Speaker of the US House of Representatives and governor of Tennessee, James Knox Polk. It was an operation done judiciously, with Jackson waiting to see if Van Buren would actually get a two-thirds majority at the convention. When Van Buren did not win on the first seven ballots, the convention adjourned for the evening. Some delegates supporting Tyler had already abandoned the convention and, in a rump meeting elsewhere in Baltimore, nominated Tyler to run as a third-party candidate.*

The next day, Polk's name suddenly became part of the discussion, and he garnered a few delegates. The New York delegation surprisingly called for a private meeting, and before the next ballot Van Buren withdrew his name and the convention gave its unanimous vote to Polk, who then chose for vice president Silas Wright, a New Yorker, as a sop to Van Buren. Then Wright declined the nomination, which Buchanan's Pennsylvania rival, George M. Dallas, accepted.

Had Jackson died a year earlier, perhaps 1844 would have been Buchanan's time, but with the nominations of both Polk and Dallas, Buchanan was trumped twice.

Buchanan shrewdly wrote to Polk, when Polk won his race easily over the Whig candidate, Henry Clay, that it was time to update the Democratic Party. "The old office holders generally have had their day & ought to be content," Buchanan wrote him the day of the election. Polk himself was still young—only forty-nine when he was elected—so this was clearly to butter up the new president, showing that the fifty-three-year-old Buchanan was still thinking young.

---

* Tyler's third-party candidacy would die the following summer.

Jackson had told Polk to spurn advances from Buchanan, maybe give him something minor, but Polk eventually gave in to Buchanan's entreaties and made him secretary of state, mostly to clear the way for his vice president, Dallas, to really take over the Pennsylvania Democrats. Polk, who was starting now finally to wean himself away from Jackson, wanted to make sure that Buchanan—and every other cabinet member—would not be a rival to him.

"Should any member of my Cabinet become a Candidate for the Presidency or Vice Presidency of the United States, it would be expected," wrote Polk to all the nominees, "that he will retire from the Cabinet." Polk wanted no patronage that would pile up into presidential caches to come out of his administration. Polk had hinted that he would be a one-term president, but that had also been the contention of Tyler, and he reneged.

Buchanan, though, gave at least the indication that he was satisfied with the plum post. "I cheerfully and cordially approve the terms on which this offer has been made," he wrote back to Polk, adding one caveat: "I cannot proclaim to the world that in no contingency shall I be a candidate for the Presidency in 1848," but he would certainly resign from the cabinet if he thought it would come about.

Buchanan's last speech as a senator was a rousing plea to annex Texas, which is what Polk dearly wanted to have happen. In it he finally articulated his feelings about slavery, since it was the proverbial elephant in the room in the Texas debate. "I am not friendly to slavery in the abstract," he said. "I need not say that I never owned a slave, and I know that I never shall own one . . . [but] the constitutional rights of the south, under our constitutional compact, are as much entitled to protection as those of any other portion of the Union." He was picking slavery and Union over his own personal beliefs. A few days later, just before Polk's inauguration, both houses passed Texas annexation and Tyler signed the resolution.

The first thing on Buchanan's agenda as secretary of state, the party giver in him awakened, was to find new and elegant digs in Washington. A friend found him a house next door to his old rival—and former secretary of state—John Quincy Adams, renting for $2,000 a year, a large sum, but one Buchanan could afford due to his profitable investments. It had loads of china for potential state dinners and he ordered a new dining table centerpiece from Paris to impress any courtly Europeans. In addition, the new home was a block from his State Department office, and a big change from his longtime boarding house living in the capital.

A century before FDR's New Deal touted change in governmental outlook, Polk started what he called the New Democracy. The point for Polk, who grew up with slave nannies, was that slavery was a nonissue. The important thing for his presidency was expansion—of the country's territory and commerce. If slavery spread or if it died, Polk intimated, he did not care.

In place of the alleged Great Men of the age, Polk filled his cabinet with people like Buchanan—specialists who could get things done, and done the way Polk wanted them to be done. Buchanan had foreign diplomatic experience and, on the side, could take care of the diplomacy in the warring factions of the Democratic Party in Pennsylvania. Financier Robert J. Walker became secretary of the treasury, for instance, and William L. Marcy of New York, who was a hawk, was thus just right for Polk's expansionist leanings as secretary of war.

Before he could get to do much as secretary of state, though, Buchanan started making noises about another job. President Tyler, in the spring of 1844, had offered Buchanan a place on the Supreme Court, perhaps just to get him out of the way of the presidential nomination. Buchanan refused it quickly, but then obviously had it on his mind for a while. The seat, previously held by Henry Baldwin, who had died, was still open in the fall of 1845, only a few months after Buchanan had taken over the State Department, and Buchanan went to Polk to say he would actually rather have the Supreme Court seat. But he told Polk he would withdraw the request if war broke out with Mexico over Texas, which was an important national and international issue.

Polk seemed about to acquiesce, but then Buchanan, as was his wont, changed his mind again. He got word that negotiations over the Oregon

Territory could be resuming, so he was willing to stay on in the State Department, especially if he could facilitate getting a few hundred thousand square miles added to the Republic.

Events turned *again*. No one satisfactory had come before the Senate for the Baldwin Supreme Court seat, so Senator Lewis Cass of Michigan, who would eventually become Buchanan's secretary of state, and Senator Thomas Hart Benton of Missouri told Polk that Buchanan should get it. Buchanan, oddly enough, had only recently been the formal escort at a Washington wedding of Jessie Benton, Thomas's favorite daughter, the wife of John Fremont, who would oppose Buchanan as the Republican presidential candidate in 1856. Washington then, like now, was nothing if not incestuous.

So now to solidify support for his latest seesaw move on the Supreme Court nomination, Buchanan held a blowout ball at a place called Carusi's Saloon, where more than a thousand of Washington's political and social finest showed up.

Buchanan employed the most prominent chef in mid-nineteenth-century America, Charles Gautier, to cater the affair. Gautier was the first of the show-off chefs in Washington—the Mario Batali or Anthony Bourdain of his era. Gautier, who had emigrated from France in 1838 and quickly become the main purveyor of haute cuisine in the United States, would decorate the inside and windows of his Ville de Paris Restaurant at Eleventh Street and Pennsylvania Avenue, a couple of blocks from the White House, every Christmas. Everyone, even those who could never afford to eat at the Ville de Paris, came by to see, as his advertising said, "a large number of superb Cakes, most tastefully and richly ornamented, ranging in weight from five pounds up to near twelve hundred pounds!" There were finely dressed dolls and other Christmas scenes—one of the big tourist attractions in the capital.

Even by Gautier's standards, the Buchanan party of January 23 was gaudy. The menu was extensive and expensive—venison, ham, beef, turkey, pheasant, chicken, oysters, and lobster for the main courses. Gautier was also a master confectioner, so he made a buffet of desserts: charlotte russe, fruit and cake pyramids, ice cream, chocolate kisses, and water ice. There were 300 bottles of wine and 150 bottles of champagne.

Everyone was there: Dolley Madison sat in her honored position, on an elevated platform at one end of the catering hall. Elizabeth Schuyler Hamilton, Alexander Hamilton's widow, now eighty-eight and more than four decades removed from his death, was visiting her old friend Dolley from New York—they were the leading movers in fundraising for the Washington Monument—and was there telling stories about her husband and the rest of the Founders. Political party did not matter. Daniel Webster, the most prominent Whig alive, was there, as was the up-and-comer William Seward, down from New York to argue a case before the Supreme Court. Mrs. John Adams, the daughter-in-law of Buchanan's old Democratic rival, former president John Quincy Adams, danced with the Whig Seward.

"He threw great parties. Hand out the cigars. Hand out the Madeira. He loved the rye whiskey and he had the money to be able to afford it," said Patrick Clarke, the director of Buchanan's estate, Wheatland. "He was a master politician in that way. He loved being around people who were in a good mood."

The one thing Buchanan did not count on was that Polk, taking a warning from his mentor, Jackson, distrusted Buchanan, and saw all this back and forth as a reason to never be sure of Buchanan's word. The office of secretary of state was different then than in the twentieth century and beyond. There was no jetting off to seventy-five countries a year and meeting with statesmen every week. It was much more an administrative post, making sure treaties were worded correctly and managing emissaries where they did travel. The more important secretary of state function, handed down from Jefferson's time in the post under Washington, was essentially being the head of the cabinet. Under a confident man like Jackson, he could be the conscience of the administration—allowed to differ with the boss to make sure every view got represented before a decision was made. Under Polk, however, who had made every cabinet member sign off that he would not challenge him for the next presidential nomination, the secretary of state was clearly to be less the secondary boss and more the administrator of foreign affairs—not quite a yes-man, but not one to tell the boss he was going down the wrong path.

Polk's greatest desire was to lower tariffs on major industries, which Pennsylvanians, fearful of how it would affect the coal and iron markets, were virulently against. The summer was approaching as the tariff bill wended its way through Congress, and Buchanan saw that if he stayed in the administration, he would be caught either alienating the president or his state's businessmen. Polk asked him to stay in the cabinet at least through the vote.

This time, though Buchanan was no doubt gnawing on his fingernails as the tariff debate continued, fate gave him a break. The vote was so close that Vice President Dallas, Buchanan's primary Pennsylvania rival, would have to break the tie. Dallas was forced to go against his state and his biggest backers there in order to vote Polk's wishes. Buchanan never had to take an official stand.

So now he figured staying in the administration would be a better deal than putting on judicial robes. No one had come close to the presidency from the Supreme Court, and Buchanan still wanted to be in the White House. Polk would not fire him, he reasoned, since he never officially contradicted the president's position on the tariff.

Buchanan's waffling this time righted him on the road to the presidency—but not quite yet. The tariff turned out to be an ephemeral issue; the manufacturing economy in the North did not collapse and, more important, the crisis moved to what was really Polk's New Democracy objective, to make sure the United States extended from the Atlantic to the Pacific and as far north and south as could be possible.

Polk had said he would accomplish his goals in one term and then leave the office. He wanted the tariff. He wanted Texas. He wanted as much land as possible in the Oregon Territory. He wanted California. He eventually got it all, but his biggest impediment was not Spain or England or the Northern and New England manufacturers. It was his secretary of state, James Buchanan.

Each time Polk made a proposal on the Texas and Mexico issue, Buchanan would suggest something different. In Oregon it was even worse. Polk's platform had a banner-rousing cheer, one known to every high school history student today: "54/40 or Fight." Polk did not seriously want to have war with Great Britain over how to split the Oregon Territory. In fact, neither country was so sure the inland and northern part of the territory was worth much. Buchanan, though, knew that Polk had to at least give a shot to gaining that 54/40 northern longitudinal parallel to please his constituents who had burned their throats shouting those numbers during the campaign.

Buchanan had started to resent his boss, especially his dictum that no cabinet member should move toward the presidential nomination while in office. The only way, Buchanan thought, to advance his presidential ambitions, then, was not to toady up to Polk's wishes all the time. Three different times, for instance, Buchanan changed his mind about what was best in Oregon. When Polk told him to press for 54/40, Buchanan said it would be better to let the British dictate terms, or at least suggest them. When Polk said, OK, let us go for the forty-ninth parallel, Buchanan said, well, why don't we try for more? Then Polk allowed Buchanan to negotiate for the bigger territory, but not to threaten war over it. Polk let the British hang for a while, and they prepared warships to start hostilities.

At that point Buchanan had publically become a strong man to some Democrats, especially those who loved winning big battles. They were the same folks who wanted a Mexican war to conquer as much territory as possible there. Polk was leery about that war as well, but figured it would be difficult to get the land to the Pacific without it. Polk would have been happy to split the difference there, too, taking the northern half of California and down to the northern part of New Mexico, instead of all the way south to the Rio Grande River and Baja California. Buchanan, it seemed, would go against Polk under any circumstances, and so induced him to have a war with Mexico, something he thought could be wrapped up in a few months.

What Buchanan did not count on, which Polk knew, was that starting the war, with its inevitable victory, would fuel the Whigs to put a winning military general at the top of their next presidential ticket. Both Winfield Scott and Zachary Taylor won big battles, which won big headlines. Polk actually had not ruled out running again in 1848, but after the war, even though he got credit for victory, he decided to cut and run. The British had backed off in Oregon and both sides were happy in the end, with the forty-ninth parallel as a border between the United States and Canada, the way it is today. The United States gave the British rights to use the Oregon Territory ports, which made cities like Seattle and Portland on one side and Vancouver and Victoria on the other thrive, especially with agricultural products from the Northwest ready for export.

With Polk bowing out—he ended up dying six months after his term, so his ill health had probably started by the time he had to decide—Buchanan again figured he was deserving of the nomination. His scheme was the usual: show complete indifference as long as possible, build up a constituency in the home state, let other people take sides in what were usually petty issues, say little controversial, and then proclaim, "Aw, shucks, well, OK," when influential, or maybe desperate, back-scenes types came calling.

This time around, it seemed that no Southerner would be in the mix, Tennessee especially having its due with Jackson and Polk already having served and Virginia with five presidents of the twelve. Buchanan's main competitors seemed to be Lewis Cass of Michigan and Stephen Douglas of Illinois, both champions of the West who could claim that the next states to come on line would support the expansionist view. Buchanan had his varied government experience going for him, but even more so, his lack of criticism of slavery gave him a constituency among Southern Democrats.

In the winter Buchanan started his other tactic, giving parties every two weeks or so where the liquor would flow, and apparently the conversation would also flow in his favor. But, to be sure, Douglas, to whom he gave an invitation each time, did not come to any, being his presidential competition. The Whigs started staying away, too—Webster willing to support him for the Supreme Court, but not for the presidency. The Pennsylvania delegation often stayed away as well, since many of them still liked Vice President Dallas to move up.

At the May 1848 convention in Baltimore, Cass did well on the first ballot, which caused Virginia, then a border state with leanings away from secession and moving in many places, especially toward its west, away from slavery itself, to abandon Buchanan for the Michigander. Taylor, though, got the Whig nomination and won the election going away. Buchanan mused later that he probably would have been defeated as well. He thought he would still have one more shot in 1852. He would go back to Lancaster, make a little money with the law, and bide his time.

Surprisingly, Buchanan was not particularly depressed about being denied the 1848 nomination. Taylor would have been a formidable opponent for anyone. The eleven elected presidents now included four major war heroes: George Washington, Andrew Jackson, William Henry Harrison, and Zach Taylor. (James Monroe had a good military record, but his election came because of his government service.) The American citizenry was Shakespearean in that regard—they were in love with their warriors, often willing to overlook their foibles. Washington had really wanted to retire; Jackson was almost misanthropic; Harrison was old and infirm; Taylor had never voted and was still a slaveholder.

Buchanan was willing to live with that, but he still thought he was the best of the civilian politicians. He was clearly, at least among Democrats, the most prepared, having served in both congressional houses, abroad in Russia, and as secretary of state. The Whigs Daniel Webster and Henry Clay could claim vast experience like his, but they had already run for president and lost. Despite his attempts for the nomination, Buchanan had no official loss on his record.

Still, he was going to have to figure out some way to bide his time and while keeping in the public and political eyes. Carriage routes and railroads had made Lancaster much more accessible to Washington, not to mention Baltimore and Philadelphia, over the last three decades since Buchanan had been there full-time, so it was hardly going to be remote while he came up with his scheme for 1852.

His living situation, though, had to change. First of all, the King Street house would be a liability. It was right in the middle of the partisan political area, and there had been fistfights and threats of worse violence among the young rivals in Lancaster. Further, many of his nephews and nieces, most of them orphans or half orphans, needed either permanent housing or at least a place they could safely go when things were dicey. The summer before the 1848 election, Buchanan heard that Wheatland, a country estate built by his old cohort William Jenkins, was available for sale. It would be perfect, he thought—a mile out of town, large enough for any of those nephews and nieces to stay in, and big enough still to entertain in, for either political or social purposes—though Buchanan's "social" entertaining always had political overlays.

He bought the estate in December and then moved in after he was done with his duties as secretary of state in March 1849. The house and surrounding grounds were in excellent shape, so Buchanan immediately started sending out invitations for politicians to come visit the new "Sage of Wheatland," as the newspapers had already come to call him.

Buchanan also searched out ways to keep himself in public circulation—not quite padding his resume, but burnishing it when he could. While he never really loved his experience at and with Dickinson College, he took the challenge, in 1851, of negotiating a peace between students and faculty there. There had been a rules rebellion by the junior class, and the faculty and administration agreed to dismiss the whole class. Buchanan forged an agreement in which the students would pledge better behavior and the faculty would let them back in on the pledge to the famous alumnus—a solution not too far different from the one his patrons made for him more than thirty years before.

Soon after that, Marshall College, named after the longtime Supreme Court chief justice, but in remote Mercersburg, wanted to merge with a more centrally located institution. Buchanan facilitated that union—with Franklin College in Lancaster. He found a large property not far from Wheatland for the new combined institution, gave a $1,000 donation to get things started, and became the chair of the board of trustees. Later on, when he was president, Buchanan rented out rooms in Wheatland to Franklin & Marshall students. This was actually not as mercenary as it sounds on the surface. Buchanan was upset that residents of Lancaster were requiring extortionate rents from Franklin & Marshall young men. Always the fair trader, he undercut those who were overcharging, but felt it was not fair just to give away the lodgings. Since he was doing a lot of financing of the school in the first place, it is probable that he donated whatever he got from his student renters back to the college, though it probably seemed strange to the public that the sitting president was renting out his house to anyone at all.

Buchanan also decided to be a gentleman farmer. He had more than a thousand strawberry plants and put trees and decorative shrubbery all around the acreage. He took a lot of sleigh rides in the snowy winter and in the spring, and started a new hobby of bird-watching out in the back grounds. He built a vaulted wine cellar in the basement of the main house and collected rare vintages. The economy was good and his investments rose precipitously, so he had to do little, if any, law work to sustain his tastes.

His parties, large and small, were legend, and even one visitor would trigger Buchanan's desire to show off his wines and liquors. He served Madeira, sherry, and rye whiskey most often—the standards of his age. The *Philadelphia Press*, when writing about his partying, said that he alone could drink two or three bottles at a sitting, mostly finishing the night with a rye or two.

"And then the effect of it!" the paper wrote. "There was no head ache, no faltering steps, no flushed cheek. Oh, no! All was as cool, as calm and as cautious and watchful as in the beginning. More than one ambitious tyro who sought to follow his example gathered an early fall." He would buy ten-gallon casks of Old J. B. Whiskey from a local distillery and joke with guests that the letters stood for James Buchanan.

From his somewhat hardscrabble beginnings a few miles to the west, Buchanan had grown into a country squire, with distinguished visitors, parties late into the night, tales swapped and cigars smoked. In a certain way, this was the height of his fame. There was no pressure to take political stands, even though certainly guests knew he was still interested in the presidency. He loved being in the know in Washington, to be sure, but he was always most comfortable in Lancaster, and it did not take long for him to believe that the purchase of Wheatland was the best one he had ever made. He had his nieces and nephews around him, and even if they needed his money to survive and thrive, he felt no compunction about giving it to them, so long as they were thrifty and moving toward good ends.

There was still one thing missing, though, and that surely was the presidency. His perennial candidacy had become a bit of a joke, especially among Whigs, of which there were still many in central Pennsylvania and nearby Maryland. Buchanan could not let that bother him. Far into the night, he wrote letters to anyone who could be of later use, so much so that Miss Hetty feared for his candles to burn him when he might fall asleep at his desk.

The nation always seemed in turmoil, and almost always it was about slavery and where that institution should go. All of the most significant bills and treaties of the first six decades of the nineteenth century were, at least tangentially, a part of that fight: the Missouri Compromise, the Louisiana Purchase, the annexation of Texas, the Mexican War and its peace settlements, the Oregon Territory compromise, the Compromise of 1850, the Kansas-Nebraska Act. Should the slave trade continue? Which states should have slavery? What should be done about runaway slaves? Could Congress regulate slavery in the territories? What was the cost going to be to keep the Union—if not, as Lincoln lamented, "half slave and half free"?

Buchanan was well aware of every move being made in Washington, and what he had done in the past was the core of that. Had the nation stayed along the Atlantic coast and slightly inland, as it was when it separated from Great Britain, it all might have been an aggravation, but nothing more. It was only when new states were being added, thus changing the makeup of Congress, that these compromises had to happen. Even that had stayed fine for the decades after the Missouri Compromise.

The large landmass the United States collected from the Mexican War and the Oregon Territory negotiation changed things. If it were not political, the vast majority of that acreage would have no reason to be slave land. The new land was not conducive to the crops that needed slave labor, and the vastness of the area lent itself more to entrepreneurial and adventurous men and families.

Political, however, is what it was. If the Southern slave states could not get the votes in Congress to stay that way, then their influence would wane immeasurably. Modern citizens may hardly believe it, but there was a general consensus in the country about slavery. Most Southerners wanted it, for practical reasons, if not also for the racist belief that the African American was inferior, at least mentally and morally. Most Northerners let the issue ride. They might have been against slavery personally, but like a tic a neighbor might have that they shrugged their shoulders about, they tolerated slavery for the places where it already existed. Clearly there were those who wanted the institution eliminated for moral reasons, but they were in an almost disdained minority.

With California coming into the Union, though, there would be one extra nonslave state. It was clear that in the long run there would be far more free states than slave. There had to be, then, a way to placate the slave owners, so that slavery itself would not be abolished in some future vote. The Compromise of 1850 was the first effort.

It was brokered primarily by Henry Clay, and though President Taylor was not a fan of it, Taylor died in office in July 1850, and his successor, Millard Fillmore, a Whig from New York at that time, pushed it through. The main points of the compromise were these: California would be admitted as a free state; Congress would pass a stricter fugitive slave law; the slave trade would stop in the District of Columbia; and Utah and New Mexico would be organized as territories, one on each side of the old Missouri Compromise line of latitude, and they would decide on their slave status when they applied for statehood.

It was a huge effort and it seemed to many at the time that it would solve the nation's seminal crisis for good. Like most wishes of the sort, it was clearly a temporary Band-Aid, and Buchanan was one of those who recognized that. If he were to even think about running for president in 1852, though, he had to come up with an opinion on the compromise. But to really put himself away from the pack, he had to think of a creative response that would be patently his.

Buchanan chose to be evasive and complex, as he often was. He noted that there was a longstanding Fugitive Slave Law, going all the way back to 1793. It was just that it was only intermittently enforced. Since that was about all the South really got from the compromise, there had to be better enforcement of it. He worried, though, that stricter enforcement would incite the people he hated most—the rabid anti-slavery abolitionists.

Strangely, Buchanan later believed that it was the abolitionists who incited the trouble that bled through Bloody Kansas, secession, and the Civil War. He thought he was the man who could keep the Union together, and to do that, he would have to condemn the abolitionists, whom he felt cared less about the Union than they did about abolishing slavery—even to the point of causing secession if necessary to that goal.

Buchanan came to the 1852 Democratic Convention in Baltimore with that stance. His major competitors were Lewis Cass of Michigan and Stephen Douglas of Illinois. A fourth favorite-son candidate, William Marcy, controlled the largest delegation, the one from New York. Horse trading dominated the early ballots, with Buchanan leading most of them, but not by nearly enough to sew up the nomination. Buchanan decided on a shrewd maneuver. He would have his emissaries put up for nomination a dark horse who would never really make inroads, and he selected handsome and young Franklin Pierce from New Hampshire.

It all backfired. By the forty-ninth ballot, the delegates had had it. The newness of Pierce energized the New York and Indiana delegates, and even those from Buchanan's own home state of Pennsylvania. The roll call was stopped for consultations, and by the end of the ballot, Pierce had all but 14 of the convention's 296 votes.

Buchanan, again, was crestfallen. He was the best candidate, and here he got only a consolation prize, the chance to put forward his friend, William King of Alabama, as Pierce's running mate. Freed of the need to be "creative" as a candidate, Buchanan became an advocate of the Compromise of 1850 as the document that could save the Union. Pierce sought Buchanan's counsel when he won the election by a landslide, but told him he wanted new blood, especially younger men, in the cabinet and in higher posts.

Buchanan still hoped he would get something in the cabinet, but it was not to be. He laughed to friends that he had moved from becoming a middle-aged fogy to an old fogy, and that he had to live with people no longer calling him "Jimmy" and now referring to him as "Old Buck." He had grown pretty fat and his blond hair was now a tuft of grey. His teeth hurt. He had spasms of biliousness. His back hurt. He had more hangovers than ever.

Pierce, though, was not going to take any chances. He went to the Old Hickory playbook and demanded that Buchanan be his minister to Great Britain. Buchanan, to be sure, realized this was a ruse to keep him out of the running for 1856, but he felt honor bound to, after waffling for a while, accept the position.

While in London Buchanan's best move was to have his niece, Harriet, come for a while. Together they charmed the monarchy and the higher governmental figures. Not much actually came of Buchanan's stay in Britain, but the queen, the prime minister, and the opposition had good social opinions of the old guy with the high collars and his well-educated and well-mannered young ward. As a bonus, Buchanan was out of the country when every other politician of note had to weigh in on the signal bit of legislation of the day, the Kansas-Nebraska Act. That he did not put any opinion on the record kept him not exactly above the fray, but at least out of it.

The stay in London energized Buchanan. He would be sixty-five in 1856, but he was not going to give up the winding road he had been taking for decades. By God, he was going to become Franklin Pierce's successor.

———

I was teaching an advanced writing class at the University of Pennsylvania in the mid-2000s when we discovered that William Henry Harrison was the only president of the United States who went to Penn. Well, sort of.

Harrison was the son of Benjamin Harrison V, who was the chairman of the Committee of the Whole that reviewed and then passed the Declaration of Independence. The elder Harrison returned home to Virginia soon after signing the document and became first governor and then Speaker of the state house.

Benjamin Harrison—his great-grandson also becoming president, bearing his name—hated war and was horrified when his son, William, wanted to become a soldier. Meanwhile, Benjamin's Philadelphia buddy, Benjamin Rush, had started the first hospital in the United States. He told William that he was not going to go to war, but to medical school with Rush, who had aligned the hospital and medical school with Benjamin Franklin's University of Pennsylvania.

A few months after young William got to Philadelphia to study with Rush, Benjamin Harrison was reelected Speaker of the state house in Virginia, but fell ill while celebrating at a dinner party and died. William went home to preside at the funeral and never returned to Penn, becoming instead a military hero, despite his father's demands.

On Presidents' Day during that class, Kia/Hyundai ran a cute TV advertisement, saying that while most businesses would promote Lincoln or Washington, Kia would be giving away souvenir William Henry Harrison towels to Presidents' Day customers. During one class we called the PR guy at the car company and put him on speaker phone. We asked him if we could get a towel, being as we were from Harrison's alma mater. The guy said, "There is one towel. It is from the ad. It is in the CEO's office. And you are not getting it."

I shrugged my shoulders, having given it, literally, the old college try. I bought a dozen white T-shirts, enough for the class, had an image of Harrison silk-screened on each and had "Our Bill" stenciled underneath.

Harrison, though his Penn connection was at best tangential and at worst dubious, was a substantial man, serving as a military governor and battlefield general off and on. The first of the Harrisons had come to the New World in 1630, and his forebears were large landholders and contributors to the colonial government.

Unfortunately, like his father, William Henry Harrison had his greatest triumph fall through or at least short, catching a fever soon after his inauguration as president and dying only a month into his term.

There is no telling whether Harrison would have been as substantial in the presidency as he was before it, but he was clearly the only president between Andrew Jackson and Abraham Lincoln to have had a shot. OK, maybe James Knox Polk, but upon later reflection, he was an opportunist who did the country no real favors. The early to mid decades of the nineteenth century were a repository of the also-run and afterthoughts of national politics: Martin Van Buren, John Tyler, Polk, Zachary Taylor, Millard Fillmore, Franklin Pierce, and our good friend James Buchanan (with the add-on of Andrew Johnson, the only president to be impeached, following Lincoln).

At the same time, however, there were giants abounding in government in the United States. There were the famous senators and diplomats Henry Clay, Daniel Webster, John Calhoun, and Thomas Hart Benton at the top of the heap, followed by Southerners like Jefferson Davis and Alexander Stephens, who became the president and vice president, respectively, of the Confederate States of America, and Northerners like William Seward, Salmon Chase, Edwin Stanton, Edward Everett, and Thaddeus Stevens, and even the overrated Stephen Douglas and John Fremont, just off that top rank.

All of the significant political events of the era were the work of the second group, not the list of woeful presidents. The Missouri Compromise, the Compromise of 1850, the Kansas-Nebraska Act, the annexation of Texas, the charting of the West, the settlement of California, the building of the railroads, the orations that resulted in either significant Supreme Court decisions or major movements, the resulting amendments of the Constitution (particularly the thirteenth and fourteenth, securing equal rights), even the idea of secession and the Confederate States of America—these were large ideas, good or bad, dreamed up, promulgated, and argued passionately by a bunch of men who never got to the White House except to visit and maybe party.

"This is certainly one of the great questions out there for scholars, why the country picked these guys and not the big politicians on the stage," Bryan Craig, the senior researcher for the Presidential Oral History Program of the Miller Center for the Study of the Presidency at the University of Virginia, told me. "I think one of the reasons is that some of the guys who won were just compromise candidates. These giants have a lot of baggage and because of that can only go so far."

Craig did a study of the 1848 election and why Clay, the most prominent man in American politics, did not get the nomination.

"Zachary Taylor was a war hero and that was huge," said Craig. "Clay had a shot at it, but he had already lost other times. By 1848 the Whigs thought he had spent his capital and could not win.

"The big giants got involved in these issues of territorial expansion and slavery, and their hands got dirty," Craig said. "I think the whole political climate at the time, the 1850s and 1860s especially, was like an earthquake. The huge shifts basically changed the landscape, and parties and people just got blown away and moved on. The men left around were those who preserved themselves, cloaked in mostly wishy-washy opinions and trying not to offend, rather than doing big things."

The presidents who came before Jackson were all either Founding Fathers or men of breeding and money, sometimes both. Jackson broke through those standards. As *New Yorker* contributor and Harvard history professor Jill Lepore wrote, Thomas Jefferson was appalled that Jackson had taken over his party. "He is one of the most unfit men I know of for such a place," wrote Jefferson of Jackson, and John Quincy Adams, his predecessor and the last in that first line of patrician presidents, lamented Jackson's "man of the people" persona. "The man spelled 'government' with only one 'n,'" the younger Adams lamented.

Jackson, being a former military man, though, started what would have seemed to be a new trend in the White House. He pushed Congress to pass what he wanted, large things and small. He micromanaged and took patronage into his own hands, rewarding and denying favors based primarily on loyalty.

In Jackson's wake others faltered. Van Buren had been an effective politician in New York, but he had no real ideas to propel the country forward, in fact presiding over the Panic of 1837, which took the United States, at least economically, back a few steps.

Caretakers instead of major thinkers then abounded in the White House, from Tyler through Buchanan. None was inherently corrupt or brainless, but all were thrust into a chair that ill-suited them. Collectively, they then took the stance that Congress was the creative branch of government, and that the executive was basically there to carry out the legislature's vision, not the other way around, as Jackson would have had it.

While Clay may have defensively said his most famous line—"I would rather be right than president"—it nonetheless was a truism. He—and Webster and Benton and Douglas—were right, or at least guiding lights, in the mid-nineteenth century, but in spite of, or maybe because of, that, they would never be president.

CHAPTER FIVE

The Election of 1856:
The Most Consequential in
American History

THE PRESIDENTIAL ELECTION OF 1856 WAS WITHOUT A DOUBT TRANS-
formational, perhaps presaging the Civil War, but certainly moving
toward the modern American political scene, with two sometimes fluid
major parties and the off-and-on happenstance of a third party with a
major theme.

The Whig Party, which had the majority in the House of Representatives as late as 1849, and only the year before the '56 election still
had twenty-two of the sixty-two United States senators, had completely
collapsed.

It was one of those perfect-storm scenarios that culminated in 1856.
The Whigs' two most prominent senators and leaders, Henry Clay and
Daniel Webster, had both died in 1852. They were nationally and inter-
nationally known figures for decades, each having served in both the
House of Representatives and Senate, served as secretaries of state, and,
between them, run for president four times.

Their losses of the presidency, and their success in pursuing other
offices, was actually consistent with Whig Party philosophy. The Whigs
took their name, if not their lineage, from the British Whig party, but
were never really related to it. At the time of the American Revolution,

many revolutionaries called themselves Whigs, for being opposed to the British monarchy, as the British Whigs were during the late eighteenth century. Clay had run for president initially in 1824 when there was only one party, the Democrat-Republicans, but when he gave his support to John Quincy Adams and, in the wake of his victory, Adams appointed Clay secretary of state, Andrew Jackson, another of the four candidates that year, became furious. When Jackson succeeded Adams, he viewed Clay as his biggest enemy and, whenever he could, pushed issues that Clay would find reprehensible.

That, in a sense, gave Clay and others who were anti-Jacksonians an opportunity to start the first new political party since the Federalists folded their hand during the Jefferson/Madison/Monroe "Era of Good Feelings" decades. The Whigs were somewhat progressive—though Clay himself had slaves—and looked to modernize society, wanted a strong central bank to foster business, and, perhaps just to be against Jackson, opposed the president's policy of moving Native Americans out of their ancestral lands and to the West. The Whigs were not particularly expansionists, fearing bad things (from slavery to war) might result from the quest for more land. They wanted to make positive modern change happen in the already existing United States and adjacent territories.

The Whigs made some good strategic moves in their presidential nominations, especially when they had former military men on their ballots. They had an ingenious strategy in 1836. Andrew Jackson's vice president, Martin Van Buren, had the blessing of Jackson, the most popular American of the era, so it seemed he could beat virtually any single opponent. The Whigs, though, decided to run four candidates, based on who was popular in different parts of the country. The theory was that if no one got an electoral majority, the election would be thrown into the House of Representatives, where the Whigs had a decent chance to get a majority of states to rally around one of the candidates. William Henry Harrison, the other popular general of the early nineteenth century, ran in the Northwest; Webster ran in Massachusetts; populist Willie P. Magnum ran in South Carolina; and Hugh L. White ran in the rest of the slave states. It did not work, since Van Buren squeaked out an electoral college victory and the Democrats won the majority of House seats anyway, but it showed cageyness.

Although their statesmen and thinkers, Clay and Webster, did not win presidential elections, they ended up nominating war heroes who did. In the manner of George Washington and Andrew Jackson, the Whigs put up Harrison again, this time alone, in the 1840 election, and he won. Unfortunately, Harrison died thirty-one days into his term. Popular mythology has long said he died from catching a cold during his inauguration, in which he delivered a two-hour address—the longest in inaugural history—not wearing a topcoat or a hat on a frigid and windy day. In reality, he did not become sick until three weeks later, more than likely related to the open sewage nearby that may have infected the White House water or food supply. Following the medical thought of the time, the fevered president was leeched and given opium and treated with strange and supposedly wonderful herbs that, to be sure, only made the disease worse. He became delirious and died in about a week.

The Constitution was somewhat vague about the succession of Harrison's vice president, John Tyler, to the presidency, merely saying that with the death of a president, the vice president would serve until a new election. Tyler, though, took the oath quickly and just acted like a president, directing policy, having cabinet meetings, and appearing at functions.

Tyler also acted mostly like a Democrat, which he had been prior to the election. He fought against having the central bank reinstated and, being a slaveholder from Virginia himself, sided primarily with any pro-slavery or inherently Southern legislation and movement. The Whigs soon threw him out of the party and rallied again around Clay and Webster. They lost the next election, however, to James Knox Polk, another of Andrew Jackson's anointed choices, but when Polk decided not to run again, the Whigs went back to the military hero mode and nominated Zachary Taylor, the hero of the recent Mexican War.

Taylor was quite an anomaly in the presidential scheme of things. He had only the vaguest of political views, being a career soldier, and because of the logistics of where he was soldiering during the more recent elections, he had not even voted until he ran for president. He was palatable to the Whig Party because he supported a strong national bank to ameliorate national debt, one of the party's main planks against the Democrats. He was also palatable because, being the hero, and the party being pragmatic, he could win the presidency. Many serious politicos in the Whig Party, though, were not crazy about Taylor, and it wasn't necessarily personal. Few knew him, Taylor not participating in politics at all and spending so much of his time in the western territories and Mexico. He was a political cipher. He was also titularly from Louisiana, and he had long been a slaveholder. At the convention the Taylor faction appeased the Northern Whigs by giving the vice presidential nomination to Millard Fillmore of New York, the chair of the House Ways and Means Committee.

The Whig presidency hit a déjà vu, though, when Taylor, like his military hero predecessor Harrison, also died in office. The long-accepted view of his death was that he ate contaminated ice milk and raw fruit at a fund-raising event for the Washington Monument on July 4, 1850, dying four days later of a digestive ailment, presumably some sort of cholera.

Yet there had always been rumors that Taylor was, in effect, assassinated by a cabal of Southern Democrats because of his lack of support for the continuation of slavery in the territories. Taylor was the last president to own slaves, but he saw the future of the West as a nonslaveholding area, and the negotiations that led to the Compromise of 1850, which brought that about, started before he died. Taylor's family allowed his body to be exhumed in 1991, and an analysis by the Oak Ridge National Laboratory determined that there was not enough arsenic in the recovered tissue to presume that assassination attempt, though he did get other drugs that probably exacerbated his gastric problem.

Fillmore was left to push the Compromise of 1850, assisting Clay and the rest of the Whig congressional delegation. Fillmore has often been vilified as an incompetent president, but David Kennedy, the Pulitzer Prize–winning history professor from Stanford (*Freedom From*

Fear: The American People in Depression and War, 1929–45), in a 2014 *Atlantic* magazine survey of the most underrated politicians in history said Fillmore was his choice: "[He] inherited the presidency, and a congressional deadlock over secession. He proved instrumental in passing the delicately balanced Compromise of 1850, a legislative package that was often maligned but that bought precious time for free states to build the material, human, and moral resources for Union victory in the next decade."

Fillmore did not save the Whig Party, though. The Southern factions still hated him and the party nominated another old general in the 1852 presidential race, Winfield Scott, who got slaughtered by Franklin Pierce, whom even his own Democratic Party was none too crazy about. Scott even lost his home state, New Jersey, and twenty-six of the other thirty as well.

It took less than two years for a new party to come out of the ashes of the phoenix that were the Whigs. The Kansas-Nebraska Act of 1854 blew up the party—those in the North and West being virulently against slavery, which the act assured would be around, perhaps everywhere, if each territory voted it in. Many of them, along with the vestiges of the Free Soil Party and a dash of Northern Democrats, met at Jackson, Michigan, on July 6, 1854, pledging themselves to Jeffersonian ideals and the thwarting of the spread of slavery. In honor of Jefferson's original name for his party, the Democrat-Republicans, they named their loud group the Republican Party, and immediately started getting candidates on ballots, at least in the Northern and Western states.

William Seward, the former powerful Whig Party senator from New York, became the most prominent Republican. He was loud and arrogant and enjoyed the company of party bosses, rather than other elected officials, but he was always acknowledged as a creative thinker and a straight shooter. Seward's particular friend was Thurlow Weed, an Albany newspaper editor and the titular boss of the Whig Party in New York. Weed had convinced Seward that 1856 was not going to be his time to run for president. He was certainly not going to win any Southern state—in fact, most of them would probably not put him on the ballot—and the party itself might be too new and confusing to voters, so that 1856 would be a loss leader of sorts. The *New York Times* thought Seward a good man, but the new party needed to run "one not identified with the political struggles and animosities of the past" in order to get a fresh start. Seward then stepped back, feeling himself passed by, at least for now.

John C. Fremont was a fresh face on the political scene, one meant for a new party. Fremont was a chance taker, a swashbuckler, a free thinker. His personality was somewhat like the future outdoorsy president Teddy Roosevelt's but, if it could be possible in a man who might be president, less tempered. His legend was enhanced by his wife, the beautiful Jessie Benton, the favorite daughter of US senator Thomas Hart Benton of Missouri, one of Washington's and the West's top dogs. In fact, had Fremont actually been elected in 1856, his legend—or even what is acknowledged to be the truth of his life—would rival Parson Weems's semifictional version of George Washington.

Fremont's nickname was "the Pathfinder," having led four expeditions to discover and track out trails all over the new West, through the mountains, along the rushing rivers, and on to what was, even in the mid-nineteenth century, the presumed paradise of California. His main trail guide was the legendary Kit Carson and his amanuensis was the woman he spirited off as his wife when she was but seventeen years old.

Like Kris Kardashian, whose fame started when she began to burnish the reputation of her Olympian husband Bruce Jenner in the early twenty-first century, Jessie Benton, knowing the way of politics from her father, saw that kind of legend in her husband. When he came home from his first expedition, she decided that, if he and it were going to be a success, he needed some public relations, so she wrote about the expedition in his voice. She was unafraid of what might seem like a dicey past. Fremont was the illegitimate son of an American woman and a man who claimed both French and Quebecois heritage, but in any case the father abandoned his family early on and died when Fremont was an adolescent. Fremont sometimes used an accent over the *e* in his last name to sound more French—read that *exotic*—and sometimes dropped the *t* at the end, perhaps to sound more like "Free Man."

Fremont was fine with his spirited wife spreading his fame and was unconcerned about details. Much of what Jessie wrote had truth as its base, but clearly enhanced some parts. The memoir, ungainly titled *A Report on an Exploration of the Country Lying between the Missouri River and the Rocky Mountains on the Line of the Kansas and Great Platte River*, though, captured the American dream and made Fremont into a celebrity, with poet Henry Wadsworth Longfellow proclaiming, "Frémont has touched my imagination. What a wild life, and what a fresh kind of existence! But ah, the discomfort."

Fremont's expeditions—there were eventually five between 1841 and 1853—jibed well with the political philosophy of his father-in-law, the influential Benton. Benton was a leader of the movement called Manifest Destiny, which promulgated the idea that the American people were an exceptional breed and deserved to rule all the land between the Atlantic and Pacific Oceans, at least in North America, pushing northward some into Canada, but clearly south into Mexico, the Caribbean islands, and Central America. The length of the expeditions clearly played havoc with Fremont's marriage, but Jessie was willing to support his cause, sometimes traveling to meet him, but often being his advocate in Washington, in their other home in New York, and wherever she could find financing for the treks.

Through his fame Fremont became military governor for the California territory for a time, and then one of its first two United States senators. He was rabidly anti-slavery, which lost him reelection to the Senate in 1852 but put him squarely in line for the nomination of the Republican Party in that group's first election in 1856. Despite his affection for his daughter and her husband, Benton, now clearly even more of an éminence grise with the death of his Senate giant cohorts Webster and Clay, stuck with the Democratic Party, thinking the new Republicans just a temporary regional faction, in effect dooming them in their first election foray.

There had never really been an anti-slavery party in the United States. Martin Van Buren, the ex-president, ran under the banner of the Free Soil Party in the election of 1848, but that party was mostly trying to keep slavery out of the territories, not eliminate it completely. The Republicans made noises of moving toward a slave-free country, but still had to be careful not to forever be a regional party, which at least for its first election it was.

Other remnants of the Whig Party started the new American Party. That party's aims were complex, its main faction calling itself the Know-Nothings. They were anti-Catholic and anti-immigrant, being particularly against the new Germans and Irish who came to the country in the 1840s. The Know-Nothings/Americans searched long for someone to head their ticket and finally settled on former president Millard Fillmore.

Fillmore was hardly a model Know-Nothing coming in, having never before promulgated those anti-immigrant views. He did, however, like being president, so he did not reject the wooing right off, as others might have. The anti-immigration movement was particularly strong in the Mid-Atlantic states and, in some cases, in cities in the Northeast and West where the Irish tended to settle.

For all their anti-immigrant and anti-Catholic stances, the Americans/Know-Nothings were curiously anti-slavery, or at least against the spread of slavery. The Kansas-Nebraska Act, passed to no great acclaim in 1854, energized the formation of the party. The act, which led to stormy times in the Kansas Territory, was definitely the burden of the Democratic Party. It essentially invalidated the Compromise of 1850, saying that each territory entering the Union would get to decide whether it wanted to be slave or free, upon application to become a state. Most earlier Democrats, and Buchanan himself, felt that the federal government administered the territories, so there was no way they could determine their free or slave status until after they were granted statehood. It was a debate that unfortunately lasted until the Civil War ended it. Since Kansas was above the line of the original Compromise of 1820, which allowed Missouri in as a slave state despite its geography, it was the most likely one to be the test case, slave versus free. The opposition to Kansas-Nebraska became a rallying point for leftover Whigs, Free Soil Democrats, and the nascent Republicans. Yet the Republicans could not capitalize on it in border and Southern states. That left open a crack for the Know-Nothings, since the party had followers in every state, but particularly in the upper South, which, though slave states, still wanted to keep the Union together, as opposed to the secessionist longings of many in the deeper South.

It was almost as if, in a sense, the nation was starting over in 1856. The alignments of the original Federalists and Democrat-Republicans no longer existed, and their successor Whigs and Jacksonian Democrats were now gone as well. Buchanan may have remembered Jackson, but his party was no longer the strong-arm, anti–national bank, expansionist, warmongering institution that it had been only twenty years before.

Each of the three parties—the new Republicans and Know-Nothings and the "old" Democrats—believed they had good chances of winning the presidential election. The major conflict in national politics was, clearly, slavery. There were people who cared about tariffs or Native American rights or even, like the Mormons and the Know-Nothings, religious freedom. There was no bigger elephant in the room, however, than slavery.

Fillmore's throw in with the Know-Nothings was proof of that. The origins of the party may have been nativism and the scourge of immigration, but Fillmore knew the big question about his candidacy would not be his stance on Catholics and their place in America, but slaves and theirs. Fillmore's strength, he thought, was that he was instrumental in getting the Compromise of 1850 through Congress, which, while no bargain, was better than the Kansas-Nebraska fiasco that came four years later. His dream was that he would vaguely buy into the Know-Nothing platform, but that was not as important as showing he was a leader who could bring sides together over the slavery issue and get back into the White House.

The Republicans made light of their expansionist and pro-business stances, but just the same, Fremont was running as an anti-slavery can-

The 1857 "Inaugural Procession" for the new president, James Buchanan, the longest and grandest inaugural parade up to that time. LIBRARY OF CONGRESS

The first photograph of a presidential inauguration, taken by John Wood, the photographer for the architect of the Capitol, which was still unfinished in 1857. Wooden slats covered the stones at the front of the Capitol to make it easier for spectators to stand. LIBRARY OF CONGRESS

The magnificent inaugural ball, with six thousand participants in a specially constructed building on Judiciary Square. Attendees devoured four hundred gallons of oysters, five hundred quarts of chicken salad, sixty saddles of mutton, one hundred and twenty-five tongues, seventy-five hams, and twelve hundred quarts of ice cream. LIBRARY OF CONGRESS

Buchanan in 1840, in the middle of his decade in the US Senate representing Pennsylvania. He almost always faced right for portraits because of vision issues that often made him look walleyed. LIBRARY OF CONGRESS

A rare full-length portrait of Buchanan, also rare in that he is facing left—not his good side. He was said to be one of the most handsome of the young men in Lancaster, but he grew stout in middle age. LIBRARY OF CONGRESS

An engraving of Buchanan sometime just before his presidency from a daguerreotype by the famous photographer Matthew Brady, who made his greater fame during the Lincoln administration and the Civil War. LIBRARY OF CONGRESS

James Buchanan on the eve of his presidency in 1857. At sixty-five he was the oldest president elected until Ronald Reagan. LIBRARY OF CONGRESS

A glass negative of Buchanan's niece, Harriet Lane, of unknown date, but probably around the start of his presidency. Lane was her uncle's First Lady—perhaps the most popular young woman in the nation. Whatever she wore, everyone wanted to wear. Wherever she went, admirers followed. She was clearly, by far, the best part of Buchanan's presidency. LIBRARY OF CONGRESS

Lane stayed popular for nearly a half century beyond her uncle's term. A Coast Guard cutter was named after her, and even after the Confederates captured it, they refused to change its name. She became a benefactor to the new Johns Hopkins hospital in Baltimore, and her name still graces a children's clinic there. She gave money for her uncle's two memorials—at his birthplace and in Washington, DC—and her portrait collection started the National Gallery of Art. LIBRARY OF CONGRESS

An 1852 campaign poster for Franklin Pierce and his Democratic running mate, William Rufus King. King lived with Buchanan in Washington for a decade and some believe them to have been gay lovers. LIBRARY OF CONGRESS

A woodcut for a campaign poster or banner for Buchanan's 1856 presidential run. He made no campaign speeches and rarely left his home in Lancaster—and his major opponent, Republican John Fremont, did the same, staying at his home in New York City practically the whole campaign. LIBRARY OF CONGRESS

John C. Fremont, "the Pathfinder," in a July 7, 1856, woodcut, three weeks after he was chosen to be the first Republican candidate for president. He was one of the biggest celebrities in the nation, having cut trails to the West in four different midcentury expeditions. LIBRARY OF CONGRESS

A political cartoon with other aspirants chasing the presidential front-runner in 1856, "Old Buck" James Buchanan. Millard Fillmore, of the Know-Nothing Party, is an emaciated loser, while Republican John Fremont rides two steeds—one being his supporter, publisher Horace Greeley, and the other representing the "wooly nag" of abolitionism. As Old Buck crosses the finish line, he says, "I could not help beating you, the American Nation wished it so." LIBRARY OF CONGRESS

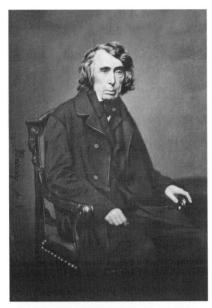

Roger B. Taney was the Supreme Court chief justice who gave Buchanan his oath of office, but also the man who wrote the decision that started his presidency to ruin—that of *Dred Scott.* LIBRARY OF CONGRESS

Buchanan and his cabinet, most of whom stayed until secession started, many being from those states seceding. From left: Jacob Thompson, secretary of the interior; Lewis Cass, secretary of state; Howell Cobb, secretary of the treasury; Buchanan; Jeremiah Black, attorney general; Horatio King, postmaster general; John B. Floyd, secretary of war; and Isaac Toucey, secretary of the navy. The cabinet met nearly every weekday, often for four hours or more. LIBRARY OF CONGRESS

A Currier and Ives woodcut presaging the Civil War. While South Carolina had seceded, it was still unsure the idea would work. Thus, Governor Francis Pickens is lighting a cannon that would fire right into his own stomach. Buchanan is throwing up his hands and pleading, "Don't fire till I get out of office." Fort Sumter is in the background. LIBRARY OF CONGRESS

Buchanan was vilified immediately after his presidency, for secession and for the Civil War. In this Unionist woodcut Lincoln defends the country while Buchanan, exiting stage left, has horns, bears a message written over him ("Something rotten in Denmark"), and is "quoted" as saying, "I am glad I am out of the scrape!" LIBRARY OF CONGRESS

As Lincoln takes over the presidency and the Civil War starts, Lincoln is presaged as a hero, here defending a still-vibrant Miss Liberty. Confederate President Jefferson Davis sits in front of a tree with a snake around its trunk, and to the left of Liberty, Buchanan sleeps while his former secretary of war, John Floyd, bags the money he supposedly grafted with bribes from military contracts. LIBRARY OF CONGRESS

The stone pyramid at Buchanan's birthplace in Cove Gap, Franklin County, Pennsylvania. It is one of the earliest memorials to a president, built with money donated by his devoted niece, Harriet Lane. LIBRARY OF CONGRESS

The log cabin in which Buchanan was born. It is now on the campus of Mercersburg Academy, about a dozen miles east of the original site. LIBRARY OF CONGRESS

Wheatland, Buchanan's beloved estate in Lancaster. He always fought the yin and yang of his character. He loved being involved in politics, but he also loved being the host of the best parties in sublime locations, as Wheatland is just outside the main town. LIBRARY OF CONGRESS

A military ceremony at the beginning of the Depression, in 1930, at the Washington, DC, memorial to Buchanan. Perhaps he wasn't looking nearly as bad as Herbert Hoover at that moment. LIBRARY OF CONGRESS

didate. The Know-Nothings, with the Democrats' acquiescence, spread rumors that Fremont was Catholic because of his father's French Canadian heritage, but few voters who may have cast a ballot for the Republicans cared at all about that. Nativism surely was an issue, but mostly to the paranoid in the cities, who feared immigrant Catholics would take their jobs. They were clearly unworried about slaves taking their jobs in the North, and were able to separate the institution of slavery as something bad from their personal fear of loss of job or station to the Catholics they saw, compared to the slaves with whom they never came in contact.

It is hard for a modern American to realize how slavery was taken pretty much as a given in the mid-nineteenth-century United States. In 1850 the census counted 23,191,876 people in the country, about the same number who live just in Texas in the twenty-first century. More than one in six of those people, 3,204,313 of them, were slaves, and the vast majority of those slaves lived in the Deep South, rather than in other more Northern slave states like Maryland and Kentucky.

By that time slavery had become a chicken-and-egg situation. Slavery had become common in Virginia and the upper South in the eighteenth century, used primarily in tobacco farming. In 1790 Virginia had 44 percent of all the slaves in the United States. The invention of the cotton gin, and the realization that the crop would thrive more in the less frost-prone Deep South, pushed the bulk of the slave trade toward Mississippi, Alabama, Texas, Louisiana, and the rest of the cotton states.

It is clear that even most slaveholders understood that the institution of slavery was not completely moral. The justifications were myriad. Slavery, for instance, was part of daily life in the Bible. Though there was no scientific proof, to be sure, slavery partisans would promulgate the "proof" that African Americans were inferior in mind and temperament. Laws prohibiting the education of blacks, slave or not, made this position more solid.

As time went on and the sections of the country developed their own demographics, the South and North became the primary division—as opposed to, say, New England and the West or the Mid-Atlantic and the Great Lakes. The accents were different. They were generally rural in the South and urban in the North. Quakers, Catholics, Jews, Mennonites, Mormons, and American Indian religions were seen often in the North, not so much in the South. Universities were Northern; military and finishing schools, Southern. Railroads and canals were more prominent in the North, and carriage routes were more Southern.

So by the 1850s, with the country decades beyond the discussions of slavery during the compromising Constitution, the two main sections and the states therein viewed themselves as different than the other. Many of those differences, though, could easily be worked around. There could be new Southern railroad routes, and Quakers started to grow in influence in North Carolina. Colleges started to spring up in the South: Tulane (or, really, its predecessor, Medical College of Louisiana) in Louisiana in 1834, Emory in Georgia in 1836, and Davidson in 1837 and Duke in 1838 in North Carolina. Once families were rooted in each section, they rarely moved away, save west, but even then still along the same north/south parallel from where they started.

Even though, then, perhaps only one in five Southern families had even one slave by the 1850s, sectional partisanship was entrenched. The one thing the South had in preponderance that the North did not was slavery. Even those without slaves there tended to live, believe, and vote as slavery partisans. The South had long had an advantage in voting, since the Constitution had allowed nonvoting slaves count as three-fifths of a person for census and, thus, congressional district enumeration. Most observers thought Kansas would never support massive slave populations because of the way land would be used for manufacturing and less labor-intensive farming, but the South needed a slave state to counteract Oregon and Minnesota and especially the growing California. For a time there were no more than a dozen slaves in the Kansas Territory as the "Bloody Kansas" crisis was building, yet the South was solidly behind Kansas being admitted as a slave state. On occasion a Northern state would vote "Southern," particularly Pennsylvania, where the last slaves were not freed until 1847, and New Jersey, which did not officially jettison slavery until 1865, two years after the Emancipation Proclamation eliminated slavery in the South.

Still, much like the Southeastern Conference against the Big Ten in football today, whatever helped the "team" got strong support from all concerned.

So slavery became the chicken, not just the egg. Southern pride got tied up in slavery, even when economic studies showed that a strict slave plantation was only slightly more efficient than a similar Northern farm with, though admittedly ill-paid, free labor. On the other hand, a loss in a slave state would diminish Southern power overall, so even people who would never be able to have a slave in their lifetimes supported legislation that would preserve slavery.

It is imperative to remember, then, that while the new Republican Party was anti-slavery, it knew it could not govern being completely abolitionist. It had taken at least three decades for William Lloyd Garrison, the most prominent abolitionist, to gain more than just a passing passel of followers. They were seen as the unjustified radical left. There were a greater number of anti-slavery advocates who thought that waiting it out was the best policy—that slavery would pretty much die out on its own, with the increase of smaller farming and concomitant industrial production not conducive to slave labor.

More strangely, there was a movement that figured slavery would die out if black people were just repatriated to Africa. It might, too, the advocates said, be good for blacks, since slave or free, they faced inevitable racism in America. Henry Clay, the Great Compromiser, was one of the three founders of the American Colonization Society, which started sending black people—not just slaves, but even freed men and families from the North—to Liberia in West Africa in 1822. Slaveholders willing to part with their chattel joined with, for the most part, religious Quakers, who would otherwise not be seen with each other, to push Clay's idea. If there were no blacks in the United States, went their convoluted argument, then slavery could die out pleasantly.

Freed blacks particularly were not all that happy with the idea. Though they had left West Africa generations before under duress, they also had the American ideal on their minds. If slavery could be eliminated, then they would have that chance for the dream, just like their white counterparts. By 1830 abolitionist leader Garrison got on board, which, ironically, started scuttling the system. The South did not mind Quakers and their soft rebukes, but Garrison was a loudmouth and excoriated slaveholders at every turn. By the 1850s Liberia was pretty much an afterthought for most blacks and whites.

Democrats went from despair at having to renominate incumbent Franklin Pierce, whose popularity plummeted with his support of the Kansas-Nebraska Act, to finding a replacement who could, maybe lumberingly, get the party across the 1856 presidential election finish line in first place. Nearly every possible Democratic presidential candidate was either a Northerner who turned Doughface and supported Kansas-Nebraska or a Southerner who was truly for it. The presumption, given Pierce or Stephen Douglas or Jefferson Davis, different though they were, was that if the party nominated one of them, the Democrats would carry Deep South states but maybe nothing else.

Except there, nearly whistling in the wind, was the greatest lumberer of all, James Buchanan. Because Pierce had exiled Buchanan to England, keeping him from being home to threaten Pierce's reelection desires, Buchanan had to take no stand at all on Kansas-Nebraska, at least publicly. He probably would have been for it, but over in England he kept his own counsel.

On the other hand, he led the charge, with Pierre Soule, the American minister to Spain, and John Y. Mason, his counterpart in France, to annex, conquer, or buy Cuba from Spain. The three met in November in secret in Ostend, Belgium. Though the idea was supposed to be publicized, if at all, as Soule's idea, the manuscripts saved from that time were clearly in Buchanan's hand. The proposal to Pierce was that the United States submit a bid of $120 million to buy the island, and to advocate, as a pitch, that America's running the place would be better for everyone—eliminating potential and real debt for Spain, enhancing American influence against Great Britain in the Caribbean, and having Cuba administered by a government next door instead of an ocean away.

It was no secret, though, that the Ostend Manifesto was no more "neutral" in the slave controversy than was the Kansas-Nebraska Act. The desire to bring Cuba to the United States was all about appeasing the slave states. Cuba could be broken up into two potential states, and since it already had slavery, they would de facto be slave states. Further, the idea that there might be a slave insurrection while Cuba was under Spanish rule scared slave owners, who thought that if that would happen, their own slaves might take a cue and revolt themselves.

In 1856 this could have been a blast against Buchanan, but since the whole scheme dissembled in the wake of Kansas-Nebraska, he never had to answer for it. Thus, the Democrats, if they nominated Buchanan, would have the perfect foil—someone who could appeal to both the North and the South, if only somewhat in either case. Despite their enthusiasm, the Republicans realized they would have to carry virtually every Northern state to win, and with Buchanan up for the Democrats, it stood to reason, even though he was not all that popular back at home, that he would probably at least be able to carry Pennsylvania.

The Know-Nothings were a curious case, however. To many people—even later historians—it would have seemed they would be fighting the Democrats in the South, while the Republicans would be doing so in the North. Over and above their anti-immigrant message, though, the Know-Nothings, who would have rather been known by their other moniker, the American Party, campaigned as the only party that could assure the Union would persist. Fillmore figured he could get Northern Whigs and what remained of the Southerners who wanted to stay in the Union to combine with border state constituencies, who were natural Know-Nothings because they feared immigration but definitely wanted to keep the Union together. Thus, the Know-Nothings campaigned not just in the South, but especially in places like New York and

New England. Their point was that if former Northern Whigs thought of the Know-Nothings as only a Southern and border party, they would just as soon throw themselves in with one of the other two parties, rather than go with a sure loser.

At the least Fillmore hoped to win enough states to deny Buchanan an overall majority of electoral votes. If, say, New York, Ohio, and a New England state could come his way, the election could be thrown into the House of Representatives, which certainly would not vote for an anathema like Fremont and might exclude Buchanan for any number of reasons, not the least of which might be his age.

The Democrats, having cast their lot with Buchanan, also said theirs was the only party that could save the Union, implying that neither of the other two parties could assure the multisectional vote to keep the country intact. Oddly enough, the man who became the vice president of the Confederacy, Alexander Stephens, was most prominent in the Union debate, and may have held the key to the election. Stephens was a Georgia Whig, a Unionist, and to be sure a member of the slavocracy. In 1852 he joined with Fillmore, then the president, and the rest of the Northern Whigs to try to make certain any compromise about slavery would appease both North and South. As the election of 1856 came closer, he proposed that whether a territory would become slave or free should come after, not before, statehood. He may have been sacrificing Kansas as a slave state, but he would be ready to support any Mexican, Cuban, or otherwise potential slave states in the future.

When Fillmore made his Know-Nothing move, though, Stephens abandoned him. He was not anti-immigrant, for at the least he would have welcomed Mexican or Cuban territory into the Union, and he had no reason to be anti-Catholic, there being so few of them in Georgia. He threw his support to the Democrats, but had Fillmore found a way to appease him, the Know-Nothings might have taken Georgia, and maybe even some nearby state, which would have either encouraged some wavering Northern state into his column or pushed the election into the House of Representatives.

Finally, though, Fillmore may have been done in by the near-impossibility of reconciling disparate groups into one during an election. Whigs and Democrats, intersectionally and within their own state or regional borders, had just been fighting each other for too long to come together, even if they essentially believed the same thing on a major issue—that Kansas-Nebraska had to go in order to preserve the Union. They also did not trust each other to get patronage right, evening it up to keep as many of their constituents as possible happy. Fillmore had given it a shot, his strategy failing only because it required that too many things break right for him.

Buchanan, despite his obvious pleasure at having the advantage going into the election, did his best to say as little as possible during the campaign. The party told him he would not be tainted by Kansas-Nebraska, at least personally, so he bowed to their request to keep it down about that. Pierce did not undercut him, as much as the lame-duck president had wanted to run again. As mentioned before, when the rumors, though false, of Fremont's alleged Catholic background flourished, Buchanan did not repeat them, but did nothing to dispel them.

Buchanan swept the South. Fillmore took Maryland, and the most southerly state Fremont won was Ohio. In fact, Fremont got more than half of his electoral total of 114 from just two states, Ohio and New York. He did not even win his own titular homes, Missouri or California, though California's electoral votes (just four) were not the bonanza they would become in the twentieth century. In the North, Buchanan won only Pennsylvania (just barely), Illinois, Indiana, and New Jersey. Douglas was a reluctant supporter—they still despised one another—but delivered Illinois's eleven electoral votes for Buchanan.

The Know-Nothings essentially self-destructed with the election results, so virtually all of the former Northern Whigs went to the Republicans. Despite Buchanan's slight foray into the Northern vote, it became apparent that the new president would have to do a lot of work to keep the Democrats viable as a national party. He could not make a mistake, or only small ones. The Republicans would probably coalesce around

William Seward of New York, who would be a good bet to win Illinois and Indiana, and maybe even Pennsylvania and New Jersey, in the next election. That result alone, especially if the abolitionist segment of the Republican vote were virulent, could augur secession.

Counter to modern presidential elections, none of the three candidates campaigned much, if at all, personally. With the exception of his usual summer spa vacation in Bedford Springs, Pennsylvania, Buchanan stayed almost entirely in Lancaster at Wheatland. He did entertain party leaders, but did not have his standard festive parties. Those leaders came and went from the mansion at a good clip, but it was mostly just looking ahead to what they supposed was going to be an easy election. Buchanan's permanent staff was just his niece, Harriet; his secretary, William V. McKean, to help with correspondence and other paperwork; and a housekeeper and two young paid servants. Buchanan did invite everyone who came on Sunday to go to the Presbyterian Church service with him, but that was about it for his public appearances. Fremont stayed primarily in New York City at his house at 56 West Ninth Street. Given that it was Manhattan, curious onlookers came by and he would greet many of them at the door, but it was hardly formal electioneering. Fillmore spent most of his time at his home as well, though he went in and out of Washington from time to time.

None of them made speeches, grandstanding or otherwise. Though it was a raucous campaign in some respects, with passions going this way and that often, the candidates were unavailable. This was standard for many of the early presidential campaigns, but by this point, the modes of transportation, be they water-borne or railroad, made travel to at least the population hubs easy.

There were, however, rallies all over the place—some reporting tens of thousands of supporters of one candidate or another, with speakers and rabble-rousers and even some brawls for good measure. Some Fremont rallies in the Midwest toward the end of the summer boasted monumental, unheard-of numbers attending political rallies: fifty thousand people in Indianapolis, thirty thousand in Kalamazoo, twenty-five thousand in

Massillon, Ohio, and Beloit, Wisconsin. Abe Lincoln spoke at a rally at the Illinois State Fair in Alton whose number was said to be more than thirty-five thousand. A procession in Jacksonville, Connecticut, was reported to be a mile and a half long.

This was transformational. Neither Washington nor Jefferson nor Jackson nor Taylor would have inspired such crowds, and the rallies often came with merriment and entertainment. Cannons blasted, brass bands played, glee clubs sang in or out of tune, uniformed men were everywhere, floats bearing beautiful women in costume and children in their arms were festooned with banners bearing slogans: "We Follow the Pathfinder," "We Are Buck-Hunting," "Kansas Will Be Free," and the inevitable "Free Speech, Free Press, Free Soil, Free Men, Fremont and Victory." There were torchlight parades all over the North and West and haranguing speakers. The idea of a sedate campaign, as Buchanan and Fremont were apparently trying to emulate, was now a thing of the past in presidential politics. The same thing happened for Democrats, though primarily in the South.

All of this cost money, and the Democrats just had more of it. The Republicans and Know-Nothings, though enthusiastic, had no entrenched organization, so fund-raising had to be started from scratch. The Democrats funneled most of their money to what would today be called the "swing states," most prominently Pennsylvania and Indiana. In those two states there would be state and local elections on October 14, three weeks before the presidential election on November 4. A never-before heard-of sum of $500,000 was allocated by the Democrats for Pennsylvania, while the Republicans could only find less than a tenth of that to spend.

There was talk of fraud, especially in Pittsburgh and Philadelphia, the money said to be "buying" people, giving them tax receipts, which would get them verification at the polls, with similar allegations in Indiana. In both states the Democratic state candidates won by slim margins—a few thousand among a couple hundred thousand votes cast.

In truth, though, the issues in these semi–border states were crucial. The industrial interests were scared that a Republican victory might lead to secession, or at least unrest, and that would be devastating to their businesses. Further, since Know-Nothings did not have many local candidates, many of them voted Democratic or stayed at home during state elections, which usually came a month before the national one in November. It was preferable to them to have local Democrats win rather than Republicans, the rival "new" party, so their national ticket would look viable.

That Buchanan was not a shoo-in in his own state would seem to be a bit ominous, but, in fact, it was only because he was on the ballot that Pennsylvania went Democratic at all. Philadelphia, Scranton, and Pittsburgh were all solidly Republican. Buchanan won in and around Lancaster and in the far western and northern rural parts of the state. More ominous were the results in the states of the more prominent Democrats. The Republicans won easily in New Hampshire, incumbent president Franklin Pierce's home state, and in Michigan, the home of Buchanan's eventual secretary of state, Lewis Cass. Illinois went Democratic, but the Republicans won the northern half of the state, which was the part, especially around Chicago, that was growing. That had to worry Senator Stephen Douglas, who reluctantly backed his rival Buchanan in hopes that he, Douglas, would have a clear path to the presidency in 1860.

It is unclear how the voting would have gone had the Know-Nothings not been around. The two combined opposition parties did beat out Buchanan's vote in New Jersey, and the Republicans won the state offices in Illinois. Pennsylvania and Indiana were clearly on their way to being Republican states before long, so if there had been more money to spread around, perhaps the Republicans would have taken them this time, too.

Nothing else really mattered as the new administration took office, nothing except keeping the Union together in the wake of Kansas-Nebraska. Tariffs, Mexico, railroad building, higher education, naval readiness, Native American affairs—they were all important issues, and may have had equal weight in another era. Once the realization set in that Fillmore was not going to win, the only solution for Unionists in those lower Northern states was to vote for Buchanan, reluctantly or not. The

Republican tide in the North, and its handmaiden, the beginning of the end of slavery, was rushing forward. There was no clear leader of the party—Fremont had not quite run his course, and William Seward seemed the likeliest, but the field could be wide open.

Buchanan could cap his long public service career with success if he could press for a solution to the slavery conundrum and keep people in South Carolina and Texas talking with those in Pennsylvania and Massachusetts. He had been given his four years. Now it was time to see what that long public service background could do with them. Old Buck would have to be a savior, a job that he might not have foreseen.

Before even taking office, he was working on that behind the scenes and pretty much alone. A few days after his inauguration, the world would find out the result he wanted, and start a four-year shudder in reaction to it.

—◆—

Few presidential campaign songs have made much of a mark, and even the ones that did were pretty much either reworkings of popular songs or those popular songs themselves.

Franklin Roosevelt had people dancing to "Happy Days Are Here Again," even when the happy days were still a bit far off from the 1932 and 1936 elections, which brought him to power and kept him in office. His successor, Harry Truman, could not help but use "I'm Just Wild About Harry." Frank Sinatra lent his voice to a version of "High Hopes," modified for John F. Kennedy's 1960 campaign. Bill Clinton rather annoyingly co-opted the soft-rock hit "Don't Stop Thinking About Tomorrow," originally done by Fleetwood Mac, whose members presumably supported his campaign, but Ronald Reagan tried to use "Born in the U.S.A." right after it came out for his 1984 campaign, and Bruce Springsteen, who was hardly a Reaganite politically, asked him to stop playing it at rallies. Maybe not so coincidentally, both John Kerry and Barack Obama used songs from that same Springsteen album—Kerry choosing "No Surrender" in 2004 and Obama, "I'm On Fire" in 2008.

The first original song that became a campaign hit was "Tippecanoe and Tyler, Too," which promoted the Whig Party ticket in 1840: William Henry Harrison, the hero general of the Battle of Tippecanoe in the Indian Wars, and his running mate, John Tyler. A jeweler from Zanesville, Ohio, not all that far from Tippecanoe, was a Whig supporter and after singing the song at home, did so at a Whig rally he went to while doing business in New York, after which it became wildly popular as a sort of novelty song. Its first verse went like this ("Van" being Martin Van Buren, the Democratic incumbent opponent):

What's the cause of this commotion, motion, motion,
Our country through?
It is the ball a-rolling on
For Tippecanoe and Tyler, too.
For Tippecanoe and Tyler, too.
And with them we'll beat little Van, Van, Van,
Van is a used up man.
And with them we'll beat little Van.

James Buchanan, though, had a little secret up his sleeve in this regard. His brother, the Reverend Edward Buchanan, was married to Ann Eliza Foster, the sister of the man who was probably the most well-known person in the entertainment business of the time, Stephen Foster.

Foster's father, William Barclay Foster, had been a Democratic state legislator in Pennsylvania and was the mayor of Allegheny, a Pittsburgh suburb. Stephen was not known to have much of a political bent, but he was apparently happy to support his relative Buchanan.

Foster's brother, Morrison, was the treasurer of a Pittsburgh group called the Buchanan Glee Club, which formed just after Buchanan's nomination in August of 1856. It was apparently a pretty rough-and-tumble band of guys, because it went around with a bodyguard of toughs numbering as many as a hundred. In one incident the club went to a Pittsburgh neighborhood where the Fosters had friends to sing some pro-Buchanan, or at least Democratic Party, songs. A member of the

Pittsburgh Fire Department, which was primarily full of Republicans, sang out of rhythm to chide the Glee Club, which caused a fight that became a near-riot, from which the Fosters escaped with the help of their bodyguards.

Given what we know of Foster's popular songs, which are nostalgic about the Old South he never knew firsthand, it is not surprising that he would feel ardent about the Buchanan Southern-leaning platform—states' rights and anti-abolitionist sentiments imbued in it. Foster was said to be anti-slavery, which he may have been, but he probably also thought African Americans to be inferior to whites—not too far different than, say, Abraham Lincoln.

Foster's "The Abolition Show" attempted to mock John Fremont's pro-abolition leanings, and tried to link the Republican Party to the "Bloody Kansas" violence.

Foster gave Buchanan the best of his 1856 output, since fully two-thirds of the songs attributed to him that year were Buchanan campaign ditties.

One Buchanan campaign song that Foster did not write was "The White House Chair," a pretty staid ballad, hardly "Born in the U.S.A." It implored the public to vote for Buchanan and the Democrats because their "creed is broad and fair":

Come all ye men of every state,
Our creed is broad and fair;
Buchanan is our candidate,
And we'll put him in the White House Chair.
For there is balm in Gilead,
We hear the people say;
Buchanan and John Breckenridge
Will surely win the day.

(Chorus)
Then come ye men from ev'ry state,
Our creed is broad and fair;

Buchanan is our candidate,
And we'll put him in the White House Chair.
Let all our hearts for union be,
For the North and South are one;
They've worked together manfully,
And together they will still work on.
We'll have no dark designing band
To rule with secret sway;
We'll give to all a helping hand,
And be open as the light of day.
We'll not outlaw the land that holds
The bones of Washington;
Where Jackson fought and Marion bled,
And the battles of the brave were won.

Fremont's campaign was a bit more, well, "creative" in its song choices. Copyright laws in the United States at the time were virtually nonexistent. Foster made most of his money on contract writing, not the millions he would have made in the modern age with licensing rights for everything.

So what Fremont's people did was often write pro-Republican lyrics to go with Foster's melodies. Presumably the thought there was that it would appear that Foster was writing tunes for Fremont, not his relative running against the Republican candidate. Here is part of one, designed to emphasize Buchanan's old age versus Fremont's relative youth, to the tune of Foster's "Camptown Races":

There's an old gray horse whose name is Buck
Du Da, Du Da.
His dam was Folly and his sire, Bad Luck
Du Da, Du Da Day.

(Chorus)
We're bound to work all night.
We're bound to work all day.

I'll bet my money on the mustang colt.
Will anybody bet on the gray?

The mustang colt is strong and young
Du Da. Du Da.
His wind is sound and his knees not sprung
Du Da. Du Da Day.

(Chorus)

The old gray horse is a well-known hack
Du Da. Du Da.
He's long been fed at the public rack.
Du Da. Du Da Day.

(Chorus)

Then do your best with the old gray hack
Du Da. Du Da.
The mustang colt will clear the track.
Du Da. Du Da Day.

Another one to show that Buchanan's "experience" was just plain old tired was a parody to a lesser-known Foster ballad, "Uncle Ned," which went in part:

There is an old donkey, a worn out Jack,
Too old to live very long.
He has no bone in the middle of his back,
Where the bones ought to grow very strong.

His legs are long when he trots after votes,
But he has no eyes for to see.
And his teeth are worn out eating public oats.
So he'll have to let the public oats be.

What's the use of a nag with so many bad ways,
So stubborn, so old, and so slow?
The best we can do is turn him out to graze,
In the fields where the short grasses grow.

Fremont's team was also not lax to take on Buchanan's bachelorhood. There was this to the tune of "The Campbells Are Coming," called "The Bachelor Candidate":

It's time to be doing, the play has begun,
There's mischief a brewing, as sure as a gun.
The Buck and Breck noodles are stupidly bent
On choosing a Bach for our next President.
A bachelor, who, like his species, you know,
Is afraid of the girls, and to union a foe.
Then up and be doing, for danger is rife—
A man is but moonshine who hasn't a wife.

Conversely, the Fremont Republicans even featured Jessie, Fremont's popular wife, just to show he was a suitable family man. "Jessie Fremont" went like this:

The sun burst has dawned over all the glad mountains.
While freedom and glory rise up hand in hand,
To meet our young chieftain from Liberty's fountain.
With Jessie, sweet Jessie, the flower of the land.

She's wife and she's prudent. She's good and she's bonnie.
For Virtue and Freedom, she makes a brave stand.
For the Chieftain's White Mansion, she's better than onie.
So giver her "God's speed," there, the flower of the land.

Let honest hearts greet her, and victory meet her.
You'll never repent it—so join hand in hand.
Till firm with our leader in rapture we seat her.
Our noble young Jessie, the flower of the land.

It does not seem likely that calling, say, Michelle Obama or Laura Bush—or even Sarah Palin—"the flower of the land" would have made it in the feminist twenty-first century, but the song does show what a celebrity Jessie Fremont had become with her frontier hero husband. The inspiration of Stephen Foster apparently made the 1856 election more prolific for campaign music than any other.

Had it only produced a better man for the office, it might have been worth it.

Chapter Six

The Worst Presidency Begins

Only a few blocks from the dramatic Gateway Arch, the most prominent tourist attraction in St. Louis, along the Mississippi River, is an adjunct to that site, not nearly so dramatic and hardly as well visited. The domed building, an architectural masterpiece when it was built in the nineteenth century, is now called the Historic Old Courthouse.

It was glorious beyond Missouri's influence, representing "America" in its grandiose physical stature and the thought that everything everywhere in the new country could be as monumental as anything that had come before it.

St. Louis thrived as the port for the fur trade, and most of the Old Courthouse's trials were due to the financial interests—or the violence—caused by the dangerous business. Certainly the city fathers who helped plan the building thought there would be stories to come out of watching trials there.

There were three tiers of balconies where spectators could view the trial area. The cornerstone was itself a masterpiece, inside and out, filled with coins and newspapers from various cities around the world when it was laid in 1839.

The pillars that held up the balconies were either stone or solid oak. From those balconies, in a huge courtroom, dozens of folks watched two trials—one in 1847 and another in 1850—of a slave, or as he hoped to be, a former slave, named Dred Scott.

Scott was born a slave in Virginia in 1799 and came with his owners, the Peter Blow family, to St. Louis in 1830. He was sold shortly after he arrived there because his owners were in the middle of a financial problem. His new owner, Dr. John Emerson, was a military surgeon stationed in Missouri at the time, but soon after was moved by the army to the Illinois Territory and then the Wisconsin Territory, where slavery had been prohibited in 1820 by virtue of the Missouri Compromise. While at Fort Snelling in what would later become Minnesota, Scott married another slave, Harriet Robinson, and they had two children. In 1842 the Emersons moved back to St. Louis. John Emerson died the next year and for a time Mrs. Emerson hired out Scott, his wife, and his children to other families.

In 1846 the Scotts filed suit against Mrs. Emerson for their freedom, contending that the nine years they had spent in free territories made them free. There was originally a mistrial at the Old Courthouse, but in 1850 the state court ruled that the Scotts were, indeed, free people based on where they had lived. Mrs. Emerson appealed the case, and in 1852 the Missouri State Supreme Court overturned the verdict.

The case had become celebrated and, ironically, the Blow family, Scott's original owner, financed his case, which was now against John Sanford, Dr. Emerson's brother-in-law and executor of his estate. (His name was misspelled on court documents as Sandford.) The federal court in St. Louis decided in Sanford's favor in 1854, but then Scott appealed the case, now approaching a decade old, to the United States Supreme Court.

By that time the courtroom where the Scott case was tried had to be remodeled; its second floor needing shoring up, so walls were put in the old large courtroom to steady that ceiling and floor. The case, as well, had changed over time, and James Buchanan would find his way to intercede in it—and on that intercession, get quickly as he could on the road to becoming the Worst. President. Ever.

—◆—

Roger Brooke Taney was a man in declining health and advanced age when he came to the podium to preside over the oath of office for James Buchanan. The new president was only a few weeks from his sixty-sixth birthday, an old man to most everyone in the country, but the long-faced, long-haired, dour-looking Taney was days short of his eightieth birthday.

Like Buchanan, he was a Dickinson College graduate, coming there at the callow age of fifteen. He was the second son of tobacco farmers in Calvert County, Maryland, just over the Mason-Dixon Line in Maryland, a slave state where Pennsylvania was not, and, with tobacco being a big slave-oriented crop, his family had a large crew of slaves.

The second son was not going to get a piece of the tobacco action, so Taney was happy to go to Dickinson and then read for the law back at home, being admitted to the bar in the last class before the eighteenth century turned to the nineteenth. He soon became one of the up-and-comers in Maryland, and in 1807 he married the sister of one of the more prominent attorneys in the state, Francis Scott Key, who would a few years later write "The Star-Spangled Banner" during the War of 1812. By that time Taney had already been elected to the Maryland State House as a Federalist, but soon after changed his party to become a Democrat-Republican, and then when Andrew Jackson appeared on the scene, Taney aligned himself with the swashbuckling "Man of the People."

In just three years, 1831–34, he served in three posts in Jackson's cabinet: secretary of war, secretary of the treasury, and attorney general. He never belied his Southern roots, as his two major cases as attorney general show. In one he "proved" why black people could not be American citizens, and the other upheld a South Carolina statute that prohibited free blacks from entering the state at all.

Soon after, Jackson nominated Taney, by then fifty-eight years old, to be an associate justice on the Supreme Court, but the nomination was blocked because the Whigs had a congressional majority. The Democrats, however, took Congress in the 1834 elections, and when Chief Justice John Marshall died in a stagecoach accident, Jackson nominated Taney to be the chief justice instead. The Whig hierarchy—primarily Henry Clay and Daniel Webster—was virulently against a clearly pro-slavery man taking over the court, and even got South Carolinian John Calhoun, who hated Jackson because he had dropped Calhoun as vice president in his second term, to come over. But Jackson prevailed with the rest of Congress and Taney was in the lifetime post by 1836.

For the decades to come, Taney almost always favored states' rights over the federal law, just the opposite of the Marshall Court, which had seemingly settled federal precedent in Marshall's decades at its helm. Oddly enough, Taney had himself given his slaves their freedom, but other people's, well, that was different.

As the sky was turning ominous at the Buchanan inauguration—the weather started out springlike and would turn to snow by evening—Taney spoke briefly to Buchanan before the ceremony itself was about to start. Buchanan had chosen to have his inauguration speech printed, at least in part, so that those in the audience would have a souvenir. Some vendors even printed it on silk.

Two parts of the speech that Buchanan actually delivered, though, were in addition to what the printed souvenirs had. One was Buchanan's pledge to serve only one term. The other was a cryptic few sentences saying that the Supreme Court would soon have a decision that would settle how slavery would be adjudicated in the territories, and that Buchanan was confident it would save the Union.

There is little question that Taney let Buchanan know the decision would be coming out soon. Some believe it happened in that short discussion with his fellow Dickinson alum on the podium, the evidence being the added lines in the speech.

Even if the word from Taney to Buchanan about the timing of the decision came earlier, Buchanan knew what the outcome from the justices—the one concerning the most famous slave in the country, Dred Scott—was going to be.

—✦—

James Buchanan had not waited to take office before setting the carousel spinning of the American presidency's worst term.

The *Dred Scott* case had been winding around the court system for more than a decade before the Supreme Court would finally hear it and end it. Because so many circumstances in the case had changed drastically in the interim—Scott's master dying, his former master's family financing his case, Scott moving back and forth between being free and slave—it was possible for the court to hear it either narrowly or broadly. Had it ruled narrowly, for instance, it might have found a technicality on which to hang Scott's own freedom or captivity without affecting most anyone else.

Buchanan, and Taney as well, thought the case should come to a sweeping resolution, one that would end the fight about slavery forever. It would supersede partisan politics if it were decreed from the Supreme Court. The people and politicians might grumble or demur, but, so the two Dickinson graduates respectively believed, it would just be done and the country could move on.

Except that Buchanan wanted to make sure the nation would see it as a Washington consensus. There were five Southern justices, counting Taney, and if the vote came out five to four, then it would appear to be just another Southern partisan deal, no more sustaining than any of the legislative compromises, provisos, or acts.

Buchanan had always claimed he was a strict constructionist when it came to the Constitution, that whatever else the United States was, it was first a union based on the principles set down by the Founding Fathers three quarters of a century before his term. Nonetheless, Buchanan wrote a note to his friend Associate Justice John Catron, who came from Tennessee, in January of 1857, two months before he would take office, asking how the *Dred Scott* deliberations were going.

Catron, surprised or not by this intercession of the (future) executive branch into the judicial, told him it looked like a close vote, and if it were, it could not be a broad-based decision. Catron suggested Buchanan have a chat with his fellow Pennsylvanian on the bench, Robert Cooper Grier. Buchanan was not above taking this advice, even if he was challenging the Constitution's separation of powers dictum here. He browbeat Grier into telling Taney he would go along with the majority, so Taney wrote the decision as broadly as possible.

Whether Taney said anything to Buchanan about the *Dred Scott* decision at the inaugural podium—its substance or its timing—matters little, for the decision came out two days later, on March 6, 1857.

It was as broad a decision as it could have possibly been. Taney's majority opinion said that Dred Scott could not have filed suit because, as an African American, he was not a citizen, slave or free. Further, the federal government had not established any power to prevent, or even allow, slavery in territories that came into existence after the Constitution. Whatever regulations there were about slavery in that document applied only to the states that existed at that time.

What this meant was that the Missouri Compromise, enacted decades before, was unconstitutional. Only once before, with the landmark *Marbury v. Madison*, when the court of John Marshall called a part of the Judiciary Act of 1789 unconstitutional, had such a ruling happened. Essentially, it said the Missouri Compromise, which held that slavery would not be allowed in any new state above the southern boundary of Missouri, was not something that Congress could pass. Slaves were slaves, no matter where they were, and the Fugitive Slave Law had to be enforced.

Korematsu v. The United States, in which the Supreme Court in 1944 upheld Franklin Roosevelt's executive order forcing Japanese Americans into internment camps during World War II, was a horrible decision, said constitutional law scholar and University of Pennsylvania professor Kermit Roosevelt, President Theodore Roosevelt's great-grandson, and thus Franklin Roosevelt's distant cousin.

"*Korematsu* is bad, but not as bad as *Plessy v. Ferguson*," said Kermit Roosevelt. *Plessy* was the 1896 case concerning a Louisiana law that required separate accommodations for blacks and whites on the railroad and in its stations. The Supreme Court ruled that "separate but equal" was valid under the Constitution, a ruling that stood until *Brown v. Board of Education* in 1954. "But *Plessy* is not even close to being as bad a decision as *Dred Scott*. That is by far the worst decision ever to come out of the Supreme Court, and I believe just about every scholar would tell you that."

And Buchanan, because of the way he influenced the case, said Kermit Roosevelt and others, is probably more culpable than the justices themselves for its scope.

In his inaugural address Buchanan apparently added a section, knowing that the decision was coming soon, saying that the question of whether those voting in the territories could reject or assent to slavery there really belonged "to the Supreme Court of the United States, before whom it is now pending, and will, it is understood, be speedily and finally settled. To their decision, in common with all good citizens, I shall cheerfully submit, whatever this may be, though it has ever been my individual opinion that, under the Nebraska-Kansas Act, the appropriate period will be when the number of actual residents in the Territory shall justify the formation of a constitution with a view to its admission as a State into the Union."

As accommodating as most Americans were to the idea of slavery, at least in the South, the codification of it in *Dred Scott* mortified Northerners, and even confused Southern Unionists. Taney's phraseology was cruel. Black people, not just slaves, were then and always had been in the United States "unfit to associate with the White race," he wrote in the opinion, "and so far inferior that they had no rights which the white man was bound to respect."

Almost immediately, the nation fell into a greater schism than had ever been seen. Southerners felt vindicated. Buchanan, their Doughface lackey in the White House, had saved the Union, or so they surmised. Not only was their land safe for slavery, they did not risk losing their slaves through escape anymore, since they would always be slaves, no matter where they ended up. Northerners were outraged, Democrat and Republican alike, since now their states were essentially slave states. They wanted no part of that—especially working men, whose wages were dependent on not having slave labor competition. There was the aggravation, too, that Northerners, rather than basically ignoring the Fugitive Slave Law, would now have to be wary of being prosecuted if they did not. It also seemed to leave open the probability that Kansas could be a slave state, since the Missouri Compromise line was no longer valid, and with Buchanan basically aligning himself with the South, slaveholders would become bolder and figure out a way to force slavery to happen in Kansas.

The *Dred Scott* decision also emboldened what had been a fringe group—the abolitionists. The only way now to stop the spread of slavery would be to abolish it completely, so they thought, and they now had a flag around which to rally. More establishment Democrats felt betrayed. Stephen Douglas's big issue of "popular sovereignty," where settlers would decide whether to have slavery as their territory turned to a state, was dead. Thomas Hart Benton, perhaps the most respected man in Congress with the deaths of Henry Clay and Daniel Webster several years earlier, wrote a book denouncing the decision, with all sorts of precedents and other arguments against it, which became a best seller. Almost every Northern newspaper, Democrat, Republican, or Know-Nothing in emphasis, opined against *Dred Scott*.

Buchanan was baffled by the reaction. He had assumed that it was the "new" compromise, replacing Missouri, which he felt outdated because so much territory had been added to the nation since then. This would give the nation time to have slavery slowly die out on its own, not in some cataclysm.

It had taken only two days for Buchanan to make a monumental misstep. Yet he had already set the stage for many more in the time before taking office.

One thing Buchanan did right for decades in Pennsylvania was act as the point man for conciliation. He was not loved in Pennsylvania, but he was respected, especially when he would show to old rivals or new that the Democratic Party could survive in a swing state of the time only when the party was more or less united. He did acknowledge that there would always be different views on some issues, but he felt that dissent would strengthen the party all the more.

When it came to picking a cabinet, though, Buchanan decided that this would not be the course. Buchanan had himself been a contrary cabinet member as secretary of state under President James Knox Polk. He knew Polk did not view him as one of his favorites and they clashed often, but he did feel he offered Polk something by making his conflicting views known.

Whether it was by design or just benign reality, Buchanan picked a cabinet that would not differ with him in any substantial way. The previous president, Franklin Pierce, would be the only president who would have the same cabinet for all four years of his term. Buchanan may well have thought having a cabinet with one voice a good thing.

Buchanan's cabinet became primarily Southerners or other Doughfaces like him. No one should have been surprised, since Buchanan had spent virtually all of his time in Washington working and socializing with Southerners, and given the long time he was there, it would have been an upset of great proportions to think he would not sympathize with them. There was not a rival or a grand thinker among his choices, and even the cabinet's seeming geographic diversity was a sham.

Howell Cobb was always one of Buchanan's favorites. Long haired and chubby, he had once had a thousand slaves on his Georgia plantation. He was a dynamo in politics, becoming Speaker of the House when only thirty-four, then later governor of Georgia before coming back to Congress. He was apparently Buchanan's chief advisor when choosing his cabinet, of which he became secretary of the treasury. Cobb was hailed as a Unionist, but to be a Unionist and a slaveholder meant that the person wanted slavery spread throughout the territories and to have Northerners accept it. Thus he was a big supporter of the Compromise of 1850 and, later, the *Dred Scott* decision.

Cobb's suggestion on secretary of state was to avoid a competent man, Robert J. Walker of Mississippi, with whom Buchanan had served under Polk; Walker was secretary of the treasury then. Cobb said Buchanan should throw a curveball and select Lewis Cass, the Democratic presidential candidate who lost to Zachary Taylor in 1848. The idea would be that Cass was growing senile and Buchanan would essentially be his own secretary of state—which turned out, as time went on, to be just as much of a disaster as his presidency itself.

The rest of the cabinet fell in line with little fervor or distinction. Jacob Thompson, who was, like Cobb, a huge slaveholder, but in his native Mississippi, became the secretary of the interior. Mostly Buchanan liked him because his wife, whom Thompson married when she was fourteen and then sent to Paris to four years for finishing, was a good partier and a friend of Buchanan's niece, Harriet Lane. Cobb pushed two other Southerners who made the cabinet: Governor John B. Floyd of Virginia at the war department and former governor Aaron V. Brown of Tennessee as postmaster general. Floyd was an incompetent, having mostly inherited his position from his father, and Brown could be trusted mostly to do what postmasters were supposed to do—fill all the post offices with patronage partisans.

Isaac Toucey, from Connecticut, became the secretary of the navy. He had family from the South and, thus, was a secure Doughface, like Buchanan. The only vaguely talented man in the cabinet was Jeremiah Black, the attorney general, who was a former chief justice of the Pennsylvania Supreme Court. He was vain and humorless, but studious and a good administrator. He hated radicalism and was a strict constitutionalist, so would be dependable to argue whatever Buchanan wanted.

The cabinet, then, was absent any genuine Northern Democrat, a slap so sound in Stephen Douglas's face it could be heard from Maine to Minnesota and definitely in Douglas's Illinois—and later on, to be sure, in Kansas.

Buchanan hated Douglas, simple as that. Douglas had nearly thwarted Buchanan's last chance to run for president by not dropping out of the race himself until the last minute at the 1856 convention. Buchanan, though, did not learn from his former political idol, Andrew Jackson. Jackson found something for everyone whom he needed to control. Jackson had exiled Buchanan to Russia to get him out of the presidential scene, but at least he allowed Buchanan to succeed at the goal of having negotiated that first commercial treaty with Czar Nicholas.

Douglas got nothing from Buchanan. Douglas loved Buchanan no more than the president loved him, but he was practical and supported Buchanan's campaign vigorously. Once Buchanan said he would be a one-term president, Douglas was immediately the front-runner for 1860 and, as such, was free to attract Buchanan or defy him when he saw it would fit his potential candidacy. He was the most popular senator in the North, or at least the Northwest, and the Democrats would need someone like that to win in 1860.

Buchanan even hated that Douglas, a widower, had married a young Washington beauty, Adele Cutts. Buchanan wrote to a friend after Mrs. Douglas's father applied for a job in the administration that if he made the appointment, "it will be my own regard for Mr. Cutts and his family, and not because Senator Douglas has had the good fortune to become his son-in-law." Even Buchanan's one move to thank Douglas for his support during the 1856 election was a snide cut—the letter he wrote in gratitude was addressed to "The Hon. Samuel A. Douglas," the first-name mix-up probably not a mistake.

Essentially, this congenial cabinet would be disastrous, too. Buchanan had always loved consensus, and he would have it—even after hours. These were social friends of the president, too. The cabinet would meet virtually daily, and for several hours. Then Buchanan, a rather lonely man without a family, would have some or all of them over for dinner at night, often with wives and family if they were around. It was both an honor and annoying—no one would ever, in a sense, leave the office.

That made for a pretty congealed and tight group, but it also meant no one was telling Buchanan when he went off kilter, as he was wont to do. He would often waffle on major issues, and could easily come up on the most ill-advised side of them.

— ~ —

As my twenty-fifth wedding anniversary approached, I tried to be creative in buying a set of gifts for my wife. For one of them, I had the idea of a silver coin, the twenty-fifth being a silver anniversary, something that had to do with twenty-five or the year of our marriage or some such.

When I got to the local coin shop, it was busy, so I idled over some of the displays in the cases. There was a set of coins from the mid-nineteenth century that caught my eye. There were large coins all through the 1840s and 1850s—up until the coins from 1857, which were, at best, half the size of the others.

"Oh, the Panic of 1857," the owner said when I asked him about the change of size. "It was really bad. The president didn't seem to have any solution except to use less gold or silver in the coins."

That president was, to be sure, James Buchanan, his minimalist solution to one of America's great financial downturns being about as anemic as it could be.

In fact, things were going well for the country for a long time before Buchanan, in effect, precipitated the Panic of 1857.

There had been a bad downturn twenty years before, with multiple causes, like war in Europe, the dissolution of the Bank of the United States, and overspeculation in, oddly enough, slaves, corn, and Western land. The great acquisition of land under Polk, from Oregon to California to Texas, reinvigorated the economy, and a boom lasted for at least a decade. Railroads were the big mover, since so many people wanted to move west into the new territories and states. Manufacturing boomed domestically, and then with foreign trade as well, since Europe had quelled many of its hostilities and American items were cheaper than those on the Continent.

Then the day before Buchanan took office, Congress passed what he wanted, the Tariff Bill of 1857, which lowered tariffs on a panoply of items from abroad—Buchanan wanted to stimulate foreign trade—but made American manufactured goods of the same sort less competitive.

Three days later came *Dred Scott*. As appalled as most of the country was about the morals of the decision, there was a practical downside, too. Now no one knew whether he or she wanted to go west, to use the railroads, to start a business that railroads might profit from. Railroad stocks started to decline in value, and then a contagion hit, and it was free fall.

By midsummer no one could take a ride on the Reading, as Uncle Pennybags does in the Monopoly game, since it had shut down, as did lines now and then famous like the Illinois Central. Several lines, like the Delaware, Lackawanna and Western and the Fond du Lac Railroad in Wisconsin, declared bankruptcy.

Thousands were thrown out of work, and banks started foreclosing on loans and property. Senator William Seward, the leader of the new Republican Party, came home from a vacation to find out he had lost most everything he owned; his stock in the Illinois Central, promoted to him by his rival Democrat Stephen Douglas, was virtually worthless. Every bank in New York City effectively closed—none would convert coins or gold into banknotes. The oldest grain company in New York, N. H. Wolfe and Company, failed in August, as did the most prominent insurance business in the country, the Ohio Life Insurance and Trust Company.

The sinking of the SS *Central America* in a hurricane in September 1857 was an event out of Buchanan's control, but it did not help matters. The ship had thirty thousand pounds of gold that had made its way to Panama from the California gold rush and was on its Atlantic Ocean voyage up to New York, when off North Carolina it came upon what would be today called a Category 2 hurricane, with winds up to 105 miles per hour. More than four hundred people on board perished and the entire load of gold sank to the bottom of the sea.

While the loss of the gold, worth about $2 million at the time, was a substantial sum, it would not have been devastating to the economy, save that Buchanan and the administration did nothing to stem the public hysteria the sinking caused. Calm words might have quelled it, but it only made for further runs on banks and, thus, more turmoil in markets.

The residue that mattered most, though, was the reaction caused by *Dred Scott*. Instead of promoting unity and opening up the West to more settlement, as Buchanan had thought, *Dred Scott* thwarted it, and brought an end to years of Northern prosperity.

Yet the South did not succumb as badly. Its agrarian culture was self-sustaining, and its cotton still had a market in Europe. That caused Northerners to further blame Buchanan for being just a Southern lackey.

His response was underwhelming, almost disdainful. He said the federal government could do nothing. As even his apologist, writer Philip Klein, noted, Buchanan was almost heartless.

> *In his Annual Message of December, 1857, Buchanan announced his policy: reform not relief. The government sympathized but could do nothing to alleviate the suffering of individuals. It would continue to pay its obligations in gold and silver; it would not curtail public works, but it would start no new ones. . . . Buchanan's personal attitude [was that] men who respected property would not put it out to work except with sound collateral; those who took the speculative risk deserved the gambler's fate. As to the innocent victims, rugged individualism would triumph over adversity; the buoyancy of youth and the energy of the people would enable them to recover. The prophecy proved correct, but not before untold thousands had suffered the misery of broken lives, imminent starvation, and despair.*

The economy would not fully recover until, alas, a few years later, it had a national war to supply.

— ~ —

Buchanan's year of infamy did not end with a busted economy's "broken lives, imminent starvation, and despair," however. He still had at least one more crisis to instigate. The Mormons were not a beloved people, but for the most part, the federal government under Millard Fillmore and Franklin Pierce tried to ignore them and let them have their Zion in the wastelands of the Utah Territory. Brigham Young, the Mormon leader, was the governor and he seemed to only ask to be left alone, which given all the things going on with slavery and the like, was just fine with most Americans.

In 1857, though, Mormon settlers wanted to start the process of becoming a state and, at the same time, were complaining that federal judges in the territory were corrupt and trying to defraud settlers of their land. The judges charged, in the other direction, that Mormons were confiscating federal documents and burning them, so the judges could not perform their duties.

Without checking any of this out, Buchanan in May appointed a new governor, Alfred Cumming, and ordered 2,500 troops, a huge number for the time, under Colonel Albert Sidney Johnson, who would later become a prominent Confederate general, to go defend American law in this wastrel state.

Needless to say, the moves riled Young and his constituents, not to mention Kansas's Governor Walker, who would be losing the Johnson troops to what seemed to him a pointless mission. He got Buchanan to let down a little bit and leave some of the cavalry in Kansas, but off went Johnson with the rest of the troops.

Meanwhile, Young had never gotten the letter notifying him that he'd been replaced as governor. This time it was a Pierce blunder, Buchanan's predecessor having annulled the Utah mail contract. Though, to be certain, Buchanan had no interest in re-upping it.

Young, hearing only that a large federal force was coming to shut him down, formed an army of his own and ordered them to burn everything—every building, every tree, every piece of hay—that the federal force might capture on the way toward the presumed invasion.

In the process Mormons allegedly slaughtered innocent wagon trains of people and animals going west, and the federal brigade, in the last miles there, was ambushed several times, losing cattle and men.

One of Buchanan's old friends, Thomas L. Kane of Philadelphia, heard of this monstrous mistake and, because he had associated with some Mormons in the past, offered himself as a freelance diplomat. Buchanan agreed but did not give Kane a salary or expenses. By the time

Kane got there and cooled things off, thousands of Mormons had lost their homes and livelihoods, scorching all, as Young had ordered, and fleeing in the face of the army.

Buchanan offered his usual solution—not much. He gave the Mormons amnesty if they would submit to federal law, but little chance of continuing the process toward statehood (Utah not becoming a state until 1896). The troops stayed, albeit forty miles away for their own safety. It took another year for the Mormons, who had lost everything because of Buchanan's overreaction to what would have been an administrative issue, to return to their scorched lands and start recovering their lives.

Year one of America's worst presidency was over.

Aaron Scott Crawford spent his time as the associate editor of the Ulysses S. Grant papers while Barack Obama was in his first term as president. The beginnings of the two administrations were parallel. Both Grant and Obama succeeded members of the opposite party—in Democrat Obama's case, George W. Bush, and for Republican Grant, Andrew Johnson, who was elected as Republican Abraham Lincoln's vice president. (Johnson, however, had been a Democrat during his previous political career and was seen that way during his presidency.)

Both Bush and Johnson finished their presidencies at a nadir—Bush with the lowest positive polling numbers in modern history and Johnson just staving off conviction in an impeachment trial by one vote. Both Grant and Obama were planning on pursuing progressive agendas, and neither had much political experience.

In measuring their entire body of POTUS work, Obama and Grant have been called among the worst presidents—as, to be sure, have Bush and Johnson—but Crawford is not so sure of those assessments.

"Grant is seeing an upsurge in popularity among historians. He certainly was progressive when it came to his views of Indians and African Americans, but in the end what brings him down is that he was a horrible administrator," said Crawford, now a fellow at the Center for Presidential

History at Southern Methodist University, noting that Grant always stayed incredibly popular among his constituency, even when corruption plagued his cabinet in his second term.

Crawford, though, finds the hatred of Obama by his critics landmark, and disturbing, and believes that history will not place Obama as among the worst presidents, if only for that.

"I think the election of Obama will be a watershed moment. It will show the absolute lapse of civility when it comes to dealing with the presidency. The hatred of Bush was intense, but the hatred of Obama came with all the extra baggage," said Crawford, a specialist in the nineteenth-century presidencies, having also worked with the James Knox Polk papers through SMU. "By that I mean race. A portion of America just could not accept that."

In the end, though, Crawford dislikes the POTUS rating game. He said he feels the quest for greatness in a president can actually detract from the need to govern, which is more important in keeping the country moving. He said academic historians are more concerned with general history—not just the president who happened to be in power at the time.

"It is a parlor game, and I do not think it is a very constructive parlor game," said Crawford. He is particularly critical of Princeton historian Sean Wilentz's 2006 *Rolling Stone* magazine story, "George W. Bush: The Worst President in History?"

"George W. Bush's presidency appears headed for colossal historical disgrace," starts Wilentz's article. "Barring a cataclysmic event on the order of the terrorist attacks of September 11th, after which the public might rally around the White House once again, there seems to be little the administration can do to avoid being ranked on the lowest tier of U.S. presidents. And that may be the best-case scenario. Many historians are now wondering whether Bush, in fact, will be remembered as the very worst president in all of American history."

Wilentz went on to claim that Bush was unique in the pantheon of historically failed presidencies because he had fallen from a position of high regard—just after the 9/11 attacks, he had a near-90 percent positive rating in nearly every poll—to the depths of disregard in a universal drought of any worthwhile moves.

"Calamitous presidents, faced with enormous difficulties—Buchanan, Andrew Johnson, Hoover and now Bush—have divided the nation, governed erratically and left the nation worse off," wrote Wilentz.

In each case, different factors contributed to the failure: disastrous domestic policies, foreign-policy blunders and military setbacks, executive misconduct, crises of credibility and public trust. Bush, however, is one of the rarities in presidential history: He has not only stumbled badly in every one of these key areas, he has also displayed a weakness common among the greatest presidential failures—an unswerving adherence to a simplistic ideology that abjures deviation from dogma as heresy, thus preventing any pragmatic adjustment to changing realities. Repeatedly, Bush has undone himself, a failing revealed in each major area of presidential performance.

Crawford said he admires Wilentz, but to rate a president not only before significant time has passed to evaluate his work, but before his term is even up, is intellectually unsound for a historian.

"These days his view of Muslims in America and immigration policy would be progressive even for a Democrat. You have to have some perspective," said Crawford. "You have to give it some time.

"Buchanan, on the other hand . . ." he said with a pause. "Probably enough time there."

Crawford may be right that rating the president is a parlor game of sorts, but the inevitability of it, be it from historians or laypeople, is assured. This book lays out the case for Buchanan's low rating, but what of the other contenders? Why do they, at least by a smidgen, but often by more, rate above Buchanan?

Often presidential ratings dismiss the presidents who served less than a full term, but that is unfair in many cases. William Henry Harrison and James Garfield certainly get a pass, since they died early in the first year of their terms. But what about Zachary Taylor, who got in six-teen months before his death, or Warren Harding, who served two and a half years before he died? Kennedy, too, made it to more than half a term, as did vice presidential successors Gerald Ford, Andrew Johnson, Millard Fillmore, and John Tyler—all often cited as lesser presidents.

Of these, Kennedy, Taylor, and Ford had some moderate successes in their presidencies—Kennedy probably even better than most—and all finished their terms still popular, or, in the case of Ford, admired for his civility. Tyler, too, established at least one precedent: that the vice presi-dent who accedes to the presidency because of the death of a president is, indeed, a president. It seems de rigueur today that the vice president become president upon his predecessor's death, but that is assured only because of the Twenty-Fifth Amendment to the Constitution, passed in 1967.

When William Henry Harrison died, Tyler was a complete after-thought. He only became a member of the Whig Party to run with his Virginia neighbor, Harrison, and his views were clearly Southern Demo-cratic, an anathema to many who held their noses and voted him in with the popular Harrison. When Harrison died, though, Tyler just marched right into the White House and got to work. Whigs started complain-ing, saying that he should be an "acting president" and that maybe there should be another quick election, as would have happened with the Whigs in Great Britain. Tyler just kept his head down, called cabinet meetings, suggested legislation, and acted presidential. His reward from the Whigs? Being kicked out of the party. He got no significant piece of legislation through Congress, but he did save the nation a presidential crisis, in his succession and the precedent it set later. Tyler had his faults, but he was clearly not the Worst. President. Ever.

Fillmore gets a lot of votes for the bottom rung, but he, too, had at least one significant upside. Despite pleas from many to avoid the entan-glement, he took up the cudgel from the Great Compromiser, Henry Clay, and got the Compromise of 1850 passed. Looking back, the act was no more than a stalling tactic to what may have been the inevitable secession of the Southern states, but it did buy time for more compromises that, unfortunately, did not happen. He followed the idea of his predecessor, Zachary Taylor, that slavery was essentially an evil, but one that would take delicacy to phase out. In later times his fairly odd first name probably was more significant in thinking him the worst—there are a lot of Jameses today, but not many Millards—but Millard Fillmore was also not the Worst. President. Ever.

Andrew Johnson was no prize as a president, but he did keep the country from buckling after the Civil War. He may have been too appeasing of the South—after all, he was the only senator who stayed with the Union from an otherwise Confederate state, representing Tennessee until Lincoln put him on the ticket in 1864. It is hard to think, though, that the Radical Republican stance—that the Southern states should pay reparations and essentially kneel prostrate in other ways in order to get back into the Union—would have been a good long-term policy. Johnson was impeached because of his policies in connection with the former Confederacy, and survived being shown the door by just one Senate vote. All the Southern states came back into the fold, and the nation held through that, too, so it is hard to call Andrew Johnson the Worst. President. Ever.

Bush and Obama may be a little too fresh to consider for the rankings, but what about Jimmy Carter and Richard Nixon, whose presidencies are often considered troubling? Nixon resigned in disgrace before he could be impeached for, and probably convicted for, the Watergate scandal. He escalated the Vietnam War, probably had something to do with the killing of Salvador Allende in Chile, and presided over the 1973 oil crisis. Still, he had plenty of achievements during his presidency: opening China to trade, laying the groundwork for the SALT anti-ballistic missile treaty, presiding over lunar landings, and establishing the Environmental Protection Agency. Nixon gets no points for Vietnam and Watergate, but he had too many other things go right thanks to his policies, not just Congress working against him, to consign him to the bottom of the POTUS heap.

Carter, too, is a yin-and-yang president, but much better seen in perspective than he was at the end of his term. Princeton University history professor Julian Zelizer wrote the biography of Carter for the Times Books American Presidents series, and later edited the one on George W. Bush. When he started the Carter book in 2008 and continued writing it through 2009, the currency of the Bush presidency weighed on his thoughts.

"Bush was clearly in decline, but it was Carter at that point who was considered a horrible president. He was seen as a failure, a model of what not to do in foreign affairs and domestically," Zelizer told me. At that time, though, Carter's post-presidency was becoming a model as well. Zelizer said it made him look at the Carter presidency not through the people who hated him, but for what ways he had a significant impact.

"Because he was such a symbol of failure, particularly with the Iran hostage situation, but also with energy crises, inflation, and rising unemployment, his accomplishments tended to be forgotten, perhaps because they were only minor things during his administration and only became larger afterwards," said Zelizer.

Carter advocated ethics reform and shepherded the electoral system away from party bosses toward more and more primaries, putting nominations more firmly in the hands of the electorate. His almost clichéd wearing of sweaters brought consciousness of conservation in energy and environment, and though he had his foreign affairs problems, he did pull off the only significant Middle East peace treaty, getting Israel's Menachem Begin and Egypt's Anwar Sadat to sign the Camp David Accords.

Further, Zelizer said, Carter was a mensch, and not completely full of himself.

"I was at the Carter Library in Atlanta doing research and went to the cafeteria there, going in the line to get my food," said Zelizer. "The woman serves me my food and I turn around, and right behind me is Jimmy Carter with his tray. He sat at one of the little round tables bothering no one, as humble as you can imagine. That captured what Jimmy Carter was."

Which was clearly not the notorious W. P. E.

Herbert Hoover had a similarly long and hardworking ex-presidency. He was always seemingly the one called on by his successors to head some committee or other, mostly those for business and economic development, and he was always willing to serve. He may not have had the human rights agenda Carter displayed, but he did not take his lackluster presidency to mean he could not make up for it with post-presidential service.

As president Hoover did preside over the worst financial crisis of the modern era. He tried desperately to think of ideas, not to forestall the Depression, because none of those ideas came then, but to ameliorate it once it happened. But none tended to work. The Smoot-Hawley Tariffs of 1930, which his economic advisors begged him not to sign, hurt American exports immeasurably, and then he raised taxes in the midst of an economic slowdown—an admirable move for a Republican in better times—which only hastened the Great Depression.

Unlike Taylor and Buchanan, though, Hoover *acted*. He was actually presented with the bubble about to burst by his predecessor, Calvin Coolidge—the stock market crash coming only seven months into his presidency—so historians have given him a bit of leeway. Further, Hoover presided over peaceful times, though he did not recognize the rise of the European right, which was starting to happen on his watch.

At least in Hoover's attempts to act, his contrition and legacy in his post-presidency, and his lack of corruption during his presidency, he was anything but Buchananesque. Hoover is not our nation's Worst. President. Ever.

For true challengers to Buchanan, it comes down to Warren Harding and Franklin Pierce, but for clearly different reasons.

Harding's peccadilloes burst back on the scene in 2015, when it was confirmed that he had a child from an affair with Nan Britton just before he became president. And he probably continued the relationship while he was in the White House. What high school history books note about Harding is mostly that the Teapot Dome and other scandals, some involving men in his cabinet, came during his term—and that he failed to see them happening, even if he had no part in them otherwise.

The book jacket copy for the definitive biography of Harding, *The Shadow of Blooming Grove: Warren G. Harding and His Times*, by Francis Russell, notes in the first paragraph that Harding was "the President who has come to be rated last in the hearts of his countrymen," calling him an "affable, goodhearted mediocrity." There's a direct quote from the text that leads off the front-flap copy—a nugget from the author's writing that the publisher must have felt would sell the book to browsers. It goes like this:

> *Harding, with his tarnished reputation, has never claimed the serious attention of historians. In this he has been the most neglected of Presidents. His centennial passed without an adequate general biography of him ever having appeared. He deserves a biography, not so much for himself—though in many ways his life was more interesting than those of more notable Presidents—but because he came at a dividing point in history when men moved forward and looked back. The first President after World War I, he was also the first President to be born after the Civil War. His election was in one sense a nostalgic imperfect haze of memory, at a moment when twentieth-century America was inevitably, if belatedly, taking form.*

In this way Harding is much like Buchanan, who was nothing if not an "affable, goodhearted mediocrity." Buchanan's election, too, was perhaps the most transforming since Washington's, and its only equal afterwards was Lincoln's in the next cycle. America was looking backward nostalgically and forward, with horror, as most electors hoped that the main problems that had plagued the nation from its start—slavery and union—could be solved.

The Harding election's issues, though, were not nearly so fraught. The election of 1920 was more about the United States on an international scene, moving from a mere adjunct to a consequential power—and then internally progressing from a rural, docile mindset to an urban, industrial, and aggressive one.

Harding was elected to be the shepherd of that piece of progress. The business of America, as it has come down, became business during Harding's regime. In his short term, gross domestic product skyrocketed from $69.1 billion in 1921 to $85 billion in 1923. His supporters wanted him to protect American agriculture and manufacturing, so he in turn supported the Fordney-McCumber Tariff of 1922, which insulated farms and factories from imports, hurting Europe at a tender moment, perhaps, but pushing the right buttons for the post–World War I era in the United States.

When it comes to scandal, though, Harding was a cross between Ulysses S. Grant and Bill Clinton. Like Grant, he did not see how some of his cronies were pillaging the coffers, especially in the Teapot Dome oil-leasing scandal. His affairs with his best friend's wife, Carrie Phillips, and Britton are reminiscent of Clinton's indiscretions. Yet Harding also brought many good people into public service. Businessman Herbert Hoover became his commerce secretary after heading European war relief efforts. Renowned legal figure Charles Evans Hughes was his secretary of state, and as secretary of the treasury Andrew Mellon was probably the most significant figure in the Roaring Twenties economic advancement. Harding did not bring William Howard Taft into public service, but he gave Taft the job in which he thrived: chief justice of the Supreme Court.

So while there is much to criticize about Harding, for the most part he did what he was elected to do and attracted an innovative group of people to government who had influence beyond his presidency. That no one wrote his biography before Russell may be an indication of how little historians thought about him early on, but he was worthy of Russell's take—a sardonic one not so different from that in this book for Buchanan. But he is not the least of the lesser presidents.

The real competition for Worst. President. Ever., then, is Franklin Pierce, and because he was Buchanan's predecessor, and in a small sense his rival, it is the fairest comparison.

Like Harding, Pierce has a paucity of biography—the only major one being *Franklin Pierce: Young Hickory of the Granite Hills*, by Roy F. Nichols, first written in 1931 and then revised in 1958. Like Russell is of Harding, Nichols is, despite being his biographer, not the biggest advocate of Pierce as a president. He acknowledges that had Buchanan's advocates played their hand a bit better during the 1852 Democratic Convention, Pierce might never have been nominated in the first place. Yet Pierce, as a compromise candidate, a Northerner with Southern views, a young guy from New Hampshire, seemed to be the proper choice at the time.

Nichols laid much of the blame for Pierce's inadequacy as president on the tragic death of his third son, Benjamin. The Pierces had had one son die in infancy and another die at age four, but Bennie, as they called him, stayed in good health, and at eleven years old he was the focus of his parents more than anything else, even though one of them was going to be president of the United States. In early January 1853, after visiting friends in Boston and staying a few days extra to attend a funeral, the Pierces headed back by train to their home in Concord, New Hampshire. No sooner had the train left the station than it tumbled off the tracks in Andover, Massachusetts, and though the elder Pierces suffered no injuries, Bennie got entangled in the wreckage and died while his parents were watching. Nichols said that Mrs. Pierce held it over Pierce the rest of her life—"His high honor," writes Nichols, "had been purchased at the price of his son's sacrifice." Nichols then makes his pitch for an excuse for Pierce's rough presidency:

> *It is difficult to express adequately the effect which this interpretation of the tragedy worked upon the President-elect. It became the fact of greatest importance in his life, troubling his conscience, unsettling him almost completely, and weakening his self-confidence for many months to come. At a time when he required peace and self-control for summoning all his powers to the big tasks awaiting him, he was distracted and worn by heart-searchings. Burdened with a dead weight of hopeless sorrow, he entered his office fearfully. He could not undertake his duties with that buoyant and confident assurance which so often in itself invites success . . . He was to work under a perma-*

nent handicap. His was not a frame of mind to command success or to invite inspiration. Much of the difficulty which he experienced in administration during the next four years may be attributed to this terrible tragedy and its long-continued after effects.

On the other hand, many presidents had death in their families, including those in Pierce's era. Willie Lincoln died in the White House less than a year into Abe Lincoln's term. John Tyler's first wife died while he was president and Millard Fillmore's was sick nearly his entire presidency, dying three weeks after he left office. It is a curious excuse to have a four-year term negated by personal tragedy. Pierce's faults may have come from his inexperience—he was the youngest elected president up until that time, at age forty-eight. His tragedy, to be sure, was palpable, but he had never really been the boss of anything—his tenure as a commander in the Mexican War was short and inconclusive, at any rate. Blaming Bennie Pierce's death for his father's less-than-mediocre presidency may be a stretch.

What is clear, though, is that Pierce's idea of the presidency was to have it be a glorified board meeting, with him as the moderator and chairman. His was the only cabinet to stay the same for the entire four years of a presidential term. It was filled, with the possible exception of Jefferson Davis, the future president of the Confederacy, with undistinguished, if functional, men. It is not hard to see them struggling daily for consensus and then ploddingly getting minor things done, but balking on major issues.

The signal moment of Pierce's presidency was the passage of the Kansas-Nebraska Act, which basically negated all the other compromises on slavery and states' rights over the previous four decades, if not all the way back to the Constitution itself, allowing slaves to be recaptured on free Northern soil and letting territories decide whether to become slave states, regardless of whether they were above or below the Missouri line that was so definite in the past.

When it came time to take a side on Kansas-Nebraska, Pierce excluded Northerners Lewis Cass, his chief noncabinet advisor, and William Marcy, his secretary of state, from the meeting with Senate sponsor Stephen Douglas, but allowed the fiery Davis, his Mississippi-bred secretary of war, to come and convince Pierce to sign on. It ended up creating the furor that caused violence throughout eastern Kansas, and the formation of John Brown's series of rebellions.

This surely trumps any of the positives of Pierce's term. The seemingly small Gadsden Purchase in the Southwest made it easier for a Southern rail route to the Pacific, a godsend when California finally opened up its markets soon after. Similarly, Pierce oversaw the opening of Japan to United States trade with the expeditions there by Commodore Matthew Perry.

Though he really blew it with Kansas-Nebraska, Pierce at least advocated that the Union was paramount, that he would harbor no secession. If Nichols is right and Pierce suffered from a type of depression throughout his term, at least he sought advice, bad though it may have been on slavery's extension, before he acted.

Pierce was no prize, but he kept the United States intact. He was never loved by the people who gave him a huge victory in 1852, with 254 electoral votes to merely 42 for his Whig opponent Winfield Scott. Those who thought at all about him by 1860 gave him at least some of the blame for the Civil War. Pierce, though, unlike Buchanan, did not blame others for it. He died an unfulfilled but contrite man. He came close, but he was not America's Worst. President. Ever.

Buchanan, then, takes that prize. Though he had some positives, they were primarily social and short lived. He was not an evil man personally and had a partying spirit when it came time for that, but even there, he could not bring himself to be even a mediocre administrator.

In short, as Robert W. Merry concludes in his section on the candidates for worst president in *Where They Stand*: "Buchanan's place in history, like Harding's, seems well established. The historians' various surveys have him vying for second from the bottom. That would seem to be a notch too high."

CHAPTER SEVEN

The Middle Buchanan Presidency: Hardly Better

MASSACHUSETTS SENATOR CHARLES SUMNER WAS SCARCELY A DOVE ON the issue of slavery when he took to the Senate chamber on May 19, 1856. He was to deliver an oration on the crisis burgeoning in Kansas, a barely populated territory west of Missouri and mostly above the boundary separating slave states and those supposed to be free as per the Missouri Compromise.

The Kansas-Nebraska Act and the Compromise of 1850 had changed the established slave/free divide and riled those in the North who wanted the institution of slavery at least contained. Sumner was of a different ilk, though, an abolitionist who wanted the institution not just contained, but eliminated for both moral and practical reasons. He was viewed by most senators as on the fringe, but his constituents in Massachusetts had come to grips with his fieriness and there was a slow, but steady, move toward abolitionism there.

The speech was not his first on the subject in his five years in the Senate, but it became his most memorable. He decided to use sexual analogies to rail against Slave Power, the slave-owning group in the South most prominent in trying to force slavery on Kansas: "Not in any common lust for power did this uncommon tragedy have its origin. It is the rape of a virgin Territory, compelling it to the hateful embrace of slavery; and it may be clearly traced to a depraved desire for a new Slave

State, hideous offspring of such a crime, in the hope of adding to the power of slavery in the National Government."

He then veered toward personal attacks. Though Stephen Douglas was one author of the Kansas-Nebraska Act, Sumner went light on him, since Douglas himself was not a slaveholder. The vituperation was greater for another author, South Carolina senator Andrew Butler.

The senator from South Carolina has read many books of chivalry, and believes himself a chivalrous knight with sentiments of honor and courage. Of course he has chosen a mistress to whom he has made his vows, and who, though ugly to others, is always lovely to him; though polluted in the sight of the world, is chaste in his sight—I mean the harlot, slavery. For her his tongue is always profuse in words. Let her be impeached in character, or any proposition made to shut her out from the extension of her wantonness, and no extravagance of manner or hardihood of assertion is then too great for this senator.

Douglas professed not to be offended, seeing the speech as just a political rant, but he presaged the offense Southerners would feel when he told an associate, "This damn fool Sumner is going to get himself shot by some other damn fool."

A few days after the speech, South Carolina representative Preston Brooks, a cousin of Butler who had contemplated challenging Sumner to a duel, instead approached the senator at his seat in the chamber, told him he thought his speech was libelous, and started to beat him over the head with his gold-topped cane. Sumner fell and was trapped under his desk as Brooks beat him so badly that Sumner was blinded by his own blood. Sumner finally was able to start staggering up the aisle to the door, but Brooks continued to beat him, stopping only when the cane broke. Brooks then rushed out of the chamber.

Sumner survived, but he had to spend several years convalescing. Brooks went unprosecuted, but each of them became heroes in their respective sections of the country.

The Kansas issue, already a mess, became a focus after the Sumner beating. With a new administration coming into the White House in a few months, there would have to be a resolution that, while probably now pleasing no one, would at least calm things down, if not in Kansas itself, then perhaps in the rest of the country.

Nobody counted on the ineptness of the newcomer in the White House.

———

By the mid-1850s Kansas had become a mini-California. Maybe there was no gold or an ocean there, as there was in California, but Kansas had millions of acres of land, most of it arable and ready for commerce.

Stephen Douglas was the chair of the Senate Committee on Territories, and thus was the creative mind in figuring out how to get them integrated into the American dream. His Kansas-Nebraska Act, at least in theory, could have been a masterstroke. It proposed two potential states, Kansas and Nebraska, and that they would be able to determine whether they would be slave or free when they were admitted into the Union.

Douglas knew that Kansas was inhospitable to slavery, that its land was not the kind suitable for cotton or tobacco or any other crop that was traditionally slave-honed in the South. Thus, he figured, a choose-your-own-status plan could placate the South without hurting the North, that the two states would eventually come to be free, but that Southerners, too, might start settling there—and maybe give up their slaves in the process.

Good in theory, and supported in bipartisan ways, Douglas's act was in practice a nonstarter. As settlers came in, many of them from slave-holding Missouri across the border, they established two governmental centers. The one in Lecompton, which got organized first, advocated slavery, while the one organized soon after to the west, in Topeka, wanted Kansas to be a free state.

There were fights back and forth between settlers of the different stripes in Kansas, people dying at random and lots of folks scared off.

The most famous event was the slaughter at Pottawatomie Creek, which happened two days after Brooks's beating of Sumner. John Brown—a man viewed as half-crazed, even by some of his supporters—and a band of seven others, including his three sons, apparently shot to death five alleged slave sympathizers and hacked their bodies into at least some parts afterwards.

With the territory in disarray, then, Buchanan had to come up with a creative solution. One of the best thoughts might have been to appoint Stephen Douglas as governor of Kansas, a job he probably would have taken. It was Douglas who started the mess, and perhaps he would have worked hard to get it resolved.

Buchanan, though, would not have been satisfied if Douglas had actually come up with a solution. He hated the senator from Illinois that much. If Douglas could have solved Kansas, or even have quelled fighting there, he would have presumably gone back to the Senate from Kansas were it to become a state. He'd be a lock as the Democratic presidential candidate in 1860, with a solid chance at being the hero keeping the country together, something Buchanan could not have countenanced.

Buchanan did appoint a competent man. Robert Walker, a native Pennsylvanian, had been the valedictorian of his class at the University of Pennsylvania and had then become a lawyer and joined his brother, who had moved to Mississippi. He became a large landowner and slaveholder and then a senator from his adopted state, before serving as secretary of the treasury under President James Knox Polk, where he became friendly with Buchanan. He retired to practice law after the Polk administration, and seemed to be the best kind of nonpartisan man to run things in Kansas after a series of ineffectual governors.

That would have been so, maybe, if Buchanan had only decided to *listen* to Walker. Buchanan seemed to think that the Lecompton group, in a sort of first come, first served idea, was the legitimate territorial government. Lecompton was almost a Potemkin Village, a ramshackle group of clapboard buildings west of Kansas City and east of Topeka, just a crossroads where slavery-sympathetic settlers happened to gather. In a lot of ways, many of these folks were less worried about slavery and more concerned with grabbing some land. Since they were from slaveholding Missouri, they were OK with the slaveholders who had set up the skeletal government, if they would secure the papers for their new lands.

Walker saw through that ruse and tried to convince Buchanan that the better idea was to have Kansas be a free state, since there were but only a dozen or so slaves even in Lecompton. Buchanan did not trust Walker's counsel. Both the Topeka and Lecompton governments claimed legitimacy, and the only way to resolve it, said Buchanan, was to have citizens vote on the Lecompton constitution, the first one of the two designed. "On the question of submitting the Constitution to the bona fide residents of Kansas, I am willing to stand or fall," Buchanan wrote to Walker.

Incongruously enough today, Lecompton proudly promotes itself as the "Civil War Birthplace" and runs annual events centered around the remembrance of "Bleeding Kansas." It commemorates, justly or not, the vote on the Lecompton constitution, which not only allowed slavery in Kansas, but made it an inviolable right until at least 1864, when, presumably, Kansas would long have been a state and its legacy would have been too ingrained to reverse.

Most anti-slavery citizens stayed home for the Lecompton election, which was only on the issue of whether slavery would be allowed in a potential state of Kansas. The Northerners of both parties were outraged that Buchanan wanted such an election. To them, any election had to be about the whole constitution, which they felt was completely invalid, given that it was promulgated by a slavery-leaning government that did not include most of the rest of the state. That a referendum later showed that 10,226 voters were against the entire Lecompton constitution, with fewer than 200 for it—thus a willingness on the part of most Kansans to just start over—seemed not to move Buchanan.

Buchanan put his reputation as a negotiator on the line with the Lecompton constitution, submitting it to Congress whole, with the slavery cause and the clearly invalid local vote intact. The Senate, highly

Democratic and heavily Southern in that regard, would pass the bill, but it was neck and neck in the House. Buchanan got his cabinet and other advisors to work, offering land grants and other goodies to the on-the-fence representatives—with accusations that some of those offers were outright bribes and even secret sexual favors from prostitutes.

In the end the House defeated the bill, and eventually a new constitution, fairly drawn, passed in Kansas, which became a state just as the Civil War started in 1861—a free state, but with as much rancor as any other before or since.

Buchanan's failed effort was generally seen as proof of his Southern sympathies. The 1858 fall congressional elections were a disaster. Democrats lost to Republicans in New York, New Jersey, Ohio, Indiana, New England, and even Pennsylvania—the most devastating being Pennsylvanian J. Glancy Jones, who had been Buchanan's most dedicated workhorse in the House.

At least Buchanan took responsibility, writing his niece Harriet, "Well! We have met the enemy," he said, "& we are theirs. This I have anticipated for three months." Even though the Democrats had a titular majority, in point of fact, there would be little from the Buchanan White House that would be easily passed after the new Congress took its seats in 1859.

⌒

As Kansas and the Panic were taking most of the air out of any seeming hope for the still relatively new administration, Buchanan tried to push onward with what he felt was his forte—the expansion of the United States as far as possible.

While he was in London as the minister to England during the Pierce administration, he and the ministers to France and Spain had met in secret to form a scheme to add Cuba to the American republic.

The document they presented to President Franklin Pierce was called the Ostend Manifesto, for the city in Belgium where they met, and based on its phraseology, was probably written whole by Buchanan.

Cuba had long been on American politicians' wish lists, but even back to the Monroe Doctrine, which advocated American dominion over the Western Hemisphere, the sovereignty of colonial powers who were already on the scene was honored. By the time of the Pierce administration, though, Spain was losing influence, having given up most of its possessions in Central and South America, and Americans were worried that more formidable countries, like France or Great Britain, would try to become stronger, too, near American shores.

For Doughfaces like Buchanan and Pierce, the overriding reason to add Cuba to the roster of states was slavery. Cuba already had a preponderance of slaves—about a third of the million people in the 1850 Cuban census were enslaved. If admitted to the Union at that point, Cuba, counting each slave as three-fifths of a person as the Constitution allowed, would have its requisite two senators, but also nine members of the House of Representatives, which would be a lot of voting power.

In addition, there was always the fear that if the weaker Spanish continued to control Cuba, there might be a slave rebellion on the island, much as the black population of Haiti created their own government. A black Cuba was one thing, but a successful rebellion there might incite American slaves to get ideas for their own rebellion. Whatever could be made of the sugar trade or any other type of economic advantage, the real goal of the Ostend Manifesto was to placate the South with the multifaceted slave argument, as one of Buchanan's paragraphs in the Manifesto read: "We should, however, be recreant to our duty, be unworthy of our gallant forefathers, and commit base treason against our posterity, should we permit Cuba to be Africanized and become a second St. Domingo [Haiti], with all its attendant horrors to the white race, and suffer the flames to extend to our own neighboring shores, seriously to endanger or actually to consume the fair fabric of our Union."

The Ostend Manifesto became one of the abolitionist movement's biggest rallying cries by the end of the Pierce administration. It was bald-faced in its thrust to bolster the Southern slavocracy, and when the Slave

Power organizations began to advocate it with vigor, it only energized the very people Buchanan feared, the radical anti-slavery groups.

Despite that, Buchanan constantly tried to find ways to annex or conquer Cuba during his administration, particularly in its early years, when he still had some cachet among Northern Democrats. He would try to convince them that placating the South was not such a bad idea, especially if the Union could be saved that way, and Cuba was an easy target. He proposed that one of his bargaining chips with Spain would be cash, which the United States surely had, and that the slave trade itself would cease.

Buchanan also looked toward Mexico and Central America for expansion of the Great Republic—Manifest Destiny redux. William Walker, the most famous of the potential conquerors then known as "filibusters," twice rolled over Nicaragua, hoping to either become its sovereign or deliver it as a slave state to Buchanan.

In what was merely for show, Buchanan sent troops down to capture Walker and his mercenaries. When Commodore Hiram Paulding dragged Walker back to New Orleans to be prosecuted, Buchanan negated Walker's arrest, saying it had taken place illegally on foreign soil, and it was Paulding who was censured. Walker did get his own come-uppance, though. He ventured back to Nicaragua, hoping to look like a savior, but was eventually assassinated by locals who were clearly fed up with him and the Buchanan administration in general.

Buchanan even promulgated petty—perhaps even silly—wars, in hopes of currying favor with expansionists, a group that was waning by the time Kansas had exhausted everyone. He fought, for instance, the now little-known Pig War on the Strait of Juan de Fuca off the Olympic Peninsula on the border of Washington and British Columbia.

On June 15, 1859, an American farming squatter named Lyman Cutlar shot and killed a pig that was rooting around his shack. It turned out that the pig belonged to the Hudson Bay Company, and the Canadians then threatened to round up and deport any Americans still living on the wrong side of the strait.

A troop of Americans commanded by then Captain George Pickett, whose charge several years later during the Battle of Gettysburg led to the Confederate defeat there, came to defend the honor of the pig-shooting squatter.

Instead of using diplomacy in what was clearly a minor incident, Buchanan dispatched General Winfield Scott with troops and warships on a six-week passage from New York to the strait by way of Panama. By the time Scott got there, there were troops and ships ready to fire at each other over, well, a pig. Scott, a former Whig and never a big fan of Buchanan anyway, proposed a joint occupation of the strait without hostility, which lasted another decade. Scott could not quite figure out what Buchanan thought might happen—maybe more territory and a better harbor in the Northwest—but he was not going to have it happen with his exhausted troops over some swine-shooting settler.

At least as embarrassing and wasteful was Buchanan's invasion of Paraguay in 1859. Yes, Paraguay. The nascent former Spanish colony had claimed land it said American citizens living there had appropriated. And truth be told, it did commit one bad act: firing on an American ship surveying the rivers of the landlocked country, killing an officer.

For that Buchanan dispatched 2,500 marines and nineteen warships, which took several weeks to get down to South America and up the Parana River to the Paraguayan capital of Asuncion. By the time they got there, even the most rabid expansionists, and those slave-holding firebrands who might have thought Paraguay ripe for a slave state, were hardly with Buchanan on the invasion. So the expedition turned around almost immediately, spending several months to get back intact.

As Jean Baker noted in her not always complimentary biography of Buchanan: "In the meantime these men and ships could have been employed in reinforcing American coastal forts, where they were needed to prevent attacks by seceding southern states, rather than fending off distant insult to the flag. Instead secession was only encouraged by the feeble response of the U.S. government."

The middle years of Buchanan's term, then, were not much better, if at all, than his initial year. He did have some work to do, however, in his last months in office to seal his fate as the Worst. President. Ever.

— ᴥ —

Maybe not quite an early-day Kennedy, Harriet Lane was among the most talked-about women in the country, if not the civilized world, by the time her uncle took office. When Buchanan was minister to Great Britain during the Pierce administration, Harriet had charmed the British royalty, at one time or another being linked to some sort of earl, prince, or nobleman. Her uncle—Nunc, she liked to call him—had taught her tact, manners, and tolerance, much-admired traits in nineteenth-century London. More than the minister himself, his niece became a pop figure of sorts, the "leading star of the social firmament," according to the editor of her hometown newspaper, the *Weekly Journal* of Mercersburg, Pennsylvania, who felt it incumbent upon himself to meet the twenty-six-year-old First Lady in person at the inaugural ball.

Lace berthas, collars covering otherwise plunging necklines atop fancy hoop-skirt dresses, became fashionable because Harriet Lane wore them. A popular song, "The Mocking Bird," was dedicated to her by the US Marine Band, which played it at White House functions. She had red hair, and it brought attention to her, enhancing her fame. A photo of her was made into a souvenir postcard, and it was collected much like modern boys keep baseball cards. A revenue cutter was named the *Harriet Lane*. In fact, it fired the first naval shot at Charleston in the upcoming Civil War—and even after the Confederate navy captured it in 1863, its name stayed the same in deference to her popularity in both the Republic and the Confederacy. A modern cutter has the *Harriet Lane* name today; its fame was enhanced in the cleanup of the 2010 Deepwater Horizon oil spill in the Gulf of Mexico.

Every newspaper and magazine reported on her, with the *New York Times* correspondent Patrick Lynch noting her renown:

Miss Lane occupies a position in the palatial residence of her eminent relative similar to that which Queen Victoria and the Empress Eugenie occupy at Buckingham Palace and the Tuileries. Nor is it, in my mind, too much for me to add that the attention of the American fashionable world will be directed to the Republican princess who presides over the social arrangements of the official residence of the President . . . Her beauty reminds me of that mixed Celt and Saxon in Ireland which Lord Byron has immortalised [sic] by calling the most exquisite in the world; and her artlessness and grace and sweetness and goodness of heart and manner make her a generous and noble American girl.

Harriet became her uncle's ward at the age of eleven, when he was forty, after both her parents had died of disease. He put her in a Virginia boarding school and then later in a Catholic one in Washington, where she met, among other daughters of politicians, Adele Cutts, the eventual young wife of her uncle's rival, Stephen Douglas. She learned all the graces and skills of young women of the time—from how to dress and bow to writing and playing piano. Whatever Buchanan did wrong in the presidency, his stewardship of Harriet was remarkable. He allowed her to be physical, climbing trees, playing sports, taking hikes on her own. He invited her to his private political meetings even when she was a teenager, and while she never gave her opinions there, he encouraged her to do so to him later on.

When they were apart they wrote letters, in appropriate uncle-niece fashion. He would correct her punctuation and grammar and she would tell him news of the town or city she was in. She was twenty-one when he brought her to London, soon after he started as the Pierce administration's minister there. She quickly became interested in both the foreign political dealings her uncle was going through and the formal goings-on in Queen Victoria's court. The queen apparently adored her and would always compliment her outfits and her demeanor both to her and to her uncle. On her way home to America, Harriet stayed with the minister to France, John Y. Mason, and came to court with him to meet Emperor Napoleon III and Empress Eugenie. After that her strolls around Paris became gawking sessions for locals. Had paparazzi been around at that time, she would have been their focus.

In the large cache of letters between Harriet and Buchanan in the Library of Congress archives, there is only one where he touts a possible romance for his niece. Just before Buchanan left for England, he stayed in New York, waiting for his ship to depart. There he was visited by John Van Buren, the widowed son of ex-president Martin Van Buren and a prominent New York lawyer and former state attorney general. The younger Van Buren himself had accompanied his father to England as a secretary when Martin Van Buren was minister there, and was a favorite of Queen Victoria in his time as Harriet would be in hers. His visit to Buchanan was, apparently, all about Harriet, not politics. The marriage of scions of two of the most prominent Democratic—not to mention presidential—families would have been eye catching, but the timing was bad, since Harriet was soon off to England herself.

Harriet was the first woman to be called a First Lady while at the White House. (Dolley Madison had the title when she came back to Washington after her husband's death.) Harriet ran the back of the house, sometimes without fervor, since it was not managing she wanted to do, but party planning. Her one big initial move was getting rid of the slaves who had served the Pierces and replacing them with paid labor, mostly German or Irish immigrants. It was daring, since the District was still very much a slave area, even if the slave trade itself was outlawed there by the Compromise of 1850.

She sometimes strayed from formalities, hiring orchestras to play at the White House gatherings, but the tenor during the mid-nineteenth century was that there would be no dancing, since some religious folks who might be there thought dancing sinful. When the teenage Prince of Wales came to Washington late in Buchanan's term, however, Harriet had the cutter named after her commandeered and hosted the biggest party of the half century in the capital, replete with an orchestra, dancing, and fine wine, not just the president's stash of Madeira. They took the cutter down to Mount Vernon, where the great-grandson of King George III got to see the home of the man who had defeated his ancestor.

The only real blemish on Harriet's First Lady-dom was her rivalry with Adele Douglas. They both were adored by most every other person of the Washington scene, but they could not get past the political and personal rift of Buchanan and Stephen Douglas. Few people chose between them, but they often gave rival parties and acted petty in that regard.

After the president's term Harriet went to Wheatland with him, and in January of 1866, at age thirty-five, she married Baltimore businessman Henry Johnston. They had met sixteen years before at the spa town of Bedford Springs, Pennsylvania, Buchanan's favorite vacation spot, and reconnected there in 1864. She moved to Baltimore and had two sons rather quickly, but always summered back at Wheatland, even after Buchanan died.

She became a big benefactor of the new Johns Hopkins University in Baltimore, particularly in its childhood medical research. Sadly, both of her sons died in early adolescence from rheumatic fever, and she and her husband then endowed a pediatric clinic in Baltimore to treat children regardless of race, a huge undertaking at the time, since Maryland was legally segregated. Unfortunately, several months later, her husband died at age fifty-three while undergoing surgery.

Harriet eventually moved back to Washington and was the Dolley Madison of her age. She gave parties and went to them, and whomever she danced with felt golden. She gave donations to many charities, having inherited a good sum from both Buchanan and her husband. Her Harriet Lane Clinic became associated with Johns Hopkins, the first clinic of its kind connected with a major hospital in the country, and it continues there into the twenty-first century.

She traveled to the social capitals of the United States, like Bar Harbor, Maine, and Newport, Rhode Island. She went to Europe and was always feted there as the First Lady. In Vienna she was so impressed with the famous Boys Choir that she gave money to start one stateside— eventually also endowing in her will what became the St. Albans School for boys in Washington, DC.

The earliest photograph of Harriet is from a party given by Sarah Polk, the wife of James Knox Polk, with Dolley Madison also in the image. Harriet was invited to many more functions by all of her successors, from the Johnsons to the Roosevelts, her last appearance at a White House function coming on an invitation from Edith Roosevelt in 1901.

Harriet's last major public appearance was her trip to England for the coronation of the then young man she had met during her uncle's term, Prince Edward; she sailed across the Atlantic at age seventy-two in 1902. She died the next year in Washington, leaving her fortune to many projects, including two monuments to be dedicated to her uncle.

Buchanan may have been the Worst. President. Ever., but there could hardly have been a better Nunc.

CHAPTER EIGHT

Mr. Buchanan's War

WHEN THE BICENTENNIAL—AND PERHAPS THE TERCENTENARY—OF
the Civil War occurs years from now, there will still be those who will rear
up and posit that the war was all about something called "states' rights"
and barely at all about slavery. They will say that the Confederate flag is
just a banner for those who identify with Southern culture, no less benign
than a high school mascot, not nearly a symbol of a society that believed
people of one skin color were so far inferior to those of another that they
should only have been chattel.

Were they able, though, to transport themselves back to the early
1860s, they would find that the only state right that any Southern secession document talked about was related to the institution of slavery, and
that short of the accent of their English and the sauces on their food, the
only thing that separated the bulk of the people in each section of the
country was their laws concerning slavery.

Now, it is true that most white folks, North and South, including
the man in the White House in 1860, James Buchanan, were convinced
that black people were not as competent in most ways as whites, but in
the Northern part of the country—and in the lands of the West moving
toward statehood—they believed that a free market system, with laborers
all getting some kind of income, was far superior to that of slavery.

At the time of the Buchanan presidency, the state of the economy
and the social status in general for the average Southerner were far
behind that of his fellow citizens to the North. According to the United

States census in 1850, there were 2,399,651 native-born whites in New England, and only 6,209 of those more than twenty years of age could not read or write. In Virginia, though, there were about one-third the number of native born whites—871,847—and twelve times the number of twenty-and-over illiterates, or 75,863 people. Virginia was an intellectual paradise compared to the states to its south. Ten percent of Arkansas's white adults were illiterate, as were 15 percent of those in North Carolina. According to historian Allan Nevins in his seminal study of the pre–Civil War era, *Ordeal of the Union*, "School appropriations were wretched, and it was said that even penal laws would hardly compel many rural parents to put their children into classes."

Though there was no particular linkage between literacy and sage farming practices, agriculture in the South was less sophisticated than in the North. "The methods of tillage were glaringly deficient in intelligence, providence, and foresight," wrote Nevins. "Slave owners seized upon most of the good land. They exhausted it by heavy crops of cotton, cane, tobacco, and corn, plowing much of the top soil into the streams. In time they sold out for a song or abandoned their holdings for taxes, moving onward. The poorer whites, in some States three fourths of the free population, took the hill land, the sterile soils, and the abandoned tracts. Meanwhile, rapid soil exploitation and Negro exploitation gave a limited number of land owners temporary wealth at the cost of sectional impoverishment."

There were estimates that as many as half of the white adult population in South Carolina was unemployed or working only a little bit and living by subsistence—hunting and foraging on their own or maybe trading with slaves. Workers in the mid-South of North Carolina and Tennessee averaged eighty cents a day, which today would be about eight to ten dollars, hardly a living even if they could raise their own food.

The Southern planters and large slave owners, who were surely as rich as any of the industrialists in the North, would point out that, according to government figures, nearly half of the nation's foreign export shipments—$71 million of $144 million—were in cotton alone, most of which was grown in the South, and almost all of that was produced by slave labor.

There were hidden issues with that, however. The slave trade itself had long been outlawed, and slave breeding was an uncertain business at best. Thus slaves alone, not to mention productive ones, cost more than in earlier years. They also had uncertain working lifetimes. Even if a slave could become productive at age ten, he or she would have, at best, thirty good working years—the average lifespan of all Americans then being about forty years. Then, too, slaves generally were, for obvious reasons, in worse health through their lifetimes than whites.

There were estimates at the time that half of some large planters' wealth was tied up in slaves. "Much of this 'wealth' represented simply the ownership of one-half the population by the other half," wrote Nevins, "but it seemed as real and profitable as houses and machines."

As unreal as the South's financial success may have been, what was indeed real was its pride. As their influence otherwise receded, Southern slaveholders' pride became somewhat defensive. The slave owners could add Texas to their roster, but, especially after the debacle of Kansas, and the demise of any of Buchanan's forays into Cuba and Central America, they would have to make their stand where they already stood.

If Buchanan did not see that early on, he surely understood it after Kansas. Still, he would go to the greatest of lengths to placate his friends in the South. At every turn he would blame the growing abolitionist movement in the North for exacerbating the differences in the sectional dispute. If slaveholders were left alone, the thinking went, the institution might die out, but at least would be contained, as the various big compromises had provided. Once anti-slavery agitators got going, they just riled up the South. It was a view he never changed, his final memoirs published after the Civil War pounding on that theme.

—◦—

There was little that Buchanan could salvage after the 1858 midterm elections. The only significant Northern winner in his party was his worst political enemy, Stephen Douglas. Despite helping make a new national political celebrity, Republican Abraham Lincoln, by having debates, an unheard-of tactic, with him during the Illinois Senate election, Douglas still came out on top. Though William Seward was still the odds-on favorite to win the 1860 Republican nomination, Lincoln, even in his defeat by Douglas, surely enhanced his standing.

For Buchanan's waning time in office, he would have a tough time passing anything significant through a Congress that was primarily either Republicans or Southern Democrats, who were getting more and more antsy to either separate or try to get concessions that were probably not possible anymore. Buchanan proposed little but still held interminable cabinet meetings almost daily, with give-and-take that no longer meant much. One cabinet debate was so frustrating to his friend Howell Cobb, the secretary of the treasury, that Cobb joked that Buchanan's waffling caused him to "oppose the administration."

If Buchanan wanted to leave a most solemn legacy—that of saving the Union—he would have to find some peace with Douglas. If he could do that and get the Democratic Party a strong and unifying candidate in 1860, at least he could escape back to Wheatland with a relatively clear mind. Buchanan may not have wanted to do that on his own, but he had long kept the Pennsylvania Democrats at least somewhat congenial, so there was a shot that it could happen.

The problem became that the people whom Buchanan listened to most feared Douglas would seek retribution on them if he got elected. Cobb and the other Southerners in his cabinet and congressmen like Jefferson Davis of Mississippi and Alexander Stephens of Georgia had Buchanan's ear. Buchanan clearly thought the elections of 1858 and the unity of the North around the Republican movement was a repudiation of him in the whole section of the country. He never liked New Englanders, for instance, and, in fact, despite having been to Scotland and Paris and St. Petersburg, had never been to Hartford or the Green Mountains, though he had taken a short sojourn in New England as secretary of state with Polk.

Where he had been a Doughface in the past, now he was virtually a Southerner, living as he did in the Southern-leaning city of Washington for so long. No matter what any of them thought of him personally, Southerners had backed him politically. He would have to stand by them as well, he decided.

Whatever Buchanan did, though, always seemed to backfire, even if it should not have even touched him. Buchanan's secretary (essentially his chief of staff) while he was minister to Great Britain was Daniel Sickles, who had held various political offices in New York. A few months before he left for London, Sickles, then thirty-three, married fifteen-year-old Teresa Bagioli and got her pregnant; he then left her at home. He brought along to Great Britain, though, a notorious prostitute he had "studied with" in New York, Fanny White, and even introduced her to Queen Victoria in court.

For the next five years, both Teresa and Sickles, by 1857 a congressman from New York, apparently had had affairs, but none really came to light until she started seeing Philip Barton Key II, the son of "Star-Spangled Banner" writer and prominent Maryland lawyer Francis Scott Key, as well as nephew of Supreme Court Chief Justice Roger Taney. The younger Key himself was a widower, but said to be the handsomest man in Washington.

In early 1859 Sickles got a letter outlining the affair and confronted Teresa with it, forcing her to admit her infidelity. On February 27 Sickles saw Key sitting on a bench near his house, apparently signaling to Teresa. Sickles rushed out and followed Key to nearby Lafayette Square, just across from the White House, and shot him dead. Dramatically, Sickles surrendered to Attorney General Jeremiah Black, who lived in the neighborhood.

The trial was the O. J. Simpson case of its time. Sickles, though confined to jail, was able to see visitors in the warden's apartment—many of whom were congressmen and other fellow dignitaries.

One of those dignitaries—he apparently could not hold himself back—was James Buchanan. The trial was expedited, and by spring the future secretary of war under Abraham Lincoln, Edwin Stanton, had become Sickles's defense attorney. Stanton introduced something that had never been used at a major trial before, the insanity defense, which worked, and when he was released, Sickles was carried from the courtroom on his friends' shoulders and Teresa reconciled with him. Sickles went on to fight as a general at Gettysburg, serve as minister to Spain, and live to the age of ninety-four.

Buchanan was vilified for his visit to Sickles, undoubtedly a friend of his from serving together in London. It is uncertain whether any other sitting president went to see a friend in jail, but newspapers, especially opposition ones, asked him why he had not, say, visited imprisoned slaves, or at least those workers in debtors' prisons.

Few people, though, ever suggested Buchanan took bribes or was in other ways politically corrupt. The same could not be said about others in his administration. When the Republicans finally took power in Congress in the middle of Buchanan's term, they appointed a fellow Pennsylvanian, John Covode, known as "Honest John," to form a committee most specifically to investigate the possible bribes Buchanan may have used to get Kansas's Lecompton constitution passed.

For five months Covode and his committee called dozens of witnesses and amassed eight hundred pages of testimony, culminating in a terse thirty-page report. Buchanan himself was exonerated of direct wrongdoing. But much of the damage was done to him because people in the administration, alleged friends of Buchanan, testified about bribes to editors to write positive stories or money paid for tips on which lands to buy or any number of smaller iniquities.

There is, without much doubt, evidence that Buchanan's cabinet, even outside of the Kansas controversy, had corruption in its veins. Secretary of War John Floyd was involved in several sketchy dealings. The department often overpaid for real estate—primarily from Democratic contributors—for its forts and armories, and then gave out sweetheart contracts for the construction of the facilities. It sold Fort Snelling, a big piece of property near the Mississippi River in Minnesota, to a partnership of Virginia

Democrats for a lowball price, and often bought armaments, some of them obsolete, from fraudulent companies. Montgomery Miegs, a Washington-based army officer who complained about all this graft, was shipped off to the Dry Tortugas off Florida—not a vacation spot at the time as it might be later—to get his voice out of prosecutorial ears. Other positions ripe for graft were the large rosters of port agents and postmasters. While some of the patronage employees in those positions actually did their work, there was too little work for the number of appointees, so there were hundreds of no-work, full-pay jobs available in the administration.

The committee did not let Buchanan defend himself, or even testify, and Buchanan challenged the committee to impeach him if they really thought he did something illegal. When the investigation was done, Buchanan pronounced that he had "passed triumphantly through this ordeal," but he was clearly embarrassed, his whole administration looking weak and at least complicit, if not actually corrupt.

Buchanan had long pledged to have a scandal-free administration, saying that if anything smelled even faintly corrupt, he would deal with it immediately. In the end, however, politics took care of that. By the midpoint of his term, he realized that the best legacy he could leave was to have the Union whole when he left office. The only way that would happen now was to placate the Southerners in his administration and in his party. If he went after someone like Floyd or Secretary of the Interior Jacob Thompson, who apparently profited from the many Kansas vote briberies, he would be "insulting" Southerners, who would then have even more reason to bolt not just the party, but the Union.

So the horizon was now clear for the final act. The time had almost come for the Fat Lady's quavering warble.

⎯⸺⎯

Though history generally accepts that the Civil War started with the firing on Fort Sumter, in reality its first battle took place in October 1859, along the rushing crossroads at the confluence of the Shenandoah and Potomac Rivers at Harper's Ferry, Virginia.

Harpers Ferry today (in West Virginia, and minus the apostrophe) has the feel of an almost-Disney version of a mid-nineteenth-century village. The buildings are lovingly restored, brick, stone, and clapboard among them. The two rivers are picturesque, rushing over rocks and eventually on toward Washington, a few dozen miles to the east. The Appalachian Trail now comes through Harpers Ferry, and hikers and bikers appear on the bends of the rivers throughout the year.

In the mid-nineteenth century, though, the town was a bustle of factories, its products wending down the rivers and out to sea. It was a natural place for the nation to have an armory in the 1850s, since it was still a break-off point for those traveling westward, and close enough to the capital to monitor.

That John Brown chose the munitions storage there to stoke his nascent slave rebellion movement was not crazy at all. There was at least a vague chance he could inspire a slave revolt if he could capture the unprotected munitions and make it out of Harper's Ferry.

It was no secret that Brown was fomenting an attack somewhere. He had met—in public, not behind closed doors—the most highly regarded people of the abolitionist movement, from Harriet Tubman to William Lloyd Garrison to Frederick Douglass, and Tubman, at least, helped him in his quest to find slaves who might like to join his rebellion. Brown had donations of armaments and money from all over the North and, though still hunted by the pro-slavery people he encountered in Kansas, he would have been easy to find.

Yet Buchanan let him ride. The president mostly deemed the American army to have the duty of protecting settlers in the West, not looking after other domestic threats. Historical estimates put the size of the army in the decade before the Civil War at about sixteen thousand men, so Buchanan may not have had much choice but to play it safe. It may have been too much to ask for Buchanan to have extra troops at Harper's Ferry, but completely ignoring such a noted figure as Brown was folly.

Even after Brown struck Harper's Ferry, it took the better part of two days for Buchanan to get a company of marines to Brown's make-shift "fort," which was pretty much an arsenal building in which he was trapped and surrounded by local farmers and workers. Even at that, Buchanan was lucky that then Colonel Robert E. Lee happened to be home in Washington on leave from his normal duty in Texas. Living as he did during his civilian years just across the river from the White House, in Arlington—where Arlington National Cemetery was later built during the Civil War, when the federal government seized his land—Lee took up his jury-rigged command and headed west along the Potomac, assisted by future Confederate cavalry hero J. E. B. Stuart, a young lieutenant at the time. Stuart tried to get Brown to surrender, but it was too late in his martyrdom for Brown to relent, and Lee's men finally killed or captured Brown's two dozen "troops."

Buchanan then receded from the fray and let Virginia politicians take over. Had he ordered Brown transferred to Washington or some other more neutral prison, and supervised an orderly trial, the incident might have been muted. The president, though, ceded the supervision to pro-slavery men, who may have followed the general rules of free trials, but in fact allowed Brown's case to become a polarizing event. Brown was quickly convicted—even though it was admitted that he never killed anyone, nor freed any slaves, the crimes of which he was accused. He was certainly not allowed the insanity defense Buchanan's friend Sickles had in his obvious murder of Philip Key.

By the time Brown was hanged in nearby Charles Town on December 2, 1859, he was a cause célèbre like no other man had been in the nation's history. Ralph Waldo Emerson and Victor Hugo and Henry David Thoreau and Walt Whitman, the literary sages of the age, all wrote about Brown, if not in glowing tones, at least in sympathy, and predicted war because of his raid and its repercussions. More than two thousand soldiers came to protect the town from a riot during the execution. Among those present were Whitman, Confederate-general-to-be

Stonewall Jackson, and Lincoln's eventual assassin, John Wilkes Booth, who apparently came to the execution disguised as a local militiaman.

Buchanan's nightmare loomed. The slave controversy, the one he had hoped would die, became virulent. Many Northerners who had tolerated slavery now saw it as a moral impairment for America, the country they had hoped would show the world the way to live.

Yet Buchanan forged on as if John Brown's body, as the song went, were not "a-mouldering in the grave." Saving the Union, it seemed, would not rank above settling last scores.

—◦—

Buchanan was still the titular leader of the Democratic Party, and as such was the last word on where the 1860 nominating convention would be held. As Elbert B. Smith, a University of Maryland historian, wrote in his 1975 assessment *The Presidency of James Buchanan*:

> *The presidential convention system has usually served America at least tolerably well, but at Charleston, South Carolina, in 1860, all of its potential frailties were united in one hideous example. Indeed, the very selection by the Democrats of Charleston as a reward to the South for good behavior in 1856 ranks with the same party's designation of Chicago in 1968 as the two most inane such decisions in American political history. A possible Southern secession from the party was universally recognized as the greatest single threat, but the convention was nonetheless held in the one city most likely to produce this result.*

Smith went on to describe Charleston that late April. Slaves were illegally imported to serve the crush of delegates—2,500 in all—and hangers-on. Northerners were not going to indulge in slave-labor service, but instead brought their own caches of liquor and prostitutes on their trains. Illegal gambling went on day and night, with bands and exotic dancers more prevalent than sane political discussion. Food came with extortionist price tags and pickpockets roamed unscathed.

If there were going to be a last bacchanalian hurrah for a unified United States, the spring convention in Charleston was not going to waste its chance.

Buchanan sat silent in Washington as the convention committed party suicide. Instead of trying to get its nominee first and finding a platform he could run on, it instead came up with a Buchanan-advised platform that could not possibly be accommodating to his enemy, and the presumed candidate, Stephen Douglas. There were a bunch of minor planks on the platform, but essentially, the party would be committed to allowing slavery in the territories and to supporting expansion of the country to Cuba and Central America, presumably also slave areas.

Buchanan would not budge to try to convince his Southern friends otherwise. One theory was that they made the platform so onerous to Northern Democrats that they would either seek a Southern replacement for Douglas or not mind the Southerners bolting and promoting a rival candidacy. Unionists among the Southerners then presumed the election would be thrown into the House, which would not find a majority candidate. The Senate would then elect a Southern vice president, who would take over as president.

This turned out to be too subtle and convoluted for the now energized forces of both Democratic factions. In time there were essentially three Democratic candidates: Douglas, nominated in Baltimore in June after the original Charleston convention recessed without a nomination; vice president John Breckenridge, the Southern choice, from a rump convention held in Baltimore the day following the regular one, after Southerners bolted; and longtime peace seeker John Bell of Tennessee, a last-ditch pitch by moderate dreamers who formed the Constitutional Union Party and nominated Edward Everett of Massachusetts for vice president.

The several months of the 1860 campaign were, then, a blur of inflamed speeches and misery for those of practical thought who hoped for the country to stay unified. With the Democrats so horribly split, no matter how much they mocked and vilified the new Republican hero, Abraham Lincoln, it would not change how the electoral college would eventually vote. Lincoln was never the favorite, but his handlers outmaneuvered every other hopeful in the party's jubilant Chicago convention—the primary one being William Seward, who had so patiently waited out his time in the original Republican election in 1856. Seward, ever practical, immediately supported Lincoln—for which Lincoln would return the favor, not just making Seward his secretary of state, but even allowing Seward to contradict him in cabinet meetings and help solve major crises during the Civil War.

Buchanan was left with dashed hopes and broken dreams. He basically stayed neutral during the election, hoping that any of the other three besides Lincoln would pull out a victory, perhaps in a divided vote that would go to the House of Representatives.

Instead, it was even more of a runaway than Buchanan could have imagined. Lincoln took eighteen states—every one of the electoral votes of the nonslave states, save three of the seven from New Jersey, for a total of 303. Bell took three border states—Kentucky, Tennessee, and Virginia. Breckenridge took the rest of the South, comprising eleven states and seventy-two electoral votes. Stephen Douglas, who had lived his whole political life pointing toward this election, took only the split vote from New Jersey and the state of Missouri, a paltry twelve electoral votes.

It was still the days of a long interim between the election and the next inauguration, so Buchanan would have to make many decisions in the four months between November 6, 1860, and March 4, 1861.

They would be, in fact, the worst of times for the worst president.

—◦—

Howell Cobb resigned from his cabinet post of secretary of the treasury on December 8, two days after a group of South Carolinians had come to the White House to tell President Buchanan that their state was moving quickly toward secession. Cobb was his most trusted advisor, but he had apparently made a deal with Attorney General Jeremiah Black that if Buchanan opposed secession, which he told the South Carolinians he would, then Cobb would resign. "The President and myself parted in the most friendly spirit," Cobb wrote his wife. "We both see & feel the necessity & both regret that it should be so."

The shuffles then started, but to seemingly no great end. Buchanan appointed the commissioner of patents, Philip F. Thomas of Maryland, to Cobb's post at the treasury. The next day, Lewis Cass, the secretary of state, resigned because Buchanan would not authorize troops to go to defend the Union forts in Charleston, particularly Fort Sumter. Buchanan was only slightly upset with this departure, since he felt Cass was incompetent. The president was virtually running the State Department himself anyway—even as incompetent as his own moves in places like Paraguay and Juan de Fuca had been. That pushed Black up to state and Edwin Stanton, more or less a Republican, who was off in California on government business, up from Jeremiah Black's assistant to attorney general. That same day, Senator John Slidell of Louisiana, another member of Buchanan's brain trust, came to the White House, and when he left, it was the last time the two ever talked.

Those three days in December depressed Buchanan—and could not have done less for those who believed the Union might somehow stand. If Cobb was gone, so was Georgia. If Slidell would no longer talk to Buchanan, then there went Louisiana. Buchanan made another slip when he allowed Secretary of the Interior Jacob Thompson of Mississippi to go to North Carolina to discuss secession with representatives there. Thompson had offered to resign before doing so, but Buchanan, apparently in hopes that he could stave off the secession of those two states, let him go.

The nation now believed Buchanan himself was an agent of secession. The most famous newspaper editor in the North, Horace Greeley, of the *New York Tribune*, ran an editorial on December 17 that said the president was, among other things, insane—perhaps not literally, but certainly figuratively in the face of crisis.

By December 20 the governor of South Carolina had sent a letter demanding that Buchanan turn over Fort Sumter immediately. Buchanan drafted a reply, reading in part, "If South Carolina should attack any of these forts, she will then become the assailant in a war against the United States . . . This would not only be a just cause of war, but the actual commencement of hostilities." The governor, knowing of Buchanan's potential reply, withdrew his letter.

It was the closest Buchanan got to being properly assertive in his lame-duck period—or maybe even before. It was his last shot at keeping the Union, and maybe if he had published the reply he never sent, it might have worked. Events were moving quickly, and someone needed to put a big boulder in their path. Buchanan could not bring himself to do so.

Cass, when he resigned, told everyone that Buchanan trembled with panic on a regular basis and spent most of his time either praying or crying. On December 20 Buchanan went to a wedding reception, apparently looking hale, but midway through the reception, there was a big commotion. Buchanan turned to a female guest and asked, "Madam, do you suppose the house is on fire?"

The woman went into a hallway and encountered US Representative Lawrence Keitt of South Carolina, who was among the staunchest of the "fire eaters," the Southerners most prone to secessionist tendencies. Keitt was already legend in Washington, though not for any legislation he fostered. Before Preston Brooks pounded Charles Sumner into submission on the Senate floor, Keitt had followed Brooks from the House over to the Senate with a loaded gun. When Sumner was on the floor nearly bleeding to death and Brooks was escaping, Keitt stood over Sumner, waving his pistol and shouting, "Let them be!" and would not allow anyone to come to Sumner's aid until Brooks was long gone. A few years later, he started a brawl in the House, calling Pennsylvania congressman Galusha Grow "a black Republican puppy" for stepping over the line that separated Democrats and Republicans on the floor. The brawl, in which about fifty congressmen participated, ended, by the way, when an errant punch knocked off the hairpiece of Mississippi Democrat William Barksdale, causing even those fire-eater compatriots of Barksdale to stop fighting and start laughing.

On this night, however, Keitt was not into fisticuffs. Buchanan and the woman saw him in the hallway, leaping up and down, shaking a paper above his head and screaming over and over, "Thank God! Thank God! Oh, thank God!" It was a telegram informing him that South Carolina had seceded. Buchanan immediately called his carriage, and when he got back to the White House, he, too, had a cable from the new South Carolina governor, Francis W. Pickens, informing him of the news.

The proclamation did not make any excuses or allege much, save that the decision was made because the state feared it would lose legal slavery. The Declaration of Causes of Secession started out with a dozen or so paragraphs comparing the state's motives to those of the colonies against the king as outlined in the Declaration of Independence, but then got to the meat:

> *An increasing hostility on the part of the non-slaveholding States to the Institution of Slavery has led to a disregard of their obligations, and the laws of the general government have ceased to effect the objects of the Constitution. The States of Maine, New Hampshire, Vermont, Massachusetts, Connecticut, Rhode Island, New York, Pennsylvania, Illinois, Indiana, Michigan, Wisconsin and Iowa, have enacted laws which either nullify the Acts of Congress or render useless any attempt to execute them. In many of these states the fugitive is discharged from service or labor claimed, and in none of them has the state government complied with the stipulation made in the Constitution. . . . Thus the constitutional compact has been deliberately broken and disregarded by the non-slaveholding States, and the consequence follows that South Carolina is released from her obligation.*
>
> *The right of property in slaves was recognized by giving to free persons distinct political rights, by giving them the right to represent, and burthening them with direct taxes for three-fifths of their slaves; by authorizing the importation of slaves for twenty years; and by stipulating for the rendition of fugitives from labor . . . They have encouraged and assisted thousands of our slaves to leave their homes;*

and those who remain, have been incited by emissaries, books and pictures to servile insurrection.

A geographical line has been drawn across the Union, and all the States north of that line have united in the election of a man to the high office of President of the United States whose opinions and purposes are hostile to slavery. He is to be entrusted with the administration of the Common Government, because he has declared that that "Government cannot endure permanently half slave, half free" and that the public mind must rest in the belief that Slavery is in the course of ultimate extinction.

It was no different in the other states when they drafted their reasons—make that *reason*, singular—for dropping out of the Union. In Mississippi's declaration there were six clauses alone that castigated the North for enticing slaves to escape and be free, even though practically no slaves from Mississippi, having to go through several other slave states to get there, actually made it to the North.

Alabama's declaration was already blaming Lincoln, even though he was not yet president, for getting rid of slavery:

Whereas, the election of Abraham Lincoln and Hannibal Hamlin to the offices of president and vice-president of the United States of America, by a sectional party, avowedly hostile to the domestic institutions and to the peace and security of the people of the State of Alabama, preceded by many and dangerous infractions of the constitution of the United States by many of the States and people of the Northern section, is a political wrong of so insulting and menacing a character as to justify the people of the State of Alabama in the adoption of prompt and decided measures for their future peace and security.

Several old heads tried to come up with solutions. Ex-president John Tyler, before he went to take his seat in the Confederate legislature, eagerly met with Buchanan—Tyler's first time back in the White House since his term was up nearly two decades before. The lame-duck president allowed him to bring together whomever he wanted, but Buchanan could not necessarily endorse anything Tyler came up with. John Crittenden of Kentucky chaired a congressional panel called the Compromise Committee of Thirteen, but it only came up with a solution that bent everything southward—allowing slavery and bolstering the Fugitive Slave Law, which no Northerner could possibly tolerate.

Buchanan went back and forth about whether to fortify Fort Sumter, trying to bluff South Carolina into maybe firing a first shot. Then he could possibly win a quick battle and put the Humpty Dumpty nation back together.

Otherwise, he kept pronouncing a dictum as confusing as it was ineffective. As a strict constitutional constructionist, Buchanan would say that no state could secede, since by signing the original pact, states gave up that right. On the other hand, he said, he as president had no power to bring them back into the Union, nor could he, without congressional approval, launch a military strike to subdue the seceding states. Congress, becoming more Republican as the Democrats from the South left their seats, might have been willing to do that, but Buchanan did not encourage it. Militias were forming quickly in the South and there was not yet conscription in the North, so each passing day made it more difficult to have a quick-ending battle in Charleston, or maybe anywhere else.

Having exhausted any chance at reconciliation before the March 4 deadline—when Lincoln would finally take over—Buchanan finally did grow despondent. He spent the bulk of his time in his last weeks writing letters and drinking his Madeira. He would often ask a congressman or two or a cabinet member to bunk in at the White House, not really for safety, but in hopes that something, anything would come about that would change the course of his term.

Buchanan had had few successes in his four years. There were mercantile forays to Japan and China, opening up those markets a bit, for instance. The northern border of the United States, the Pig War notwithstanding, was stable. There were a few technological advances—the first oil well was drilled, Elisha Otis developed a safe elevator, the transatlantic cable was laid, the Pony Express got its start—but even these were somewhat thwarted because of the depression that followed the Panic of 1857, the abrupt end to a dozen years of plenty, caused by Buchanan's fostering of the *Dred Scott* decision.

The night before Lincoln's inauguration, Buchanan held one last cabinet meeting. The next morning, as Buchanan was preparing for the inauguration, Major Robert Anderson sent an urgent message. After weeks of assuring everyone he was safe as commander of Fort Sumter, he now said it would take twenty thousand troops there to secure the fort in case of attack, another miscalculation on Buchanan's part that would blow up a month later when the fort was, indeed, attacked. There was nothing he could do now.

Buchanan ordered his carriage and went off to pick up Lincoln at his hotel. On the ride he was said to have a cheery expression as he told Lincoln, "My dear sir, if you are as happy in entering the White House as I shall feel on returning to Wheatland, you are a happy man indeed."

Lincoln is said to have replied, "Mr. President, I cannot say that I shall enter it with much pleasure, but I assure you that I shall do what I can to maintain the high standards set by my illustrious predecessors who have occupied it."

Along the way, for what was said to be the first time, sharpshooters spied from rooftops and platoons of soldiers lined the route to the Capitol. As they neared the inaugural stand, the man who would often be called the Greatest. President. Ever., and the one who was surely the Worst, saw swinging from the dome an empty crane, and lying in anguished repose on the ground nearby was *Freedom*, the large bronze statue it was to have carried.

When James Buchanan started his presidency, there was no country more fascinating to other nations than the United States. Alexis de Tocqueville's cross between a travelogue and a political treatise, *Democracy in*

America, intrigued Europeans, who had previously thought of the United States as an obscure piece of land too far away to think about.

It took until the late 1840s for the adventure bug to bring Europeans as tourists to the growing country across the Atlantic, and everyone seemed to have an opinion—some haughty and critical, others wide-eyed and praising—on what America was and Americans were.

Despite, or maybe because of, its other cranky issues, the United States had an almost uninterrupted economic boom for the decade or more before Buchanan took office in March of 1857. New cities grew up where only crossroads had been before, not just in the growing West, but even in the East—"One flourishing town after another," wrote the scientist and traveler Charles Lyell of his trek through upstate New York. "Utica, Syracuse, Auburn." There were no beggars or people shoeless unless they wanted to be. "Everywhere the most unequivocal proofs of prosperity and rapid progress in agriculture, commerce, and great public works."

It was only eighty years since the Declaration of Independence was signed and a dozen years fewer since George Washington first occupied this strange office of "president," unknown before in the civilized world. Not anyone could be king in other nations, but, it appeared, anyone could be the guy who ran the United States, as fourteen before Buchanan had been.

Because of that, it seemed to Europeans visiting, there had developed some human traits that were undeniably American. And Americanism, if there could be such a thing, had been born. "Whether foreign visitors landed at New York, Philadelphia, or Boston, they were struck by the bustle, enterprise, and rough-and-ready cheerfulness of the people. Men talked of money, and had it," wrote Allan Nevins in his seminal study of the period, *Ordeal of the Union*.

Almost everything seemed permissible, almost anything possible. It was frequently noted that the analyst shocked by some gross defect could find a compensating grace registered with equal energy. America offered an

appalling total of violence, yet it had the most vigorous pacifist move-
ment in the world. It was cursed by gross intemperance in the large
cities and along its borders, yet great areas proscribed liquor with inex-
orable severity. It seemed in some places the most licentious of lands,
in others the most puritanically strait-laced. Americans were frank to
confess themselves materialistic and addicted to money-hoarding, yet
they were equally the most idealistic and philanthropic of peoples. The
nation at times witnessed deplorable exhibitions of religious bigotry,
but it prided itself, with justice, upon the general tolerance of its laws
and traditions. The whole gamut of human failings and attainments
seemed expressed with more emphasis and color than in older nations.

Americans loved themselves, loved the way they were, and looked to continue to be that way. Walt Whitman's words in "Song of Myself" were the
song of every true American: "Do I contradict myself? / Very well then I
contradict myself / (I am large. I contain multitudes.)" There was nothing
that stopped an American. If he did not make it in one neighborhood,
he would find another. The Mormons, for instance, plagued Buchanan
during his term, having found paradise and alleged freedom in Utah, not
without violence and bloodshed, but they had not started that far west.
Founder Joseph Smith had his first vision near his home in Palmyra, in
western New York, but as animosity gathered, or wanderlust ensued, his
followers moved to Harmony, Pennsylvania; then Kirtland, Ohio; then
Jackson, Missouri; then Nauvoo, Illinois; then across the plains toward
Utah—all within a generation.

The vastness of the country and its youth, both as a nation and in
its people, encouraged innovation and self-reliance. In Great Britain
and Spain and France, the point seemed to be to preserve what was
there. In America change itself was a value. Things were supposed to be
bigger, better, different, wondrous—and standing still was really flow-
ing swiftly backward. Nevins noted that even in language, Americans
were decidedly new and non-European. Everything was "powerful" or
"magnificent" or "mighty" and everything, good or bad, from a factory to

slavery, became an "institution." American humor bespoke exaggeration or aggrandizement—fish would be gargantuan; lakes, ocean-like; noses, like elephant trunks; drippy pumps, virtual Niagaras. There was nothing so big an American could not visualize.

This collective aggrandizement also made an American fearless, and that influenced the violence that was unavoidable in the American mid-nineteenth-century character. Dickens's boys in *Oliver Twist* would "pick a pocket or two," as the song went, for Fagan in London, but in America they would be prone to fighting, even killing, for what they wanted and thought they deserved. Chicago, Philadelphia, Washington, and New Orleans had major riots during the 1850s. Duels and honor killings proliferated, even among the country's leaders. Aaron Burr's shooting of Alexander Hamilton gave rise to Andrew Jackson's duel killing of Charles Dickinson. Senator William L. Yancey of Alabama killed his uncle and never served a day for it. Senator John T. Wigfall of Texas went to a friend's wedding, walked down the street afterward, and had an argument with the groom and killed him.

This strain of violence seemed distinctly American to Europeans. First of all, there was that ever-expanding frontier. There was always someplace to escape to, and from. After a while violence became its own entertainment. Davy Crockett's sometimes fictional endeavors—"Killed him a b'ar / When he was only three," as the song from the Disney show about the frontiersman went—were the first best sellers from the West, full of killing and shooting and dueling and, eventually, Crockett's own death at the Alamo. Prize fighting thrived and duels were spectator sports. The myriad immigrant and even Native American tribes contributed conflicts over territory and riches constantly.

No one particularly argued over the meaning of the Second Amendment in the 1850s, as they do today, but it is true that almost every family had a deadly weapon of some sort. There was even one-upmanship in styles—Jim Bowie's knives were the fashion for a time, then Colt's 45s, then sword canes, and even cutlasses. The vastness of the country led to the surety that law enforcement was, if not impossible, then much more difficult than in relatively crowded Europe. In the big cities, police forces finally became more organized, but not until the latter part of the 1850s. The Civil War itself got organized so quickly because so many individuals in the South had their own rifles and were ready to do battle without having to start manufacturing to arm up.

At the same time, Europeans marveled at the idealism almost inherent in the American psyche. That strain came with the first colonists: James Oglethorpe in Georgia, William Penn in Pennsylvania, Roger Williams in Rhode Island, William Bradford in Massachusetts, the planters and religious folks all up and down the coast—each had their own ideas of success. As was said of the Quakers, they came to America to do good—and they did well. Jews, who had been oppressed everywhere, felt ambitious by the mid-nineteenth century in the United States. Each Protestant sect started its own schools, figuring that education was the way to perfection for their children. The present was important, surely, but the future was where the American people would become dominant.

Americans were relentlessly optimistic, even in their materialism and their individualism. Yet despite that individualism, Americans were unusual—especially in relation to Europeans—in their belief in democracy. John Jacob Astor could come from nothing to amassing $25 million and Stephen Girard immigrated with empty pockets to become the richest man in the hemisphere. There were no kings or serfs, just possible success stories.

The one peculiarity in all of this, though, was the tolerance of slavery, both in the North and South. With all the screeds about equality, liberty, and democracy, fully one-sixth of the nation's residents were enslaved. The other governmental peculiarity, the forming of "states" from "territories," with states having more rights—something that really did not exist in Europe—happened in lockstep with the recognition of slavery. Since the Missouri Compromise in 1820 let in Missouri as a slave state while Maine came in nonslave, the states were created in pairs—one free and one slave—for the next several decades. Michigan was paired with Arkansas in 1836–37. Florida and Texas were paired with Iowa and Wisconsin in the mid-1840s, making it fifteen of each. California, though, broke the tie in 1850, which brought on the pressure to finally decide how to deal with slavery from then on. While it had not been a back-burner issue, there had been a general agreement that it was part of the American fabric, that Americans accepted slavery, even in the face of the rest of the civilized world getting rid of it.

So the other thing that Americans brought with them, the burden on the opposite side of liberty, was the superiority of white over black. Few white men thought black men their equals, whether they believed in slavery or not. Liberty and democracy had their limits in the United States, and to be an American was to accept that. Women, too, were second-class citizens, but that was the case elsewhere as well.

As the decade went onward, it became apparent that there would have to be some grand reconciliation of this part of Americanism. Whether Abraham Lincoln's "house divided" speech was a mere political ploy or a heartfelt philosophical musing, it caught the public's ear and clarified what all Americans knew. Delivered at the Illinois State House upon his acceptance of the Republican Party's nomination for the 1858 US Senate race against incumbent Democrat Stephen Douglas, Lincoln meant the speech to differentiate himself from Douglas, and it surely did:

A house divided against itself cannot stand. I believe this government cannot endure, permanently, half slave and half free. I do not expect the Union to be dissolved—I do not expect the house to fall—but I do expect it will cease to be divided. It will become all one thing or all the other. Either the opponents of slavery will arrest the further spread of it, and place it where the public mind shall rest in the belief that it is in the course of ultimate extinction; or its advocates will push it forward, till it shall become lawful in all the States, old as well as new—North as well as South.

James Buchanan was only one year into his term as president when Lincoln spoke those words, but both men had to be listening to the nation's heartbeat. Lincoln eventually lost the Senate race to Douglas, but he saw what Americans might become, and how the world's perception of them might change. The excitement with which de Tocqueville and his contemporaries described the denizens of the new nation would soon simmer, and Buchanan would be instrumental in fostering that disappointing change.

CHAPTER NINE

The Legacy of the Least
of the Lesser Presidents

IT WAS A SNOWY MIDWINTER SATURDAY MORNING WHEN I PARKED THE car along Sixteenth Street in Washington, DC, the White House in the haze in the distance a little less than a mile away. Meridian Hill Park, which more than a hundred years before was a mansion estate plot, was on the east side of the street for a few blocks.

The only other people roaming through the park were a young couple and their female friend. Every so often, they would stop at a scenic spot and the friend would take a photo of the couple kissing, most likely for a preview wedding album.

I was there for a different reason, but they seemed to know where they were going. I asked them if they knew where the Buchanan statute was. They just shrugged. "Buchanan the president?" the young man asked. "Seems unlikely here, don't you think?"

Yet down from a rise at the southeast corner of the park, there it was. A long curve of granite at the midpoint of which is an eight-foot-high bronze of Buchanan sitting in repose on a pedestal. At one end of the curve is a stone statue of a mythical male Justice; on the other, a female Diplomacy, both stripped to the waist. On a side panel is a quote from his old friend Jeremiah Black, calling him "The incorruptible statesman whose walk was upon the mountain ranges of the law."

When I got to the monument, the snow seemed to be weighing on Buchanan's shoulders a bit, as if he knew I was there, like Brutus for Caesar, come to bury, not to praise him.

Buchanan's beloved niece, Harriet Lane Johnston, left a bequest in her will to erect two monuments to her uncle, one at Stony Batter, the site of his birth, and the other in Washington. She died in 1903 and gave the money to the Commonwealth of Pennsylvania for the one at Stony Batter, and to Congress for that one in Washington. The will gave each fifteen years to commission those monuments. Famed Washington banker Lawrason Riggs, a friend, bought the property in Stony Batter and took charge of that monument—a thirty-one-foot-high pyramid made from fifty tons of native stones and mortar. Riggs arranged for thirty-five workmen to make the pyramid and built a small railroad to get the stone from a nearby mountain to the site. The Pennsylvania General Assembly used Johnston's bequest to oversee the whole thing, and the eighteen-and-a-half-acre Buchanan Birthplace State Park opened in 1911.

It was not so easy in Washington, as nothing seems to be. There were outdoor commemorations of presidents when Johnston's bequest became known. The first had been a statue of Andrew Jackson on horseback in Lafayette Square, across from the White House, started in 1847, and the next year, the Washington Memorial's cornerstone was laid, but that obelisk was not completed until 1885, its construction suspended for more than two decades for lack of funds. The City of Washington erected a statue of Abraham Lincoln at City Hall in 1867, two years after his assassination. In 1902 the Army of the Tennessee finally raised enough money to start a statue of Ulysses S. Grant on horseback by the Capitol, but it ended up taking sculptor Henry Merwin Shrady nearly twenty years to complete.

These four were either great military heroes or an assassinated martyr, almost secondarily presidents, and even then people were less than enthusiastic to finance such projects. Though Johnston's bequest would cover at least the cost of the Buchanan monument itself, there was no rush by congressmen to commemorate an obscure and, frankly, thirty-five years after his death, a clearly unloved and unremembered president.

As the fund languished and time ticked away, several bills were introduced in Congress to erect a better memorial to Lincoln, three of them failing until President William Howard Taft shepherded a $300,000 grant through in 1910.

By that time the Johnston grant had been forgotten. With the fifteen-year deadline to use the money approaching, someone discovered the grant proposal, and a few weeks before it would expire, in the spring of 1918, the commission was approved. Even then, it took until 1930 to get a site, an architect, and a sculptor to finish the job, still beating out the next honored monumental president, Thomas Jefferson, who got his rotunda thirteen years later.

While he had a substantial advocate in his niece, who was certainly more popular than her Uncle Nunc both during his career and after his death, Buchanan, even in the rest of his life after the presidency, was never again popular.

"Frankly, he was just vilified," said Patrick Clarke, the director of Wheatland, Buchanan's Lancaster estate. "It was not just historians who are not kind to Buchanan. The hatred was really intense when he first came home to Lancaster. It is particularly intense in 1863, when the battle of Gettysburg occurs just a few miles from here."

Clarke related the story of John F. Reynolds, the son of Buchanan's great friend, also named John Reynolds, from his early days in Lancaster. In 1837, when he was in the United States Senate, Buchanan recommended the son to West Point, where he started a brilliant and meteoric military career. When the Civil War started, he became a brigadier general and was assigned to the main battle group, the Army of the Potomac. Reynolds was captured once by the Confederate army, but through a Confederate military friend with whom he had served before the war, he was exchanged for another prisoner. Soon after a disastrous battle at Fredericksburg, Virginia, in the spring of 1863, Lincoln was looking to replace Joseph Hooker as his military leader and interviewed Reynolds, who refused the job when Lincoln said he could not shield him from politicians who might object. George Meade, another Pennsylvanian, took over instead.

On the first day of the battle of Gettysburg, though, Reynolds, while leading his troops, was shot in the back of the neck and killed. There are now three memorials to Reynolds at the Gettysburg battlefield and another of him on horseback on the apron of Philadelphia's City Hall, but there was a less fortunate fallout at Wheatland.

"The entire family blamed Buchanan for his death," said Wheatland's Clarke. Ellie Reynolds had been as close to Buchanan's niece Harriet Lane as a sister, and the younger John was at least as beloved to Buchanan as his own nephews.

"The father, John Reynolds, was dead, but the family always blamed Buchanan for the Civil War itself. Now their most favored son was gone. The father was so close to Buchanan that he was the first line signer on his petition to become a Mason, which is a really big deal. After that all of the siblings of General Reynolds turned their backs on Buchanan."

The prologue of Philip Klein's sympathetic biography is a scene of Buchanan pondering his fate at his home at Wheatland a few days before Gettysburg. Probably fictionalized, it told the tense story of how people then thought of Buchanan.

Occasionally small squads of horsemen came galloping out from town and headed for the Susquehanna River ten miles to the west. Most of the riders seemed intent on their own business; but where the pike ran past the spacious grounds of Wheatland, home of former President Buchanan, some would shout, "You damned rebel!" or "I hope they burn you out like they did Thad Stevens."

Buchanan had walked down from his house to the spring on the lower lawn which bordered the pike, his favorite spot in the evening. He liked to look over the low stone parapet into the clear water and watch the moss and white sand swirling gently in the undercurrent. Nowhere else in the world had he ever found the sunsets more relaxing

or the world more serene than here, under the willow by his Wheat-
land spring. But not so this night. Would Wheatland be standing
tomorrow, or in ashes? Would he be alive, or dead, or some kind of
ridiculous trophy of this senseless, unthinkable war? He did not know,
nor did he really care very much. . . .

After entering the house, Buchanan went directly to the study and
began to write. If the rebels came, they would find him at work—
preparing his story of Mr. Buchanan's Administration on the Eve
of Rebellion.

—◦—

Buchanan would not die or be captured; he would live on beyond the
end of the war. He worked on those memoirs of his presidency but did
not publish them until after the Civil War ended, even though most of
the book was done by 1862. He said he felt honor bound not to have
his successor, Lincoln, burdened by his thoughts while prosecuting a
war. Buchanan, while he hated that there was a war, supported Lincoln
through it, hoping each day it would end and find the Union resurrected.

He wrote the book, as the title implies, in the third person. It is dull
but full of detail. Buchanan used mostly official sources and what he had
accrued and saved from friends' and officials' correspondence to him. He
hectored some of those people to send him copies of whatever they had,
and many of them did not want to be bothered—there was a war going
on, after all.

Over the last few decades, there has been an expectation that former
politicos of all kinds, but certainly ex-presidents, will publish memoirs,
but prior to Buchanan, only Thomas Jefferson had any real success at
autobiography, publishing one at age seventy-seven in 1821. Most presidents, in fact, did not live long enough after their public service to get
around to doing so.

Buchanan's book is notable, really, for just one thing: that he blamed
Northern anti-slavery agitation for the Civil War and the heightening of
the conflict during his administration. It was not an untrammeled path,

since there was a cadre of both moderate and fire-eating Democrats who felt that way. The North had accepted at least Southern slavery for so long that it had become expected in many corners that it would always be that way. When it became clear, though, that eventually, with all the westward expansion, the South would turn from an equal section to a minority one, abolitionists, who had just been a nuisance, started really bothering Southerners. The schism became greater, and eventually irreconcilable, and according to Buchanan's view, it was primarily the fault of the agitators from the North.

Modern histories about the Civil War make this interpretation seem inane. Slavery was in the South, and the South wanted to keep it at least that way. The obsession of the slaveholders, combined with the pride the bulk of the South felt in its traditions, divided the Union. As much as most anti-slavery voices in the North wanted the institution ended, they did not want to jettison the South, just reform it. It was like, perhaps, the spouse who wants to change the other's habits, not divorce. The idea of secession was completely Southern. The idea of hanging on to an immoral and, eventually, unsustainable institution was Southern. And even if the progressively louder anti-slavery voice annoyed them, it was Southerners who were looking to leave and fight over it if necessary.

Buchanan had originally sought to have someone else write the book, and first asked his former attorney general and secretary of state, Jeremiah Black, to do it, offering him a good sum, $7,000. Black, however, soon found that he disagreed with Buchanan's assessment of so many points, particularly that Buchanan wanted to say that he was fully behind Lincoln once the war started. "I am willing to vindicate the last administration," wrote Black to his former boss, "but I can't do it on the ground which you now occupy." So Buchanan decided to go it on his own.

To the extent that Buchanan's memoirs were taken seriously and became part of the political air after the war, he was the voice of the Northerners-started-it strain of Civil War analysis. His reputation, what there was left of it, was even more destroyed during the war, since even

those who blamed Lincoln primarily for it never absolved Buchanan—
and at least Lincoln regained the Union in the end.

Buchanan still wanted someone to write his authorized biography
after the war and employed two different Philadelphians, James Shunk
and William Reed, to do it at different times. Shunk and his wife lived at
Wheatland for much of a year, taking notes from interviews with the former president, but never wrote their book. Reed, a Philadelphia publisher,
then took over, but procrastinated and never sought the Shunks' notes.

Long after Buchanan's death, the Johnstons—his niece, Harriet, and
her husband—started shopping around for writers. Eventually, they settled
on George Ticknor Curtis, a lawyer who had written a couple of historical
books. Ironically, he had been Dred Scott's defense lawyer in the Supreme
Court case, but letters back and forth in the collection of the Library of
Congress about the book negotiations never mention this. The two-volume
Life of James Buchanan, published in 1883, fifteen years after the subject's
death, is a bit of a mess, loaded down with irrelevant or obscure letters.
Presumably Curtis felt he had to include everything that the Johnstons had
given him, since they were his patrons. It seems clear that a lawyer wrote
it, not a stylist or even a creative author. It would take until 1962 for the
next biography, that by Philip Klein, to appear. Klein's writing is fluid, but
he does not present an engaging story. He was a historian and, like Curtis,
seems to want to include every last item to show his meticulousness. It is
an apologia, and making through its more than five hundred pages, a reader
who did not otherwise know American history would think that Buchanan
was high on the presidential slopes of Washington and Jefferson, not in the
valley with Pierce and Harding.

The biography Jean H. Baker wrote in 2004 for the American Presidents series is short and, if not David McCulloughesque, certainly read-
able. It stands to reason, though, that it would never have been assigned
unless it had to be; Buchanan was, after all, one of the presidents and had
to be included in the series.

In 2014 the Corcoran Gallery in Washington closed, and in 2015 its
17,000 holdings got new homes. More than 6,500 of them went, as would

be appropriate, to the National Gallery of Art, its sister Washington, DC, museum. One of the pieces the National Gallery rejected, though, was a portrait of Buchanan by George Peter Alexander Healy. It could have been an oversight, but it really was an insult. The death bequest of his niece, Harriet Lane Johnston, established the whole idea of the vague collection in the Smithsonian becoming, as Johnston had in her will, a "National Gallery of Art." Included in Johnston's bequest was her personal art collection, which included as a favorite piece the Healy portrait.

It is safe to say, then, that, save for the diligence of his niece, and her long life and social prominence in Washington, combined with Philip Klein's obsession with a relatively famous man in his hometown, there would be little legacy at all for Buchanan. In 1938 the postal service issued a presidential series of stamps, with a bust of Buchanan facing right on a dull gray background. It was, appropriately, a fifteen-cent stamp for the fifteenth president, but no doubt barely used since no postal fee amounted to fifteen cents or any multiple of it during its time in circulation. There was also a perfunctory 1986 series of presidential twenty-two-cent stamps, which featured every chief executive up until that time, but few of them, as well, reached actual circulation.

That said, looking at Buchanan's presidency is not a futile gesture. For a year in the late 1990s, my wife had a fellowship at Stanford University—where, by the way, one of Buchanan's competitors for assailable presidencies, Herbert Hoover, an alumnus, is revered. It was the height of the first Silicon Valley tech company boom, and one of the mantras was that failure was a good thing. If an entrepreneur had not failed, he had not tried to "expand the envelope," as another cliché of the time went. There was not a successful Silicon Valley icon, not Hewlett and Packard, not Steve Wozniak, and surely not Steve Jobs, who had not experienced significant failure.

So maybe it is a good thing to view Buchanan's series of failures as a worthwhile study of how to become a better president. And presidents who want to be a political party's standard-bearer should take heed. A lasting result of Buchanan's presidency was the severe diminution of—

almost the dissolving of—the Democratic Party. Before Buchanan, fully two-thirds of the presidents—ten of fifteen—were Democrats, some winning by extraordinary margins. James Monroe, for instance, won all but one vote in the Electoral College. The party split into three factions in the 1860s election, which assured Lincoln the presidency. Yet worse was that in the next half-century, there was only one Democratic president—Grover Cleveland. The rift in the party exacerbated by Buchanan was transformational. Even after substandard presidencies, like those of Andrew Johnson and Ulysses S. Grant, Republicans succeeded Republicans. There has never been a presidential legacy like that.

In toto, much of Buchanan's failure seems to come from his obtuseness and his cleaving to some vague idea of what he thought a strict reading of the Constitution was, which meant that the president was mostly an administrator and that Congress and the states should dictate the direction of the country. To be sure, he deviated from that whenever he wanted to—particularly in his influencing of the *Dred Scott* case.

Still, in the contrarian mode I often find myself, it would not be a bad thing for the next presidents, before they come into office, to inspect not just Washington or Lincoln, but Buchanan as well. Most presidents will not ever have the chance to be those two guys we mostly celebrate in February on Presidents' Day. Those potential presidents are probably up from ordinary or, at most, upper-middle-class beginnings, have gotten decent educations, and are also immersed at some point in partisan politics. That is not Washington or Lincoln, but more like Buchanan. Chances are, they have made intractable enemies—or at least enemies they are so obsessed with that they cannot get them off their minds—as Buchanan had with Stephen Douglas. They have probably made friends with doctrinaire people, as Buchanan did with his Southern friends. They have probably served in posts they eventually thought were insignificant—like Buchanan in Russia—and maybe pulled off an upset in policy or election, as Buchanan seemed to do in that Russian ministry.

If those folks can learn from someone who reached their station, then Buchanan may be the one. It would be hard to aspire to, say, a middle-of-the-road presidency like that of Calvin Coolidge or James Monroe. What egotist like a potential president wants to end up midrange? It is easy, though, to hope that a potential term would *not* be like Buchanan's.

When Buchanan died he was the last surviving member of the United States House of Representatives session that began in December 1821, halfway into the term of James Monroe., He breathed his last just before U. S. Grant was elected. Thus his public life spanned many ups and downs of the nation. He spent his last years much as any senior who was the head of a family did: He checked on every relative's and friend's finances down to the penny. He gave secret bits of money to those he found in need. He walked a lot in his garden. He traveled a little—mostly to Philadelphia to see old friends or Baltimore to see his niece or Bedford Springs, where he had taken the waters for years. He even once went to the Jersey Shore—and had a Jersey Shore–type experience, getting struck by gout, and he could not drink his favorite, Madeira, his whole painful time there.

Though a good crowd, perhaps several thousand, came to his funeral in Lancaster, no one gave memorable remarks. One speaker quoted in the *Lancaster Intelligencer* spouted a feckless cliché: "Starting at Stony Batter, a barefoot boy climbed to the highest office in the world. A rail-splitter of Illinois did the same thing. The effect of such an example is incalculable. A Republic is the only place on earth where such a thing is possible."

A sigh. A raised eyebrow in sardonic measure. A weary tribute to the Worst. President. Ever.

ACKNOWLEDGMENTS

As any researching nonfiction writer, I bend appreciatively to those who wrote the material listed on these pages. Even where I disagreed—and there were many instances where I did—I am thankful that the writers pointed out facts and opinions valuable to me. And to the historians who talked with me about the presidency and Supreme Court decisions, particularly Julian Zelizer at Princeton and Elliot Roosevelt at Penn, I owe a special debt.

I am particularly appreciative of the kindness of Patrick Clarke, the director in charge of Wheatland, President Buchanan's home in Lancaster, PA. Though he knew what I was up to—the vilification of the man whose legacy he is charged to protect—in emails, phone calls, and one long visit to the estate, he answered all of my questions and, even at times, agreed that Buchanan could have been a better president.

I thank my editor, Keith Wallman, for his perspicacious comments and support as I wrote and afterwards. My agent, Jane Dystel, was her usual tough cookie, but tough love is how I respond best, and she has spurred me on in this and other books and proposals.

I know it is soppily sentimental, but I rarely write a piece, certainly not a book, without thinking how my wife, Susan Warner, and my daughters, Ella and Sylvia Strauss, will eventually read it. They may often look at me and my obsessions—and the presidency is certainly one of them—with crossed eyes, but I write for them nonetheless, hoping the words will please them.

I am not a great believer in an afterlife, but if there is one, I know my dad, Sam Strauss, and my mother, Edna, are smiling that I finally wrote something historical—or as my mom, not without a bit of irony, would say, "hysterical." I can see my dad, the book in his hands, his glasses atop the front of his bald head, dozing off with a grin, knowing all those treks to all those historical sites were finally worth it.

Endnotes

Chapter One

1 *There had been one minor slipup*: Philip Klein, *President James Buchanan: A Biography* (University Park: The Pennsylvania State University Press, 1962), 271.

1 *Dolley Madison . . . America's Princess*: Cokie Roberts, *Capital Dames: The Civil War and the Women of Washington, 1848–68* (New York: HarperCollins, 2015), 9.

2 *After her husband's own presidential term*: "Dolley Madison," National First Ladies' Library, www.firstladies.org/biographies/firstladies.aspx ?biography=4.

2 *William Henry Harrison died*: Joseph Nathan Kane, *Facts About the Presidents* (New York: Permabooks, 1960), 107–57.

3 *Most tragic of all*: Roy Franklin Nichols, *Franklin Pierce: Young Hickory of the Granite Hills* (Philadelphia: University of Pennsylvania Press, 1958), 224–25.

3 *For the most part*: Jean H. Baker, *James Buchanan* (New York: Times Books, 2004), 25.

4 *He had first come*: Ibid., 1.

4 *Only about three in a hundred*: Ibid., 21.

4 *When Buchanan was first elected*: Klein, *President James Buchanan*, 37.

5 *Washington was ill developed* (and on): Margaret Leech, *Reveille in Washington 1860–65* (New York: Harper & Brothers, 1941), 10–14.

5 *"Our Democratic Queen"*: Klein, *President James Buchanan*, 272.

6 *The idea of one inaugural ball*: Joint Congressional Committee on Inaugural Ceremonies, www.inaugural.senate.gov.

6 *A huge temporary structure*: Kane, *Facts About the Presidents*, 165.

6 *The feast was a gastronome's delight*: Ibid., 165.

6 *Lynch, the* New York Times *correspondent*: George T. Curtis, *Life of James Buchanan, Fifteenth President of the United States* (New York: Harper & Brothers, 1883), Vol. 2, 187–96.

8 *He came from little*: Author interviews with Patrick Clarke, director of Wheatland, December 2015 and January 2016.

9 *Its leading popularizer being George Gallup*: Erin Overbey, "George Gallup and the Mystery of Polls," *New Yorker*, October 26, 2012.

10 *Abraham Lincoln when he got a letter*: Letter dated Monday, October 21, 1861; Abraham Lincoln Papers, Library of Congress.

11 *Edward Dickinson Baker*: "Senator Killed in Battle," United States Senate Stories 1851–1877, www.senate.gov/artandhistory/history/minute/Senator_Killed_In_Battle.htm.

12 *All the presidents elected*: Kane, *Facts About the Presidents*, 107–57.

13 *Smitten by the charisma*: Baker, *James Buchanan*, 75.

13 *Buchanan's post-presidency memoir*: James Buchanan, *Mr. Buchanan's Administration on the Eve of the Rebellion* (New York: D. Appleton & Co., 1866).

14 *Buchanan presided over the Panic*: Walter Stahr, *Seward: Lincoln's Indispensable Man* (New York: Simon & Schuster, 2012), 168.

17 *To call Buchanan America's worst president*: Robert W. Merry, *Where They Stand* (New York: Simon & Schuster, 2012), 51–66.

18 *Eight major surveys*: Ibid., 244–45.

19 *Merry then takes*: Ibid., 248–50.

20 *I once spent*: Robert Strauss, "He's Rounding Third," *Los Angeles Times*, July 11, 1993.

21 *The late David H. Donald*: Michael J. Birkner, ed., *James Buchanan and the Political Crisis of the 1850s* (Selinsgrove, PA: Susquehanna UP, 1996), 107.

21 *George Ticknor Curtis wrote*: Curtis, *Life of James Buchanan*.

22 *He saw Buchanan*: Klein, *President James Buchanan*.

22 *John Updike said it was*: Updike, *Buchanan Dying: A Play* (New York: Random House, 1974), 151.

23 *"Most historians agree Buchanan was a failure"*: Clarke interviews.

24 *People would come to the grounds*: Ibid.

25 *Long before he became president*: Merry, *Where They Stand*, 99–103.

25 *He brazenly opposed*: Baker, *James Buchanan*, 40.

26 *Polk, in his diary*: Marquis James, *The Life of Andrew Jackson* (New York: Bobbs-Merrill, 1938), 771.

26 *Buchanan might have been prescient*: Kane, *Facts About the Presidents*, 166.

Chapter Two

28 *Log cabin birthplace*: Franklin County, Pennsylvania, tourism website, www.explorefranklincountypa.com/early-history.

29 *The elder Buchanan*: Klein, *President James Buchanan*, 1–3.

29 *At least one account*: Ibid., 3.

29 *There are few signs announcing it*: Author visit to Stony Batter, PA, October 2015.

29 *He decided it was time*: Klein, *President James Buchanan*, 4.

30 *James the younger was the second born*: Ibid., 3–5.

30 *Various relatives and friends*: Updike, *Buchanan Dying*, 160–61.

30 *"My father was a man"*: Curtis, *Life of James Buchanan*, 2.

31 *"My mother . . . was a remarkable woman"*: Ibid.

31 *"She was a woman"*: Ibid., 3.

32 *For those in south-central Pennsylvania* (and additional details about Buchanan): Klein, *President James Buchanan*, 7–12.

33 *The new president, Jeremiah Atwater*: Ibid., 8.

34 *"Without much natural tendency"*: Ibid., 9.

35 *On September 19, 1809*: Ibid., 12.

35 *Buchanan's father had occasion*: Ibid., 13.

35 *Buchanan was not in Lancaster by chance*: Clarke interview, January 2016.

36 *Lancaster was no half-baked place*: Lancaster website, www.lancaster
history.org.

36 *Smaller than the population of*: United States Census, www.census
.gov.

37 *Just as he was about to step out*: Clarke interview.

37 *Western state of Kentucky*: Klein, *President James Buchanan*, 15.

38 *"I went there"*: Ibid., 15–16.

38 *The northern part of Lancaster County*: Ibid., 16.

39 *"I determined"*: Ibid.

40 *Buchanan joined the Washington Association*: Ibid., 17.

40 *The next day, August 25* (and ensuing story): Ibid., 17–19.

42 *"I hope you will make the best"*: Ibid., 18.

42 *The scheme was*: Ibid., 20.

43 *According to Buchanan's own private papers*: Curtis, *Life of James
Buchanan*, 17.

44 *Buchanan was overjoyed*: Klein, *President James Buchanan*, 22.

44 *He and Lancaster's prothonotary*: Ibid., 16.

45 *Buchanan was said to be distinguished looking* (and other physical and
social traits): Baker, *James Buchanan*, 19.

45 *"A perpetual attitude of courteous defence"*: Klein, *President James
Buchanan*, 21.

46 *The speech he planned*: Ibid., 20.

47 *His father, once again*: Ibid., 22.

47 *Buchanan started plugging away at his law practice*: Ibid., 23–25.

48 *So the Democrats took another tack* (and details about the defense of
Judge Franklin): Ibid., 24–26.

50 *Local downtown Lancaster taverns*: Ibid., 27–28.

50 *Molton C. Rogers*: Clarke interview.

51 *By October*: Klein, *President James Buchanan*, 27.

51 *Rogers started dating*: Ibid., 28.

51 *The grocer's son* (and further details of the courtship and breakup
with Ann Coleman, as well as her death): Ibid., 28–35. (Baker and

others have these same facts, but it is clear that Klein is the main source for them.)

56 *For the rest of December*: Ibid., 35.

57 *The statistics are all over the place* (and further statistics mentioned): Kane, *Facts About the Presidents*, 391–432.

62 *On December 9, 1981*: *Philadelphia Daily News*, December 9, 1981, and other news reports through 1983.

63 *How she was sunbathing*: Author phone interview with Frances Payne Tyler, February 2015.

CHAPTER THREE

65 *Even Cyrus Jacobs*: Klein, *President James Buchanan*, 35.

65 *Now when the Federalists of Lancaster were looking*: Ibid., 35.

66 *That "slave," a woman named Hannah*: Ibid., 36.

66 *One of Buchanan's best traits*: Leonard White, *The Jacksonians* (New York: Macmillan, 1954), 13.

66 *Buchanan won and Findlay lost*: Klein, *President James Buchanan*, 36.

66 *During the Jeffersonian Democratic era*: White, *The Jacksonians*, 145.

66 *When his father died*: Baker, *James Buchanan*, 22.

67 *Buchanan came to a Washington*: Daniel J. Boorstin, *The Americans: The National Experience* (New York: Random House, 1965), 349.

67 *John Randolph, the venerable Virginia congressman*: Klein, *President James Buchanan*, 38.

67 *Lowndes was ill* (and the rest of the story of Buchanan's initial speech in Congress): Ibid., 39–41.

68 *Buchanan had already started thinking*: Ibid., 42–43.

69 *Buchanan, though, wanted to make sure first*: Ibid., 43.

69 *The Federalists were clearly on the wane by then*: Boorstin, *The Americans*, 339.

69 *He ran on a ticket*: Klein, *President James Buchanan*, 49.

70 *By late 1824*: White, *The Jacksonians*, 3.

70 *In an election that seemed more European*: Klein, *President James Buchanan*, 49.

70 *He asked Jackson*: Ibid., 50–52.

71 *Buchanan had always been a good budgeter*: Baker, *James Buchanan*, 16.

72 *Seeing Adams as a temporary obstacle* (and details about the Amalgamation Party): Klein, *President James Buchanan*, 53–56.

72 *Then a bombshell came*: Ibid., 57–59.

73 *Buchanan was now a firm Jacksonian Democrat*: Ibid., 60–61.

74 *He gave three speeches*: Ibid., 61–62.

74 *The Marietta Pioneer* (and details about the rest of the 1828 campaign): Ibid., 62.

75 *In the spring of 1830*: Ibid., 73.

75 *The original thought of backroom* (and details about the 1828 presidential election): White, *The Jacksonians*, 13–14.

75 *Because his wife had died*: Kane, *Facts About the Presidents*, 90–91.

76 *That tariff tiff*: Boorstin, *The Americans*, 216.

77 *He ended up his decade in Congress*: Klein, *President James Buchanan*, 74–77.

77 *In a final rush*: Ibid., 76.

78 *Jackson had a bit of a surprise*: Baker, *James Buchanan*, 30.

78 *Jackson dispatched one of his closest advisors* (and story of Buchanan's attempt to get out of ministership): Klein, *President James Buchanan*, 78–80.

79 *Petticoat Affair*: Frederic D. Schwarz, "1831: That Eaton Woman," *American Heritage* 57, no. 2 (April/May 2006).

79 *Jackson was the Don Corleone of his day*: Klein, *President James Buchanan*, 79.

80 *"Jackson really disliked Buchanan"*: Clarke interview, January 2015.

80 *By all accounts*: Clarke interview.

80 *Beginning in early April 1832*: Klein, *President James Buchanan*, 81.

80 *Buchanan's imprimatur*: Ibid., 82.

81 *Buchanan found, though* (and details of Russian negotiations): Ibid., 82–86.

81 *I must submit*: Ibid., 84.

83 *You may judge of my astonishment*: Ibid., 88.

84 *Along the way* (and greater discussion of Buchanan's trip home from Russia and negotiations in Great Britain): Ibid., 95–96.

84 *When Jackson sends him to Russia*: Clarke interview.

84 *Buchanan came back to Lancaster*: Klein, *President James Buchanan*, 100–101.

84 *"The emperors and empresses"*: Ibid., 96.

85 *Bachelorhood in middle-class and upper-class America*: Clarke interview.

86 *According to Judge Thomas Kittera's diary*: Klein, *President James Buchanan*, 31.

87 *Letters between Buchanan and Mrs. George Blake*: Ibid., 47.

88 *Klein also points to letters*: Ibid., 101.

89 *Buchanan and William Rufus DeVane King*: Baker, *James Buchanan*, 25–26.

89 *"They certainly didn't have the word 'gay' back then"*: Lou Chibbaro, "King Was Likely Gay Vice President," *Bay Area Reporter*, October 6, 2011.

89 *Another piece of "evidence"*: Klein, *President James Buchanan*, 149.

90 *King died only weeks*: Nichols, *Franklin Pierce*, 234.

90 *As a moderate Democrat* (and further biographical details on King): "William Rufus King, 13th Vice President (1853)," US Senate biography, www.senate.gov/artandhistory/history/common/generic/VP_William_R_King.htm.

91 *The Encyclopedia of Alabama says*: "William Rufus King," *Encyclopedia of Alabama*, www.encyclopediaofalabama.org/article/h-1886.

91 *After King's election* (and story of name change of King County, Washington): King County website, www.kingcounty.gov/depts/records-licensing/archives/research-guides/history-links.aspx.

92 *Gay activist Larry Kramer*: Larry Kramer, *The American People, Vol. 1: Search for My Heart* (New York: Farrar, Straus and Giroux, 2015), 244.

93 *Biographer Jean Baker*: Baker, *James Buchanan*, 21–22.

93 *Dolley Madison's niece, Anna Payne*: Klein, *President James Buchanan*, 156.

94 *There has certainly also been*: Kramer, *American People*, 245.

CHAPTER FOUR

95 *Passive-aggressive move*: Klein, *President James Buchanan*, 93.

95 *The Democratic faction*: Ibid., 99.

95 *Two big political issues*: Richard B. Morris, *Great Political Decisions* (Philadelphia: Lippincott, 1960), 110–51.

96 *Jackson himself was in a bind*: Klein, *President James Buchanan*, 105.

97 *"James Buchanan always did things the slow way"*: Ibid., 107.

97 *The Whigs and Anti-Masonic Party*: Ibid., 108.

97 *While Buchanan had done nothing of significance*: Ibid., 108–9.

98 *Most of the more prominent Doughfaces*: Birkner, ed., *James Buchanan and the Political Crisis*, 68–87.

98 *In fact, only a few years before*: Klein, *President James Buchanan*, 124.

99 *About this same time in 1934*: Ibid., 100.

99 *Chair of the Senate Foreign Relations Committee*: Ibid., 113.

99 *Buchanan made a deal with his best buddy, King*: Ibid., 130–35.

100 *As their 1840 presidential candidate* (and details about Buchanan during that election): Ibid., 132–35.

101 *He had never had his name*: Baker, *James Buchanan*, 32–33.

102 *The secretary of state, Abel P. Upshur, was killed*: Klein, *President James Buchanan*, 158.

102 *Van Buren's newfound popularity* (and more on 1844 Democratic Convention): Ibid., 159–60.

103 *Buchanan shrewdly wrote to Polk* (and more on being named secretary of state, as well as last Senate speech): Ibid., 163–64.

104 *His last speech as a senator*: Ibid., 164.

104 *The first thing on Buchanan's agenda*: Ibid.

105 *The point for Polk*: Morris, *Great Presidential Decisions*, 152–58.

105 *Before he could get to do much* (and the saga of waffling back and forth between Supreme Court and secretary of state): Klein, *President James Buchanan*, 167–70.

107 *"He threw great parties"*: Clarke interview, January 2016.

108 *Polk's greatest desire*: Morris, *Great Presidential Decisions*, 152.

108 *The vote was so close that Vice President Dallas*: Klein, *President James Buchanan*, 173.

109 *Each time Polk* (and saga of Polk versus Buchanan in Oregon negotiations): Ibid., 178–82.

110 *Buchanan again figured he was deserving*: Ibid., 192.

110 *Buchanan started his other tactic*: Ibid., 203–4.

111 *Taylor would have been a formidable opponent*: Baker, *James Buchanan*, 45.

112 *The King Street house*: Klein, *President James Buchanan*, 206.

112 *While he never really loved* (and details about Dickinson and Franklin & Marshall works): Ibid., 210.

113 *Buchanan was upset*: Clarke interview, February 2015.

113 *Buchanan also decided* (and more on initial time at Wheatland): Klein, *President James Buchanan*, 206–7.

113 *And then the effect of it*: *Philadelphia Press*, January 24, 1860.

114 *The Compromise of 1850*: Boorstin, *The Americans*, 273.

116 *Buchanan chose to be evasive and complex* (and his views on the Compromise of 1850): Klein, *President James Buchanan*, 211–15.

116 *The 1852 Democratic Convention*: Ibid., 219–20.

118 *Harrison was the son of Benjamin Harrison V*: Robert Owens, *Mr. Jefferson's Hammer: William Henry Harrison and the Origins of American Indian Policy* (Norman: University of Oklahoma Press, 2007), 3.

120 *"This is certainly one of the great questions"*: Author interview with Bryan Craig, Miller Center for the Study of the Presidency, University of Virginia, January 2016.

120 *Jackson broke through those standards*: Jill Lepore, "Bound for Glory," *New Yorker*, October 20, 2008.

121 *Caretakers instead of major thinkers*: Craig interview.

CHAPTER FIVE

122 *The Whig Party*: Michael F. Holt, "Another Look at the Election of 1856," in Birkner, ed., *James Buchanan and the Political Crisis*, 40.

124 *In reality, he did not become sick*: Kane, *Facts About the Presidents*, 114.

124 *Harrison's vice president, John Tyler*: Ibid., 120.

124 *Taylor was quite an anomaly*: Nichols, *Franklin Pierce*, 180.

125 *Yet there had always been rumors*: Eric Harrison, "Zachary Taylor Did Not Die of Arsenic Poisoning, Tests Indicate," *Los Angeles Times*, June 27, 1991.

125 *Fillmore has often been vilified*: David Kennedy, "The Big Question," *Atlantic*, November 2014.

126 *It took less than two years*: Boorstin, *The Americans*, 384.

126 *William Seward, the former powerful Whig Party senator*: Stahr, *Seward*, 144–48.

127 *John C. Fremont was a fresh face*: Boorstin, *The Americans*, 226–28.

127 *Jessie Benton, knowing the way of politics* (and story of John Fremont's expeditions): Roberts, *Capital Dames*, 26–33.

129 *Martin Van Buren, the ex-president*: Klein, *President James Buchanan*, 205.

129 *The Know-Nothings/Americans searched* (and details of Millard Fillmore's candidacy with them): Holt, "Another Look," 52–56.

131 *In 1850 the census counted*: United States Census, www.census.gov.

133 *Henry Clay, the Great Compromiser*: Boorstin, *The Americans*, 186.

134 *Except there, nearly whistling in the wind*: Holt, "Another Look," 59.

134 *The three met in November in secret* (and story of Ostend Manifesto): Nichols, *Franklin Pierce*, 595–96.

135 *The Know-Nothings were a curious case*: Holt, "Another Look," 48–56.

137 *Buchanan swept the South*: Klein, *President James Buchanan*, 257–60.

138 *With the exception of his usual*: Ibid., 258.

139 *Neither Washington nor Jefferson* (and details of Buchanan's campaign): Ibid., 255–58.

142 *James Buchanan, though, had a little secret* (and story of campaign songs): PBS, "Stephen Foster Backs Buchanan," *The American Experience: Stephen Foster*, www.pbs.org/wgbh/amex/foster/peopleevents/e_politics.html.

Chapter Six

148 *Only a few blocks from the dramatic Gateway Arch* (and story of Old Courthouse, St. Louis): "Old Courthouse," National Park Service, www.nps.gov/jeff/planyourvisit/och.htm.

148 *Scott was born a slave* (and history of the *Dred Scott* decision): Paul Finkelman, "Scott v. Sandford: The Court's Most Dreadful Case and How It Changed History," *Chicago-Kent Law Review* 82, no. 1 (Symposium: 150th Anniversary of the *Dred Scott* Decision, December 2006).

149 *Roger Brooke Taney was a man*: "Roger B. Taney," *Wikipedia*, https://en.wikipedia.org/wiki/Roger_B._Taney.

151 *Buchanan had chosen*: Elbert B. Smith, *The Presidency of James Buchanan* (Lawrence: University Press of Kansas, 1975), 23–27.

151 *The* Dred Scott *case had been winding* (and details of Buchanan's intercession with justices): Baker, *James Buchanan*, 83–86.

153 *It was as broad a decision*: Smith, *Presidency of James Buchanan*, 24–29.

153 *"Korematsu is bad"*: Author interview with Kermit Roosevelt, University of Pennsylvania Constitutional Law professor and presidential descendant, January 2016.

154 *In his inaugural address*: Smith, *Presidency of James Buchanan*, 27.

154 *Almost immediately, the nation fell*: Ibid., 28.

155 *Buchanan was baffled*: Ibid., 31.

156 *When it came to picking a cabinet*: Klein, *President James Buchanan*, 275.

156 *The previous president, Franklin Pierce*: Kane, *Facts About the Presidents*, 158.

156 *Howell Cobb was always one*: Klein, *President James Buchanan*, 276.

157 *The rest of the cabinet fell into line*: Smith, *Presidency of James Buchanan*, 19.

157 *Buchanan hated Douglas*: Ibid., 20.

158 *"It will be my own regard"*: Ibid., 21.

158 *"The Hon. Samuel A. Douglas"*: Ibid.

158 *The cabinet would meet*: Klein, *President James Buchanan*, 279.

159 *There had been a bad downturn*: Ibid., 120.

159 *Tariff Bill of 1857*: Smith, *Presidency of James Buchanan*, 121.

160 *By midsummer no one could take a ride*: Klein, *President James Buchanan*, 314.

160 *Senator William Seward, the leader*: Stahr, *Seward*, 168.

160 *The sinking of the SS* Central America: Nina Strochlic, "The Curse of the South's Shipwrecked Gold," *Daily Beast*, August 19, 2015.

161 *In his annual message*: Klein, *President James Buchanan*, 314.

161 *The Mormons were not a beloved people* (and more about the Mormon crisis): Smith, *Presidency of James Buchanan*, 121; Klein, *President James Buchanan*, 315.

162 *Thomas L. Kane of Philadelphia*: Klein, *President James Buchanan*, 316–17.

163 *Aaron Scott Crawford spent his time* (and direct quotes that follow): Author interview with Crawford, postdoctoral fellow at the Center for Presidential History at Southern Methodist University, January 2016.

164 *"George W. Bush's presidency appears headed*: Sean Wilentz, "George W. Bush: The Worst President in History?" *Rolling Stone*, April 21, 2006.

165 *Crawford said he admires Wilentz*: Crawford interview.

166 *Tyler was a complete afterthought*: Chris DeRose, *The Presidents' War* (Guilford, CT: Lyons Press, 2014), 22–31.

166 *Fillmore gets a lot of votes*: Merry, *Where They Stand*, 95–96.

167 *Andrew Johnson was no prize*: Ibid., 104–7.

168 *"Bush was clearly in decline"* (and direct quotes that follow): Author interview with Julian Zelizer, author of *Jimmy Carter* (in the American Presidents series for Times Books), January 2016.

169 *Herbert Hoover had a similarly long . . . ex-presidency*: Merry, *Where They Stand*, 92–93.

170 *The definitive biography of Harding*: Francis Russell, *The Shadow of Blooming Grove: Warren G. Harding and His Times* (New York: McGraw-Hill, 1968), inside front cover, 1.

170 *The Harding election's issues*: Merry, *Where They Stand*, 107–9.

171 *The real competition*: Ibid., 96–99.

172 *"His high honor"*: Nichols, *Franklin Pierce*, 225.

173 *The signal moment*: Ibid., 407.

174 *"Buchanan's place in history"*: Merry, *Where They Stand*, 103.

CHAPTER SEVEN

175 *Massachusetts senator Charles Sumner* (with account of Sumner's beating): Allan Nevins, *Ordeal of the Union, Vol. 2* (New York: Charles Scribner's Sons, 1947), 444–45.

176 *"The senator from South Carolina"*: David Herbert Donald, *Charles Sumner and the Coming Civil War* (New York: Alfred A. Knopf, 1960), as outlined in "Charles Sumner," *Wikipedia*, www.wikipedia.org/wiki/Charles_Sumner.

177 *By the mid-1850s*: Klein, *President James Buchanan*, 286.

177 *Stephen Douglas was the chair*: Nevins, *Ordeal of the Union, Vol. 2*, 420.

178 *The most famous event was the slaughter*: Klein, *President James Buchanan*, 254.

178 *Robert Walker, a native Pennsylvanian*: Baker, *James Buchanan*, 96.

179 *"On the question of submitting"*: Smith, *Presidency of James Buchanan*, 37.

179 *Incongruously enough today*: Lecompton, Kansas, website, www.lecomptonkansas.com.

179 *Most anti-slavery citizens* (and the account of Lecompton constitution en toto): Smith, *Presidency of James Buchanan*, 39–46.

180 *The 1858 fall congressional elections* (and letter to Harriet Lane after): Klein, *President James Buchanan*, 330.

180 *The document they presented*: Ibid., 239–41.

181 *For Doughfaces like Buchanan and Pierce*: Nichols, *Franklin Pierce*, 366–71.

181 *"We should, however, be recreant to our duty"*: Ibid., 596.

182 *William Walker, the most famous*: Smith, *Presidency of James Buchanan*, 72–73.

182 *The now little-known Pig War*: Ibid., 71.

183 *Buchanan's invasion of Paraguay*: Klein, *President James Buchanan*, 323–24.

183 *As Jean Baker noted*: Baker, *James Buchanan*, 111–12.

184 *Harriet Lane was among the most talked-about women*: Klein, *President James Buchanan*, 273.

184 *"Leading star of the social firmament"*: "Harriet Lane," National First Ladies' Library, www.firstladies.org/biographies/firstladies.aspx ?biography=16.

184 *Lace berthas became popular*: "Harriet Lane," National First Ladies' Library, www.firstladies.org/biographies/firstladies.aspx?biography=16.

185 *"Miss Lane occupies a position"*: Patrick Lynch, *New York Times*, March 6, 1857.

185 *Harriet became her uncle's ward*: "Harriet Lane," National First Ladies' Library.

185 *She was twenty-one*: Baker, *James Buchanan*, 60.

186 *A possible romance for his niece*: Letter from Buchanan to Harriet Lane, August 3, 1853.

186 *Prince of Wales*: Roberts, *Capital Dames*, 83.

187 *The only real blemish*: Ibid., 35.

187 *After the president's term*: Klein, *President James Buchanan*, 437.

187 *Harriet eventually moved back to Washington*: Roberts, *Capital Dames*, 404.

188 *The earliest photograph*: "Harriet Lane," National First Ladies' Library.

CHAPTER EIGHT

189 *At the time of the Buchanan presidency*: United States Census, 1850, www.census.gov.

190 *"School appropriations were wretched"*: Nevins, *Ordeal of the Union*, *Vol. 2*, 53.

190 *"The methods of tillage"*: Ibid., 54.

190 *"Half of the white adult population"*: Ibid., 56.

190 *Nation's foreign export shipments*: Ibid., 58.

191 *"Much of this 'wealth'"*: Ibid., 60–70.

192 *Though William Seward*: Stahr, *Seward*, 168.

192 *Cobb joked that Buchanan*: Smith, *Presidency of James Buchanan*, 37–39.

192 *A short sojourn in New England*: Klein, *President James Buchanan*, 202.

193 *Daniel Sickles* (and story of Key's murder): Baker, *James Buchanan*, 60; "Daniel Sickles," *Wikipedia*, https://en.wikipedia.org/wiki/Daniel_Sickles.

194 *A fellow Pennsylvanian, John Covode* (and details on the committee report): Smith, *Presidency of James Buchanan*, 99, 104, 177.

196 *It was no secret*: Smith, *Presidency of James Buchanan*, 89.

197 *Even after Brown struck*: Ibid., 90–91.

197 *Virginia politicians take over*, Ibid., 92.

197 *Cause célèbre like no other man*: Ibid., 94–95.

198 *"The presidential convention system"*: Ibid., 105.

199 *Instead of trying to get its nominee first*: Ibid., 106.

199 *Buchanan would not budge*: Klein, *President James Buchanan*, 340–43.

199 *Essentially three Democratic candidates*: Ibid., 342–43.

199 *A blur of inflamed speeches*: Ibid., 347–49.

200 *Seward, ever practical*: Stahr, *Seward*, 354–55.

200 *Lincoln took eighteen states*: Kane, *Facts About the Presidents*, 174.

200 *Howell Cobb resigned*: Smith, *Presidency of James Buchanan*, 143.

201 *"The President and myself parted"*: Klein, *President James Buchanan*, 371.

201 *The shuffles then started*: Ibid., 372.

201 *Buchanan made another slip*: Ibid., 373.

201 *The nation now believed*: Ibid., 374.

201–2 *Buchanan drafted a reply*: Ibid., 375.

202 *He went to a wedding reception*: Ibid.

202 *Keitt was already legend*: Ibid., 253–54.

203 *"An increasing hostility"*: "Declaration of Causes of Seceding States," Civil War Trust, www.civilwar.org/education/history/primarysources/declarationofcauses.html.

204 *It was no different in the other states*: Ibid.

204 *Several old heads tried to come up with solutions*: Smith, *Presidency of James Buchanan*, 162.

205 *Otherwise, he kept pronouncing a dictum*: Klein, *President James Buchanan*, 355–63.

205 *Buchanan finally did grow despondent*: Ibid., 400ff.

205 *Mercantile forays to Japan and China*: Baker, *James Buchanan*, 108.

206 *The night before Lincoln's inauguration*: Klein, *President James Buchanan*, 402.

206 *Buchanan ordered his carriage* (and details on final ride to Lincoln inauguration): Smith, *Presidency of James Buchanan*, 190–91.

207 *"One flourishing town after another"*: Nevins, *Ordeal of the Union, Vol. 2*, 35.

207 *"Whether foreign visitors"*: Ibid., 36.

208 *The Mormons, for instance, plagued Buchanan*: Boorstin, *The Americans*, 62–65.

208 *Nevins noted that even in language*: Nevins, *Ordeal of the Union, Vol. 2*, 46.

209 *They would be prone to fighting*: Ibid., 65.

209 *No one particularly argued*: Ibid., 69.

210 *Americans were relentlessly optimistic*: Ibid., 51.

210 *The tolerance of slavery*: Ibid., 74.

211 *"A house divided against itself"*: June 16, 1858, Springfield, Illinois, speech; transcript at Abraham Lincoln Online, www.abrahamlincolnonline.org/lincoln/speeches/house.htm.

CHAPTER NINE

214 *Buchanan's beloved niece*: "Harriet Lane," National First Ladies' Library.

214 *There were outdoor commemorations*: John Kelly, "Naming Andrew Jackson's Horse in Lafayette Square," *Washington Post*, August 3, 2010.

215 *The commission was approved* (and direct quotes that follow): Clarke interview, January 2016.

216 *The prologue of*: Klein, *President James Buchanan*, xvii.

217 *Buchanan would not die or be captured*: Ibid., 417.

217 *Buchanan's book is notable*: Ibid., 419.

218 *Buchanan had originally sought*: Ibid., 416–20.

218 *"I am willing to vindicate"*: Ibid., 416.

219 *Long after Buchanan's death*: Harriet Lane Papers, Library of Congress.

219 *In 2014 the Corcoran Gallery*: Randy Kennedy, "Corcoran Gallery Art Transforms National Gallery," *New York Times*, February 6, 2015.

220 *The postal service issued*: "US Presidents on US Postage Stamps," *Wikipedia*, https://en.wikipedia.org/wiki/U.S._presidents_on_U.S._postage_stamps.

221 *When Buchanan died* (and details on his last days): Klein, *President James Buchanan*, 427–28.

222 *Starting at Stony Batter*: Ibid., 428.

Bibliography

American Heritage Editors. *The American Heritage Book of the Presidents and Famous Americans.* New York: Dell, 1967.

Baker, Jean. *James Buchanan.* New York: Times Books, 2004.

Binder, Frederick Moore. *James Buchanan and the American Empire.* Selinsgrove, PA: Susquehanna University Press, 1994.

Birkner, Michael J., ed. *James Buchanan and the Political Crisis of the 1850s.* Selinsgrove, PA: Susquehanna University Press, 1996.

Boorstin, Daniel J. *The Americans: The National Experience.* New York: Random House, 1965.

Buchanan, James. *Mr. Buchanan's Administration on the Eve of the Rebellion.* New York: D. Appleton and Co., 1866.

Buchanan, James. Papers. Dickinson College Archives and Special Collections. http://archives.dickinson.edu/search/node/buchanan%20type%-3Adigitized_resources.

Catton, Bruce. *The Coming Fury.* New York: Doubleday, 1961.

Chibbaro, Lou. "King Was Likely Gay Vice President." *Bay Area Reporter,* October 6, 2011.

Clarke, Patrick, director of Wheatland. Personal interviews with author, December 2015, January 2015 and 2016, February 2015.

Craig, Bryan, senior researcher at Miller Center for the Study of the Presidency, University of Virginia. Personal interview with author, January 2016.

Crawford, Aaron Scott, postdoctoral fellow at Center for Presidential History, Southern Methodist University. Personal interview with author, January 2016.

Curtis, George Ticknor. *The Life of James Buchanan, Fifteenth President of the United States*. New York: Harper & Brothers, 1883.

"Declaration of Causes of Seceding States." Civil War Trust. www .civilwar.org/education/history/primarysources/declarationofcauses .html.

DeRose, Chris. *The Presidents' War: Six American Presidents and the Civil War That Divided Them*. Guilford, CT: Lyons Press, 2014.

Finkelman, Paul. "*Scott v. Sandford*: The Court's Most Dreadful Case and How It Changed History." *Chicago-Kent Law Review* 82, no. 1 (December 2006).

Harrison, Eric. "Zachary Taylor Did Not Die of Arsenic Poisoning, Tests Indicate." *Los Angeles Times*, June 27, 1991.

Holt, Michael F. "Another Look at the Election of 1856." In *James Buchanan and the Political Crisis of the 1850s*, ed. Michael J. Birkner. Selinsgrove, PA: Susquehanna University Press, 1996.

James, Marquis. *The Life of Andrew Jackson*. New York: Bobs-Merrill, 1938.

Kane, Joseph Nathan. *Facts About the Presidents*. New York: Permabooks, 1960.

Kelly, John. "Naming Andrew Jackson's Horse in Lafayette Square." *Washington Post*, August 3, 2010.

Kennedy, David. "The Big Question." *Atlantic*, November 2014.

Kennedy, Randy. "Corcoran Gallery Art Transforms National Gallery." *New York Times*, February 6, 2015.

Klein, Philip Shriver. *President James Buchanan: A Biography*. University Park, PA: The Pennsylvania State University Press, 1962.

Kramer, Larry. *The American People. Volume 1: Search for My Heart*. New York: Farrar, Straus and Giroux, 2015.

Leech, Margaret. *Reveille in Washington, 1860–65*. New York: Time, 1941.

Lepore, Jill. "Bound for Glory." *New Yorker*, October 20, 2008.

Merry, Robert W. *Where They Stand: The American Presidents in the Eyes of Voters and Historians*. New York: Simon & Schuster, 2012.

Moore, John Bassett, ed. *The Works of James Buchanan*. Philadelphia: Lippincott, 1908.

Morris, Richard B. *Great Presidential Decisions*. Philadelphia: Lippincott, 1960.

Nevins, Allan. *Ordeal of the Union*. 2 vols. New York: Charles Scribner's Sons: 1947.

Nichols, Roy Franklin. *Franklin Pierce: Young Hickory of the Granite Hills*. Philadelphia: University of Pennsylvania Press, 1958.

Overbey, Erin. "George Gallup and the Mystery of Polls." *New Yorker*, October 26, 2012.

PBS. "Stephen Foster Backs Buchanan." *The American Experience: Stephen Foster*. www.pbs.org/wgbh/amex/foster/peopleevents/e_politics.html.

Roberts, Cokie. *Capital Dames: The Civil War and the Women of Washington, 1848–68*. New York: HarperCollins, 2015.

Roosevelt, Kermit, professor at University of Pennsylvania. Personal interview with author, January 2016.

Russell, Francis. *The Shadow of Blooming Grove: Warren G. Harding in His Times*. New York: McGraw-Hill, 1968.

Schwarz, Frederic D. "1831: That Eaton Woman," *American Heritage* 57, no. 2 (April/May 2006).

Smith, Elbert B. *The Presidency of James Buchanan*. Lawrence: The University Press of Kansas, 1975.

Stahr, Walter. *Seward: Lincoln's Indispensable Man*. New York: Simon & Schuster, 2012.

Strauss, Robert. "He's Rounding Third." *Los Angeles Times*, July 11, 1993.

Strochlic, Nina. "The Curse of the South's Shipwrecked Gold." *Daily Best*, August 19, 2015.

Tyler, Frances Payne, granddaughter-in-law of John Tyler. Telephone interview with author, February 2015.

Updike, John. *Buchanan Dying: A Play*. New York: Random House, 1974.

White, Leonard. *The Jacksonians*. New York: Macmillan, 1954.

Wilentz, Sean. "George W. Bush: The Worst President in History?" *Rolling Stone*, April 21, 2006.

Zelizer, Julian. Personal interview with author, January 2016.

Index

Q
Queen Victoria, 185–86, 193

R
Radicals, 68
Ramelton, Ireland, 84
Randolph, John, 67, 80
ranking of presidents, 17–21,
    164–66
Reading Railroad, 160
Reagan, Ronald, 13, 20, 141
Reed, William, 219
Reigart, E. C., 74
Report on an Exploration of the
    Country Lying between the
    Missouri River and the Rocky
    Mountains on the Line of
    the Kansas and Great Platte
    River, 128
Republican Party, 10, 14, 126,
    128–30, 133, 138, 139–41,
    160
Reynolds, Ellie, 216
Reynolds, John, 51, 81, 215–16
Reynolds, John F., 215–16
Ridgely, Charles Sterret, 41
Riggs, Lawrason, 214
Robinson, Harriet, 149
Rogers, Molton C., 50–52
Rolling Stone, 164
Roosevelt, Edith, 188
Roosevelt, Franklin, 18–20, 23,
    141, 153

Roosevelt, Kermit, 153
Roosevelt, Theodore, 127, 153
Ross, Betsy, x
Rowan, John, 38
Rush, Benjamin, 33, 118
Russell, Francis, 170–71
Russia, 78–84, 95–96, 99, 101, 157

S
Sadat, Anwar, 168
SALT treaty, 167
San Diego State University, xi
Sanford, John, 149
Schlesinger, Arthur M. Jr., 18, 23
Schlesinger, Arthur M. Sr., 18
Scott, Dred, 8, 14, 26, 148–49,
    151–53, 219
Scott, Winfield, 110, 126, 174,
    183
secession, 16–17, 116, 200–205,
    218
Selma, AL, 90–91, 98
Senate Committee on Territories,
    177
Senate Foreign Relations
    Committee, 99
Sergeant, John, 67, 84
Seward, William, 12, 107, 119,
    126–27, 138, 141, 160, 192,
    200
Shadow of Blooming Grove, The,
    170
Sherwood Forest, VA, 62

ABOUT THE AUTHOR

Robert Strauss has published more than one thousand stories in the *New York Times* and has also written for the *Washington Post*, the *Los Angeles Times*, *Fortune*, *Slate*, and many college alumni magazines and other publications. He is an instructor of nonfiction writing at the University of Pennsylvania and the author of *Daddy's Little Goalie*, a funny and sentimental memoir about being the father of girl athletes. He is a former reporter for *Sports Illustrated*, feature writer for the *Philadelphia Daily News*, TV critic for the *Asbury Park Press*, and news and sports producer for KYW-TV, then the NBC affiliate in Philadelphia. He was also the co-owner of Jerry's, a "Best of Philadelphia" restaurant in his native city. Strauss holds a BA in Philosophy from Carleton College. He lives in Haddonfield, New Jersey, with his wife, Susan Warner. They are the parents of two daughters, Ella and Sylvia.